CONNECTIONS
English Language Arts

Grade 7

Perfection Learning®

Editorial Director:	Sue Thies
Editors:	Andrea Stark, John T. Ham
Proofreading Coordinator:	Sheri Cooper
Art Director:	Randy Messer
Designers:	Tobi Cunningham, Emily Adickes
Contributors:	Carmel McDonald, Jen Yocum

Reviewers:

Karen Dierks
Media Specialist, ESL certified
ELA and Social Studies
Shawnee Mission Schools
Overland Park, Kansas

Danielle Emery, M.Ed.
Secondary ESL Coordinator
Lewisville, Texas, ISD

Lauri Garbo, M.Ed.
English Department
Gulf Coast High School
Collier County School District, Florida

Carmel McDonald
Instructional Coach
Paragon Charter Academy
Jackson, Michigan

Matthew T. Meldrum
Secondary Language Arts Curriculum
    Specialist
Austin Independent School District
Austin, Texas

Lisa Scribellito Milligan, MA.Ed.
Special Education/Reading
    /ELL Teacher Ed
White High School
Jacksonville, Florida

Kendall Mott
DL Spanish Instructor
Region 5 Education Service Center
Beaumont, Texas

Shelli Shaw
Instructional Officer for Secondary
    Reading Intervention
Katy Independent School District
Katy, Texas

JoAnn Williams
Secondary ELA/Reading Interventionist
Alief Independent School District
Houston, Texas

When ordering this book, please specify:
ISBN: 978-1-5311-2717-6 or **R7345**
ebook ISBN: 978-1-5311-2718-3 or **R7345D**

Contents

Read, Reread, and Read Again

Welcome to *Connections!* Think about an amazing movie you have seen—one you couldn't stop thinking about when you left the theater. Have you talked about the movie with your family or friends? Have you watched the movie again after first seeing it in the theater? Do you see something new each time you watch it?

Complex texts are like movies. You can't grasp all of the details in one read. Each time you read, you'll discover something new.

Connections will encourage you to develop a habit of reading a text several times. With each read, you will dive deeper into the text. You'll move from key ideas and details to discovering how authors create meaning by using special types of language to communicate their thoughts. With each read of the selections in *Connections*, you will be asked to focus on a central question: *What? How? Why* or *Why Not?*

First Read Focus on *What?*

What are the key ideas?

Ask: What is this mostly about? Which ideas are most important?

Who is writing and why are they writing?

What words or phrases stand out as important?

Second Read Focus on *How?*

How does the writer support his or her purpose?

Ask: How do details develop the central idea?

What special types of language (figurative language, repetition, rhyme) does the writer use to create meaning?

How do the sentences/paragraphs in the text relate, or fit together? How does the structure of the text emphasize the ideas? Do I see causes/effects? problems/solutions? claims/reasons?

Third Read Focus on *Why* or *Why not?*

Why is this text important or meaningful to me—or to others?

Ask: What can I learn from this text that will help me understand the world?

What can I learn that will make me a better writer?

Why is (or why isn't) this nonfiction text convincing? Why is (or why isn't) this work of literature meaningful?

How does this text connect to other texts? Where have I seen this theme before? How do other presentations of this text (movie, artwork, etc.) or ideas in this text communicate the theme in similar or different ways?

Learning to read and reread texts for meaning will make you a confident, successful reader as you encounter ever more challenging texts.

Unit 1

Essential Question
How do you know right from wrong?

Most people believe that they have a clear sense of right and wrong. Consider sayings such as "two wrongs don't make a right" and "it's black and white." Seems clear, right? But when you delve further into morality for specific situations, things become less clear. Stealing is wrong and against the law, but stealing to defend yourself or save yourself from starvation is understandable and pardonable. Destroying property is also wrong in most people's minds, unless you break down a door to help someone escape from a fire. Thus, some crimes are justifiable.

Another influencing factor is age; a child is not held to the same standard as an adult in social situations or according to the law. Parents can sometimes be held accountable for their children's actions though, so are parents the largest influence on a child's moral development?

If you had to teach someone right from wrong, where would you begin? At what age do children begin to understand that they have a choice between good and evil? In fact, how do people in general learn about what is the right thing to do versus the wrong thing? How do they decide what to do when faced with a moral dilemma—like whether to tell a lie to protect someone they love?

In this unit, you will explore the question: How do you know right from wrong? You will explore the morality of people's actions and decisions. Activities will provide opportunities to write, speak, and debate about right and wrong. You will also read and discuss issues related to the ethical treatment of animals. As you work through this unit, you may make surprising discoveries about the nature of right and wrong and how point of view impacts ideas about morality.

GOALS

- To identify and summarize central ideas
- To make inferences based on textual evidence
- To analyze point of view and theme
- To evaluate claims, reasons, and evidence in an argument
- To compare evidence in two texts
- To write an argumentative essay

Chapter 1

Identifying Key Ideas and Details

Preview Concepts

Who is your favorite superhero? Who is your superhero's villain or nemesis? What are the differences between the hero and the villain that identify them as good and bad? Write a response below.

CHAPTER GOALS

In this chapter you will

- develop a summary.
- determine the meaning of technical terms.
- identify claims and support.
- participate in a roundtable discussion or write an argumentative essay.

Share your answers with a partner. Then discuss the following question:

- Which two qualities are the most important for the hero to possess to be considered a good guy? Why?

PREVIEW ACADEMIC VOCABULARY

affix

antonym

claim

evidence

reason

root word

suffix

synonym

Making Connections

Read the following moral dilemma.

You have witnessed a man rob a bank, but then, he did something completely unusual and unexpected with the money. He donated it to an orphanage that was struggling to take care of the children. With this money, the orphanage could keep its doors open and continue taking care of the needy children. Would you:

a. Call the police and report the robbery, even though they would likely take the money away from the orphanage, or

b. Do nothing?

1. With a partner, discuss what you would do. Explain reasons for your choice of action.

2. What does your choice say about your moral beliefs or what is right and wrong?

3. What does your choice say about your belief in laws vs. your belief in fairness?

4. Do you think your ability to choose between right and wrong is something you learned from your family and society or it is something that developed in your brain over time? Or is it both?

> **MAKING CONNECTIONS**
>
> In this passage you will be reading a text that presents a claim about the human brain and morality.

First Read: Summarizing a Text

The following article comes from *Frontiers for Young Minds*, an online science journal. The authors are a professor of psychology and psychiatry and a developmental neuroscientist. In other words, one is an expert on how the mind works, and the other is an expert on how the brain develops. Before you read, consider the style of writing you expect from this informational genre.

Objective: As you read, underline the key idea of each paragraph. Write questions you have about morality in the My Thoughts column.

excerpt
Our Brains Are Wired for Morality: Evolution, Development, and Neuroscience

by Jean Decety and Jason M. Cowell, edited by Paul Glimcher

My Thoughts

1   How do we distinguish good from evil, right from wrong, just from unjust, and vice from virtue? An obvious answer is that we have learned to do so through socialization, that is, our behaviors were shaped from birth onward by our families,
5   our preschools, and almost everything we contacted in our environments. Morality is an inner sense of rightness about our behavior and the behavior of others. How we feel, think, and act about the concepts of "good" and "bad" are all parts of our morality. For example, hitting another person for any
10   reason is seen as bad, while sharing something we like with another child who is sad is considered good. Morality is so deeply rooted in the fabric of our everyday lives that it seems hard to imagine a society without any moral rules. Indeed, observations made by scientists who study different societies
15   around the world have shown that, despite cultural and individual differences, all human beings have some sense of right and wrong.

When we use the word "morality" we are generally talking about ideas of justice, fairness and rights, and the rules we

20   have about how people should treat one another. Consider the
following: as a reward for finishing your homework, you have
been given 10 marbles that you really like. You are then told
about a poor child who would not be able to get any marbles,
even though he did his homework too. However, you have

25   the option to give some of your marbles to the poor child.
What would you choose to do? Most children would naturally
share some of their marbles with a poor child and would also
be surprised if another child received more than 10 marbles
after doing the same amount of homework! This shows that

30   children understand both fairness and justice. As humans,
when we consider how we or others should share something
we have been given, we tend to take into account both how
much of a reward someone deserves for the "work" they did
and whether rewards are evenly split between individuals.

35   Humans are an extremely social species. We are dependent
on each other and cannot survive and flourish without
interacting with others. Newborns only survive to adulthood if
given enough care, and societies succeed through cooperation.
Almost all of our actions and thoughts are about others or are

40   in response to others. We cooperate with and help people who
are not related to us at a level that is unmatched in the animal
kingdom.[1] Since humans are, by nature, both helpful and
selfish, we think that morality evolved to support our helpful
social interactions with others and control our somewhat

45   selfish tendencies.

       However, it would be misleading to see morality as only
a result of evolution. Although some human traits, like skin
color, are determined by our genes alone, morality is quite

My Thoughts

_____

_____

_____

_____

_____

_____

_____

_____

_____

_____

_____

_____

_____

_____

_____

_____

_____

_____

_____

_____

_____

_____

_____

[1] Tomasello, M., and Vaish, A. 2013. *Origins of human cooperation and morality.* Annu. Rev. Psychol.
64:231–55. doi: 10.1146/annurev-psych-113011-143812

different in that it is also determined both by our nature and
50 the society in which we live. Many moral rules and values vary
between different cultures and also change over time. For
instance, bull fighting is seen as a cruel form of entertainment
or even as animal torture in North America and most European
countries, but it is still very popular in Spain and Colombia
55 where it is considered a form of expression, despite the
obvious suffering of the animals. An example of a shift in
morality over time is our attitude toward slavery. Most people
in the world today think that it is immoral to own slaves but
that was not the case a century ago.

60   Thus, our morality has been formed over thousands of
years from the combination of both our genes and our culture,
rather than just one or the other. This genetic and cultural
evolution has shaped our brains to care for others, react to
those who try to harm us, and to create moral rules that help
65 us to live together successfully.[2]

        There are three main lines of evidence that support the
view that our brains are wired for morality. (1) The "building
blocks" of morality have been observed in non-human animals,
(2) even very young babies appear to exhibit some **basic
70 moral evaluations**, and (3) the parts of the brain involved in
moral judgments are beginning to be identified.

CITATION: Decety J and Cowell J (2016) Our Brains are Wired for Morality: Evolution,
Development, and Neuroscience. Front Young Minds. 4:3.
doi: 10.3389/frym.2016.00003
Copyright © 2016 Decety and Cowell

[2] Decety, J., and Wheatley, T. 2015. *The Moral Brain: A Multidisciplinary Perspective*. Cambridge: MIT
Press.

basic moral evaluations: considered to be an early form leading to mature morality in babies and
involves basic appraisals of the social interactions of others

---

My Thoughts

FIRST RESPONSE: KEY IDEAS AND DETAILS

Based on your first read of the article, what do the authors believe about the way people make moral decisions? Write your answer in your journal. Share your answer with a partner.

TECH-CONNECT

Post your response on your class website, according to your teacher's instructions, or tweet it to your teacher.

Focus on Summarizing a Text

A good summary explains the key ideas in an article without repeating the entire article. Writing a summary is a little like packing a suitcase. You can't include everything you want to, so you have to decide what's the most important. Sometimes it isn't easy!

When summarizing, use the following guidelines:

- Be objective. Do not include your personal opinions.

- Include only essential information. If you remove the information and it doesn't change the passage's overall meaning, it is probably not essential.

- Use your own words to retell the central idea.

You identified sentences containing key ideas during the First Read, so let's pack the summary suitcase. In the left-hand box below, write the sentences with the most important ideas you underlined during the First Read. In the "suitcase" on the right, rewrite these sentences in your own words. Not every key idea will fit. Remember to be objective, restating what the author says without changing the meaning.

Key Ideas	My Summary
1. An obvious answer is that we have learned to do so through socialization, that is, our behaviors were shaped from birth onward by our families, our preschools, and almost everything we contacted in our environments. 2.	

Key Ideas	My Summary
3.	
4.	
5.	
6.	

⌐Write Based on the graphic organizer on the previous page, write a summary of the article. Your summary should include the authors' beliefs about the source of morality. Here are some sentence frames to help you get started. Use specific evidence from the article in your answers.

- In "Our Brains Are Wired for Morality," the authors describe . . . .
- They state that morality is shaped by . . . .
- But they believe it is also . . . .
- They support this position by referring to . . . .

CONNECT TO ESSENTIAL QUESTION

Criminals receive jail sentences based on the severity of their crimes. How do you decide which wrong acts are worse than others? Or what a fitting punishment is?

⌐Second Read: Understanding Technical Terms

Objective: Read the article a second time with a partner, taking turns reading paragraphs. Circle words and phrases that are confusing or unfamiliar. Underline context clues that help you infer the meaning of these unfamiliar or unclear terms.

Focus on Understanding Technical Terms

This article includes many scientific terms. Articles about scientific or historical topics often include technical terms that are important to understand the topic. Sometimes an article includes footnotes that define key terms. Always use this feature when reading challenging texts with technical terms.

One way to figure out the meaning of unfamiliar words and phrases is to use context clues. Context clues are the words and phrases that surround the unfamiliar word. Context clues have four main types:

Synonym: another word or phrase has a similar meaning to the unfamiliar word.

> The frigid wind slipped through the gaps in the makeshift shelter, making an *icy* current of air swirl around our feet.

Antonym: another word or phrase has an opposite or contrasting meaning to the unfamiliar word.

> The new tiger at the zoo was wary of emerging from the den at first, but she soon became more *trusting* of her surroundings.

Inference: the word's meaning is not directly stated but can be figured out by the context.

> The castaway's *gaunt, skeletal frame* and *lack of energy* showed him on the brink of starvation.

Definition: the unfamiliar word is defined in the sentence (or in a nearby sentence).

A <u>speedometer</u>, *an instrument for measuring a vehicle's speed,* comes standard in vehicles today, and the idea of measuring speed has been around since early Romans estimated their speed and distance by marking the wheels of their chariots and counting the revolutions.

REFLECT

What is your earliest memory of knowing you did something wrong?

Fill in the following table, first with your own definition and then confirm the definition by checking a dictionary. At the bottom, use the blank spaces for any words or phrases you identified in the article that are not listed in the table.

Word(s)	What I think it means from the context and my background knowledge	Dictionary definition
morality		
tendencies		
culture		
genetic		

☾Speak and Listen Share your answers to the definitions chart with a partner. Discuss the following questions:

1. Which word or phrase is most important to understanding the passage's key ideas? Why?
2. Why would the authors be interested in whether morality has evolved or is cultural?

TECH-CONNECT

Search online for one of the words used in the passage. Click on three links for websites and notice how the word is used in context. Add this new information to your knowledge of how to use the unfamiliar word.

▶Third Read: Identifying Claims, Reasons, and Evidence

The authors state, "There are three main lines of evidence that support the view that our brains are wired for morality." This sentence explains what the authors intend to prove: that morality is built into the brain. During this read, you will read another excerpt from the same article.

Objective: Reread the final paragraph of the first excerpt on page 12. Then read the three headers from the article below. How do the headers help you understand and predict what this article is about? As you read, think about the following questions:

- What reasons do the authors give to support the ideas that "our brains are wired for morality"?

- What evidence do they use to support their reasons?

Underline sentences that state the authors' reasons that support their central claim. Then double underline sentences that provide evidence to support the reasons.

excerpt

Our Brains Are Wired for Morality: Evolution, Development, and Neuroscience
by Jean Decety and Jason M. Cowell

My Thoughts

1 **Building Blocks of Morality in Non-Human Species**

   Natural observations of animals in the wild and research

   in laboratories show us that a number of "building blocks"

   of moral behavior can be found in animals. For instance,

5 many animals exhibit behaviors that benefit other members

   of their species. Such prosocial behaviors (meaning behaviors

   that are good for others), like helping each other and caring

for offspring, have been seen in rodents and primates. Rats
will help other distressed rats that have been soaked with
10 water, and [they] will also choose to help a cage mate that is
in distress before obtaining a food reward. Chimpanzees will
help each other and share with each other, but only when they
benefit from the sharing, as long as the costs are minimal and
the needs of the other chimpanzees are clear. Chimpanzees
15 also collaborate and form alliances in fights or when hunting.
Capuchin monkeys have even been shown to react in a negative
way when they see other monkeys being treated unfairly. . . .

Evidence for Moral Behavior in Babies

When we see early signs of morality in young babies,
20 this provides strong evidence for the evolutionary roots of
morality, because babies have not yet had much time to be
influenced by their environment. Psychologists who study
human development have shown that human babies enter
the world ready to pay attention and respond to social stimuli,
25 such as voices and faces, and that babies begin forming social
relationships during the first year of life. Young children
provide comfort and assistance to both other children and
adults in emotional distress. For instance, when they see their
mothers in pain, 18-month-old toddlers show comforting
30 behaviors (such as hugging, patting, and sharing toys). As
infants develop and become more able to analyze what is
going on around them, they even have the ability to recognize
when a person in their environment is treating another person
badly. At a young age, infants are quickly able to figure
35 out whether the consequence of a behavior is good or bad,
suggesting that their genes are involved and that experience
and learning are not the only causes of moral development. . . .

My Thoughts

The Role of The Brain in Morality

. . . An area of the brain called the ventromedial prefrontal

40 cortex has been found to be important for certain aspects of

human morality. If this brain region is damaged early in life

(before 5 years of age), the person is more likely to break

moral rules or inflict harm on others, suggesting that the

ventromedial prefrontal cortex helps us to understand what

45 is and is not moral. Patients who have damage to this brain

region or who have had it removed also tend to experience

less **empathy**, embarrassment, and guilt than people without

damage to this region.

---

empathy: the ability to understand others' feelings

Focus on Identifying Claims, Reasons, and Evidence

A claim is a statement or assertion that something is true. A claim is based on an opinion and is sometimes directly stated and other times must be inferred. Authors support their claims with reasons that explain why their opinion is valid. Reasons should be "sound." This means that the reasons are logical. They fit with the claim being made.

In a strong argument, reasons are then supported by evidence. Evidence includes facts (statistics or data) and opinions and testimony from experts. Evidence should be relevant and sufficient. *Relevant* means the evidence is clearly connected to the reason. *Sufficient* means there is enough evidence to prove that the claim is true.

Fill in the chart below. The reasons are listed. Fill in the evidence from the article.

> **CONNECT TO ESSENTIAL QUESTION**
>
> How do expectations for understanding right from wrong change with age?

Claim: Our brains are wired for morality.	
Reasons	**Evidence**
1. The "building blocks" of morality have been observed in non-human animals.	• Rats help other rats that have been soaked with water. • •

continued on next page

| Claim: Our brains are wired for morality. ||
Reasons	Evidence
2. Even very young babies appear to exhibit some basic moral evaluations.	• • •
3. The parts of the brain involved in moral judgments are beginning to be identified.	• • •

(Speak and Listen With a partner, share your answers to the claims and evidence chart. Use the following questions in your discussion.

1. Which reasons have the strongest evidence?
2. Does some evidence seem weaker than other evidence? Identify the strongest evidence.
3. What evidence do you think could have been added to strengthen a particular reason?

If you add or change information in your chart based on your discussion, use a different color pen or pencil.

Language: Prefixes, Suffixes, and Root Words

Earlier in the chapter, you learned about using context clues to determine word meanings. Another way to figure out unfamiliar word meanings is to analyze word parts and their meanings.

A root word is the base word. It contains the basic meaning of the word. A prefix is a word part added to the beginning of a word that changes its meaning. A suffix is a word part added to the end of a word that changes its meaning. Knowing what common prefixes and suffixes mean can help you figure out a word's meaning.

Look at the charts below to become familiar with a few common roots, prefixes, and suffixes.

Root	Meaning	Example
aqua	water	aquarium
bio	life	biography
gen	birth, kind	generate, genre
graph	writing	graphic
hydr	water	hydrate
luc	light	translucent
log/logue	word, study	dialogue, biology
omni	all	omniscient
phil	love	philanthropy
struct	build	construct
vid/vis	see	video, visual

Prefix	Meaning	Example
auto-	self	autobiography
co-	joint, together with others	cooperate
dis-	not, none	disinterest
mis-	wrongly	misspeak
sub-	under, below	submarine
un-, non-	not, opposite of	unbelievable, nonsense

Suffix	Meaning	Example
-able	capable of	achievable
-al	relating to or characterized by	three-dimensional
-ic	having characteristics of	Celtic
-ion	act or process, condition	calculation
-ology	study of	geology

continued on next page

Read these sentences from the article and use the information in the charts to determine the word meanings.

1. Chimpanzees also <u>collaborate</u> and form alliances in fights or when hunting.

2. The "building blocks" of morality have been observed in <u>non-human</u> animals.

3. This genetic and cultural <u>evolution</u> has shaped our brains to care for others, react to those who try to harm us, and to create moral rules that help us to live together successfully.

4. Indeed, observations made by scientists who study different societies around the world have shown that, despite <u>cultural</u> and individual differences, all human beings have some sense of right and wrong.

Project-Based Assessments

Roundtable Discussion

Participate in a roundtable discussion on the following question, based on your reading of the chapter text.

> Is morality mostly learned from social interactions, or is it built into our genes?

In a roundtable discussion, all students are equal and everyone participates. Arrange your seats in a circle so that all participants can see one another. The teacher or a discussion leader may sit in the middle. Come to the discussion with an open mind and be prepared for a challenge! You will be evaluated on the following:

Expectations for Discussion	
Listening	**Speaking**
Listen respectfully.	Speak at least two times.
Look at speaker.	Ask questions.
Follow text references.	Explain and give reasons to support your opinion.
Take notes on what the speaker is saying.	Refer to the text to support conclusions.
Write follow-up questions.	Use a tone of voice and language appropriate for an open exchange of ideas.
Reflect on what others say and be open to changing your mind based on new evidence.	Invite comment.

As you participate in the discussion, you will need to support your conclusions with details from the passage. In your response journal, create the following chart to refer to during the discussion.

Detail from the text	How it supports your opinion

Instructions for a Roundtable Discussion

1. The discussion leader (or teacher) begins by asking the following question:

> Is morality mostly learned from social interactions or is it built into our genes?

2. Allow each member a chance to reply to the question.

3. Take notes on comments you disagree with or have questions about. Record what was said and who said it.

4. Go around the circle again and allow everyone to ask a follow-up question or make a comment. Questions should be directed to the person who made the original comment. Try phrasing your questions and comments in this way:

   • Explain what you mean by . . . .

   • I agree/disagree with ____ because . . . .

   • Why do you think . . . .?

5. Close the discussion by having everyone respond to the following question:

> Which aspects of morality seem to be inborn, and which ones are learned?

REFLECT

Why do people sometimes do the wrong thing even when they know it is wrong?

Use the following guidelines for your roundtable discussion.	
To receive the highest score, the discussion must meet all of these criteria.	During the discussion, you should • listen carefully when others are speaking and make notes about what they say. • offer thoughtful feedback and encourage everyone to participate. • share reasonable opinions and support your opinion with examples from the text. • demonstrate an understanding of the text. • speak to the question or point in a clear, concise manner.

Argumentative Essay

Write an essay in which you argue whether humans are by nature more or less moral than animals.

Use these steps to help you:

1. Write a central idea statement that includes your claim about whether humans are more or less moral than animals.

2. Develop an outline to organize your main reasons to support your claim. Include direct quotations and evidence from the article.

3. Write your essay. Include an introduction and conclusion.

4. Ask two classmates to read your essay and give feedback. Revise your essay based on their suggestions.

5. Check your essay for mistakes in grammar, usage, spelling, and punctuation.

Use the following guidelines for your argumentative essay.	
To receive the highest score, the discussion must meet all of these criteria.	Your argumentative essay • makes a claim about whether humans are by nature more or less moral than animals. • supports the claim with more than one reason. • includes support in the form of direct quotations and evidence from the article. • includes an introduction and a conclusion. • is clearly organized with good transitions between sentences and paragraphs. • uses correct grammar, word usage, punctuation, and spelling.

On Your Own: Integrating Ideas

1. Experts in morality often talk about the "trolley problem." Imagine this situation: A runaway trolley, or train, is about to hit five people who are stuck on the tracks. You are standing nearby. You can pull a lever that will switch the tracks so the trolley changes direction. But if the trolley switches tracks, it will hit a single person. Is it morally acceptable to pull the lever in order to save the five people? What if you have to push a single person in front of the trolley to stop it? Discuss the trolley problem with a small group.

2. The question of whether morality is more built-in or learned is only one example of a larger question in science. The debate is often called "nature versus nurture." Watch the About.com video "What Is Nature Vs. Nurture?" on YouTube and discuss it with friends or family members.

Connect to Testing

In this chapter, you practiced summarizing a text; determining word meanings from context; and analyzing claims, reasons, and evidence in an argument. When you take assessments, you will be tested on these skills. Answer the following questions.

1. **Part A:** Read this sentence from the text. Then answer the question that follows.

> Psychologists who study human development have shown that human babies enter the world ready to pay attention and respond to social <u>stimuli</u>, such as voices and faces, and that babies begin forming social relationships during the first year of life.

What is the meaning of *stimuli* as it is used in the text?

A. things that are seen or heard

B. rules that govern behavior

C. parents or other caretakers

D. method of decision-making

Part B: Which words or phrases from the text in Part A best help the reader understand the meaning of the word *stimuli*?

A. *Psychologists who study human development*

B. *ready to pay attention*

C. *begin forming social relationships*

D. *such as voices and faces*

EXPLANATION

Part A: Choices B and D are incorrect because the sentence makes no mention of moral rules.

Study the other answer choices. Choice C seems plausible, but choice A fits better with the context clue *such as voices and faces*.

Part B: The phrase *such as voices and faces* suggests that babies respond to sounds and images. The best answer is choice D.

2. **Part A:** Which of the following best summarizes the central claim of the text in this chapter?

   A. Morality is an inner sense of right and wrong.

   B. Humans are an extremely social species.

   C. Morality evolved to support social behaviors.

   D. The human brain is set up to understand right and wrong.

   Part B: Provide two examples of textual evidence to support your answer to Part A.

3. Which of the following quotations is evidence used by the authors to support the central claim of the article?

   A. *How we feel, think, and act about the concepts of "good" and "bad" are all parts of our morality.*

   B. *For instance, bull fighting is seen as cruel form of entertainment or even as animal torture in North America and most European countries, but it is still very popular in Spain and Colombia . . .*

   C. *This genetic and cultural evolution has shaped our brains to care for others, react to those who try to harm us, and to create moral rules that help us to live together successfully.*

   D. *For instance, when they see their mothers in pain, 18-month-old toddlers show comforting behaviors (such as hugging, patting, and sharing toys).*

4. Read the following paragraph from the excerpt in the chapter. Then answer the questions that follow.

      However, it would be misleading to see morality as only a result of evolution. Although some human traits, like skin color, are determined by our genes alone, morality is quite different in that it is also determined both by our nature and the society in which we live. Many moral rules and values vary between different cultures and also change over time. For instance, bull fighting is seen as a cruel form of entertainment or even as animal torture in North America and most European countries, but it is

continued on next page

still very popular in Spain and Colombia where it is considered a form of expression, despite the obvious suffering of the animals. An example of a shift in morality over time is our attitude toward slavery. Most people in the world today think that it is immoral to own slaves but that was not the case a century ago.

Part A: What is the key idea of this paragraph?

A. Some people argue that morality is purely genetic, but the authors disagree.

B. Humans are naturally moral, but cultures decide what behavior is moral.

C. Some cultures are more moral than others, and cultures become more moral over time.

D. The way a culture treats animals is key to understanding the culture's morality.

Part B: Which of the following provides the best evidence for the answer to Part A?

A. *morality is quite different in that it is also determined both by our nature and the society in which we live.*

B. *For instance, bull fighting is seen as a cruel form of entertainment or even as animal torture in North America and most European countries*

C. *An example of a shift in morality over time is our attitude toward slavery.*

D. *Most people in the world today think that it is immoral to own slaves but that was not the case a century ago.*

5. Read this sentence from the text. Then answer the question that follows.

Since humans are, by nature, both helpful and selfish, we think that morality evolved to support our helpful social <u>interactions</u> with others and control our somewhat selfish tendencies.

Part A: What is the meaning of *interactions* as it is used in the text?

A. relations

B. difficulties

C. rules

D. benefits

Part B: Which of the following provides the best evidence for the answer to Part A? Choose two.

A. *by nature*

B. *morality evolved to support*

C. *helpful social*

D. *with others*

E. *somewhat selfish tendencies*

Chapter 2

Analyzing Theme Through Story Elements

Preview Concepts

Conflict is the struggle the characters in a story must overcome. Conflict makes a story interesting, moves the plot, adds suspense, and reveals the true personalities of the characters.

With a partner, study the following types of conflict found in stories. Then identify examples of this conflict from books or stories you have read. If you have studied other types of conflict, add them to the first row.

Main Types of Conflict in a Story	
person vs. person	Harry Potter vs. Voldemort
person vs. nature	
person vs. self	

CHAPTER GOALS

In this chapter you will

- analyze how conflicts interact in the story.
- identify the theme of a story.
- understand the point of view of a character in a story.
- rewrite a story from a different point of view.

PREVIEW ACADEMIC VOCABULARY

conflict

first-person point of view

narrator

point of view

theme

third-person limited point of view

third-person omniscient point of view

Making Connections

Read the following story.

Once there ruled in the distant city of Wirani a king who was both mighty and wise. And he was feared for his might and loved for his wisdom.

One night when all were asleep, a witch entered the city, and poured seven drops of strange liquid into the city well, and said, "From this hour he who drinks this water shall become mad."

Next morning all the inhabitants, save the king and his lord **chamberlain**, drank from the well and became mad, even as the witch had foretold. The people in the narrow streets and in the market places began to whisper to one another, "The king is mad. Our king and his lord chamberlain have lost their reason. Surely we cannot be ruled by a mad king. We must dethrone him."

That evening the king drank from a goblet full of water from the well. He gave it to his lord chamberlain to drink as well.

And there was great rejoicing in that distant city of Wirani, because its king and its lord chamberlain had regained their reason.

—"The Wise King" by Kahlil Gibran

---

chamberlain: a manager of a royal household

With a partner or small group, answer the following questions.

1. What is the conflict in the story?

2. How is the conflict resolved?

3. What is the king like? How does his reaction to the conflict reveal his character?

MAKING
CONNECTIONS
_____

In this chapter you will analyze conflicts in a story to understand its theme.

4. Use your answers to questions 1–3 to write an explanation of the theme.

First Read: Analyzing Plot and Conflict

Leo Tolstoy was a Russian author who is best known for his complex and sprawling novels *War and Peace* (1869) and *Anna Karenina* (1877) that explore truth and morality. Today Tolstoy is still considered one of the greatest writers of all time. In this story, a king longs to make good decisions so he asks the advice of a hermit.

Objective: As you read, think about how the actions of the characters move the plot forward. Draw arrows in the text from an action that results in a reaction.

excerpt
Three Questions
by Leo Tolstoy
translated by L. and A. Maude

	My Thoughts

1   When the King approached, the **hermit** was digging the ground in front of his hut. Seeing the King, he greeted him and went on digging. The hermit was frail and weak, and each time he stuck his spade into the ground and turned a little

5   earth, he breathed heavily.

     The King went up to him and said: "I have come to you, wise hermit, to ask you to answer three questions: How can I learn to do the right thing at the right time? Who are the people I most need, and to whom should I, therefore, pay

10   more attention than to the rest? And, what **affairs** are the most important, and need my first attention?"

     The hermit listened to the King, but answered nothing. He just spat on his hand and recommenced digging.

     "You are tired," said the King, "let me take the spade and

15   work awhile for you."

     "Thanks!" said the hermit, and, giving the spade to the King, he sat down on the ground.

     When he had dug two beds, the King stopped and

---

hermit: one that retires from society and lives in solitude especially for religious reasons
affairs: matters of concern

20 repeated his questions. The hermit again gave no answer, but rose, stretched out his hand for the spade, and said:

"Now rest awhile—and let me work a bit."

But the King did not give him the spade, and continued to dig. One hour passed, and another. The sun began to sink behind the trees, and the King at last stuck the spade into the

25 ground, and said:

"I came to you, wise man, for an answer to my questions. If you can give me none, tell me so, and I will return home."

"Here comes someone running," said the hermit, "let us see who it is."

30 The King turned round, and saw a bearded man come running out of the wood. The man held his hands pressed against his stomach, and blood was flowing from under them. When he reached the King, he fell fainting on the ground moaning feebly. The King and the hermit unfastened the

35 man's clothing. There was a large wound in his stomach. The King washed it as best he could, and bandaged it with his handkerchief and with a towel the hermit had . . . So the King, with the hermit's help, carried the wounded man into the hut and laid him on the bed. Lying on the bed the man closed his

40 eyes and was quiet; but the King was so tired with his walk and with the work he had done, that he crouched down on the threshold, and also fell asleep. . .

"Forgive me!" said the bearded man in a weak voice, when he saw that the King was awake and was looking at him.

45 "I do not know you, and have nothing to forgive you for," said the King.

"You do not know me, but I know you. I am that enemy of yours who swore to revenge himself on you, because you

My Thoughts

_____
_____
_____
_____
_____
_____
_____
_____
_____
_____
_____
_____
_____
_____
_____
_____
_____
_____
_____
_____
_____
_____
_____
_____
_____

executed his brother and seized his property. I knew you had

50 gone alone to see the hermit, and I resolved to kill you on

your way back. But the day passed and you did not return.

So I came out from my ambush to find you, and I came upon

your bodyguard, and they recognized me, and wounded me. I

escaped from them, but should have bled to death had you not

55 dressed my wound. I wished to kill you, and you have saved my

life. Now, if I live, and if you wish it, I will serve you as your most

faithful slave, and will bid my sons do the same. Forgive me!"

The King was very glad to have made peace with his enemy

so easily, and to have gained him for a friend . . .

60 Having taken leave of the wounded man, the King went

out into the porch and looked around for the hermit. Before

going away he wished once more to beg an answer to the

questions he had put. The hermit was outside, on his knees,

sowing seeds in the beds that had been dug the day before.

65 The King approached him, and said:

"For the last time, I pray you to answer my questions, wise

man."

"You have already been answered!" said the hermit, still

crouching on his thin legs, and looking up at the King, who

70 stood before him.

"How answered? What do you mean?" asked the King.

"Do you not see," replied the hermit. "If you had not

pitied my weakness yesterday, and had not dug those beds for

me, but had gone your way, that man would have attacked

75 you, and you would have repented of not having stayed with

me. So the most important time was when you were digging

the beds; and I was the most important man; and to do me

good was your most important business. Afterwards when that

My Thoughts

man ran to us, the most important time was when you were
80 attending to him, for if you had not bound up his wounds he
would have died without having made peace with you. So he
was the most important man, and what you did for him was
your most important business. Remember then: there is only
one time that is important—Now! It is the most important time
85 because it is the only time when we have any power. The most
necessary man is he with whom you are, for no man knows
whether he will ever have dealings with anyone else: and the
most important affair is, to do him good, because for that
purpose alone was man sent into this life!"

My Thoughts

_____

_____

_____

_____

_____

_____

_____

FIRST RESPONSE: KEY IDEAS AND DETAILS

What is the story mainly about? What further questions do you
have after reading? Write your answers and questions in your
response journal. Share your answer with a partner.

TECH-CONNECT

Post your response
on your class website,
according to your
teacher's instructions,
or text or tweet it to
your teacher.

Focus on Analyzing Plot and Conflict

Stories have different elements, including character, plot,
conflict, and setting. These story elements work together to create
the central idea, or in literature, the theme. Plot is often a series
of actions and reactions. One event causes a second event, which
results in another event and on it goes.

Fill in the following graphic organizer with the king and hermit's
actions and reactions during the story. The first action is done for you.

King's Action/Reaction	Hermit's Action/Reaction
1. The king asks the hermit three questions.	2.
3.	4.
5.	6.

King's Action/Reaction	Hermit's Action/Reaction
7.	8.
9.	10.

Conflict is important to a story because it moves the plot forward and adds suspense to the story. To understand conflict in a story, ask: What is the character(s) struggling with? Many times there is more than one conflict.

CONNECT TO ESSENTIAL QUESTION

Is seeking revenge a justified action?

Conflicts in the story	Type of conflict (person v. person, person v. self, person v. nature)	Resolution
1.		
2.		
3.		

Speak and Listen Share your answers to the conflict chart with a partner. Then answer the following question:

How do the different conflicts interact? For example, how does the resolution of the king's conflict with his enemy impact the resolution of the other conflicts in the story? How does the conflict create suspense?

REFLECT

When you need advice, to whom do you go?

Second Read: Identifying Theme

Read the story a second time or listen as your teacher reads it aloud.

Objective: Think about how the plot reveals the theme. Underline lines from the text that reveal the theme. Write two or three questions you have in the My Thoughts column.

Focus on Identifying Theme

Identifying theme leads to a deeper understanding of literature. Study the following explanation of a theme.

What is theme?
Theme
• is the central idea of a story, poem, or other piece of writing.
• is stated as a sentence that expresses a general, universal truth explored by the author.
• is usually inferred rather than directly stated.
Theme is NOT
• the topic. Examples: love, friendship, war.
• a summary of what happens.
• the purpose.
• the moral.
• the conflict or problem.

Use these steps to determine theme:
1. Summarize the plot, paraphrasing the events in logical order. Write a short description of the events in the story.
2. Identify the conflicts in the story, including the central problem or obstacle the main character is trying to overcome. How do the conflicts resolve?
3. Consider how the main character changes. The theme is often revealed through changes in the main character. Consider what lesson the main character learned or how his or her thinking about life changed.
4. Look for repeated ideas throughout the passage.

Remember, all of the above must be supported by evidence from the text. Longer stories, poems, and novels may have more than one theme.

Fill in the chart below to help you identify the theme in the passage. Some sentence starters are included for you.

Steps to finding theme	Your response
1. Summarize the plot. Write a short description of the events in the story from beginning to end.	
2. Identify the conflicts. (See your answers to the First Read.) What central problem or obstacle is the king trying to overcome? How does the conflict resolve?	
3. Does the king change or grow throughout the story?	
4. What repeated words or ideas do you see?	
Review your responses to 1–4 above. Then finish the following sentence: The theme of "Three Questions" is	

(Speak and Listen Share your theme statements with a partner. Are your statements similar or different? Respectfully explain reasons for your answer. Be open to changing your theme statement based upon your partner's evidence.

Third Read: Understanding Point of View

Objective: Read through the story again. Think about how the characters view each other.

Focus on Understanding Point of View

In literature the term *point of view* can have multiple meanings.

First, point of view is the perspective from which a story or poem is told. The story in this chapter is told from a third-person point of view, so readers learn about the characters and events from a narrator outside the story.

The chart below identifies common points of view used in literature along with the related pronouns so you can tell which point of view is being used in a story or poem.

Point of view	Pronouns used
First person—narrator is a character in the story	*I, my, mine*
Second person	*you, your*

Third person
 	
    limited—narrator is outside the story but only reveals the thoughts of a single character
 	
    omniscient—narrator reveals the thoughts of multiple characters
	he, she, him, her, it, hers, they

The second meaning of point of view refers to the opinion or perspective of a character in a story. Readers infer the characters' points of view based on what they say and do and how they respond to other characters in the story.

In the story in this chapter, the events and interactions revolve around the king and the hermit. Complete the graphic organizer below to analyze how the hermit views the king.

The hermit's speech or action(s)	What it shows about how the hermit feels about the king
Seeing the King, he greeted him and went on digging.	

The hermit's speech or action(s)	What it shows about how the hermit feels about the king
The hermit listened to the King, but answered nothing. He just spat on his hand and recommenced digging.	
"Thanks!" said the hermit, and, giving the spade to the King, he sat down on the ground.	
"Do you not see," replied the hermit. "If you had not pitied my weakness yesterday, and had not dug those beds for me, but had gone your way, that man would have attacked you, and you would have repented of not having stayed with me.	

Speak and Listen Refer to your answers in the chart, and discuss the following questions with a partner:

- Does the hermit's view of the king change during the story?
- Why does the hermit finally answer the king's questions?

Write Following your discussion, write a paragraph answering the questions above.

REFLECT

What response would you give to the king's questions?

Language: Using Commas To Set Off Nonrestrictive Phrases and Clauses

Restrictive (or essential) phrases or clauses are necessary to understand the meaning of a sentence. They are not set off from the rest of the sentence by commas and often begin with the words *that* or *who*.

The man <u>who came running out of the trees with a large wound</u> was the King's enemy.

continued on next page

Nonrestrictive (or nonessential) phrases or clauses can be taken out of the sentence without affecting its meaning. Nonrestrictive elements should be set off by commas. Read this sentence that has a nonrestrictive element set off by commas.

> The King, puzzled by the hermit's silence, kept digging with the spade.

A clause is nonrestrictive/nonessential if it can be removed from the sentence without changing the basic meaning of the sentence.

Here are some examples of sentences with restrictive and nonrestrictive elements.

> **Restrictive:** A story that was written about King Arthur won first prize.
> **Nonrestrictive:** King Arthur, whose adventures were many, may have actually lived during the Dark Ages.

> **Restrictive:** Early medieval monarchs were rulers who were responsible for their people's protection.
> **Nonrestrictive:** Early medieval monarchs, who came to power through various means, were responsible for their people's protection.

> **Restrictive:** The girl who played the part of Joan of Arc is Amir's sister.
> **Nonrestrictive:** Joan, who is reading a book about Robin Hood, enjoys legends.

Read the following sentences, inserting commas where appropriate. Write correct next to sentences that are correctly punctuated.

1. A hermit is a person who chooses to live alone.

2. In early Christian times a person who lived apart from society in order to focus on his/her devotion to God was a hermit.

3. The ancient castle which has never been found might be a legend.

4. Rahul who wants to be an archaeologist wrote about the search for Camelot

5. The grave discovered by the lost tourists did not contain the body of King Arthur.

Project-Based Assessments

Change the Point of View

Three Questions is told from an outside narrator's point of view. Rewrite the story from another character's perspective, using first-person point of view. Make sure the characters are true to their descriptions in the text. Before you begin, think about how the characters interact. Consider how they feel about the events in the story and each other. Follow these steps:

- Add a character's inner thoughts and feelings where appropriate.

- Make sure the main events of the story remain. Stay true to the characters' personalities and emotions. Think about what the king, the hermit, or the wounded man might be thinking when they interact with each other.

- Use the following rubric to guide your writing.

Use the following guidelines for your new point of view story.	
To receive the highest score (4.0), the story must meet all of these criteria.	Your story • is true to the plot, characters, and theme of the passage. • is clearly organized and easy to follow. • uses a variety of sentence types and lengths and has engaging and interesting writing. • contains specific words, creating details that draw the reader into the story. • uses correct grammar, spelling, and punctuation.

In groups of three or four, conduct a peer review of your paragraphs. Follow these steps.

Steps for Peer Review

1. Select a timekeeper. Stick to the time. Each writer gets five minutes.

2. One person begins by reading aloud his or her story while other group members listen.

3. Pause. The same reader reads the story aloud a second time. (Don't skip this step.)

4. The group members listen and write notes or comments.

5. The writer asks, "What part was most clear to you?" Each member responds. Writer jots notes on the draft.

6. The writer asks, "Was there any part that confused you?" Each member responds. Writer jots notes on the draft.

7. Go to the next member in the group and repeat steps 2-6.

As soon as possible after the peer review, make any necessary revisions. Make sure to use proper grammar, punctuation, and spelling.

On Your Own: Integrating Ideas

1. Read more of Leo Tolstoy's stories by searching for his name online at gutenberg.org.

2. Read a children's book *Three Questions* by Jon J. Muth. Think about how the author transforms the story for the intended audience. You can also find a video of someone reading the book on YouTube.

3. Leo Tolstoy wrote, "Happy families are all alike; every unhappy family is unhappy in its own way." Do you agree or disagree? Go to ted.com and watch a TED talk by Robert Waldinger about a study on happiness done by Harvard researchers.

Leo Tolstoy telling a story to his grandchildren.

Connect to Testing

In this chapter, you analyzed story elements, such as conflict, plot, theme, and point of view, and how they interact. When you take assessments, you will be tested on these skills. Answer the following questions.

1. **Part A:** Which statement best expresses a theme of the text?

   A. Treat others well.

   B. Be alert at all times.

   C. Stay close to enemies.

   D. Seek forgiveness.

EXPLANATION

You can eliminate choice B because it has no support in the passage.

Choice C is incorrect because although the passage features the wounded man as an enemy, the king was unaware of this fact when he was bandaging him, so this incident in the passage does not relate to keeping enemies close.

Choice D seems possible since the bearded man asks the king's forgiveness and receives it, but the idea of forgiveness is only found in this one interaction, so there is little textual support for it. Also, the king himself is seeking knowledge, not forgiveness.

Choice A is the best answer because the idea of treating others well is found throughout the passage.

Part B: Support your answer to Part A with at least two details from the text.

2. The king's three questions in the passage reveal his

    A. doubt in his own judgment.

    B. desperation to change his destiny.

    C. desire to make wise decisions.

    D. determination to leave a strong legacy.

3. Which is the best summary of this passage?

    A. A king discovers the value of knowledge by interacting with a hermit.

    B. A king learns a lesson in forgiveness when he visits a hermit's house.

    C. A king learns a lesson about making wise decisions by visiting a hermit.

    D. A king discards his royal rank and helps a hermit with manual tasks.

4. **Part A:** In the excerpt, for what did the king forgive the wounded man?

Part B: Explain the answer to Part A using evidence from the text.

5. Read this paragraph from the text. Then answer the question that follows.

"Do you not see," replied the hermit. "If you had not pitied my weakness yesterday, and had not dug those beds for me, but had gone your way, that man would have attacked you, and you would have repented of not having stayed with me. So the most important time was when you were digging the beds; and I was the most important man; and to do me good was your most important business. Afterwards when that man ran to us, the most important time was when you were attending to him, for if you had not bound up his wounds he would have died without having made peace with you. So he was the most important man, and what you did for him was your most important business. Remember then: there is only one time that is important—Now! It is the most important time because it is the only time when we have any power. The most necessary man is he with whom you are, for no man knows whether he will ever have dealings with anyone else: and the most important affair is, to do him good, because for that purpose alone was man sent into this life!"

What theme does the author convey in this paragraph? Cite two pieces of textual evidence to support your answer.

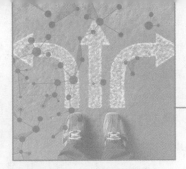

Chapter 3

Understanding Point of View Through Inferences

Preview Concepts

Think about the last time you visited a zoo. Then answer the following questions.

1. Describe the animal enclosures. Were they cages with bars or spaces that imitate the animals' native habitats?

2. Did the animals seem content and happy?

3. Have you ever been to a zoo or petting zoo where the animals did not seem healthy or happy? Describe your experience.

4. Based on your experiences, are zoos important and necessary in teaching the public about animals and protecting endangered animals from extinction, or should the animals be free to live out their lives in the wild?

Discuss your answers with a partner.

Making Connections

As you read the following passage, underline lines from the text that indicate the author's opinion about zoos.

> . . . . in Denmark, the human/animal role of zoos is already being reversed. At Zootopia, BIG, the architecture firm, designed a 300-acre zoo without bars, fences or glass, which it said makes for the "best possible and freest possible environment for the animals." The first phase is scheduled to open in 2019. It's not a preserve—as those who want zoos shut down have called for—but it is an advancement in how people think of holding captive animals. Zootopia's layout would let animals roam land that encircles a doughnut-hole observation center. And though people can walk through tunnels and poke their heads up for a closer look, in this design it's not dangerous animals like the silverback gorilla that are caged, it's the humans.
> —"Do We Need Zoos?" by J. Weston Phippen, *The Atlantic*

1. What is the author's point of view about zoos? What evidence supports your inference?

2. How would people who are against zoos feel about Zootopia? Support your inferences with evidence from the text.

MAKING CONNECTIONS

In this chapter you will read an informational article about zoos and infer the author's point of view.

3. How would people who support zoos feel about Zootopia? Support your inferences with evidence from the text.

Discuss your answers with a partner. Summarize your discussion in your response journal.

First Read: Making Inferences

In this article, the author details scenarios featuring zoo animals and asks readers to judge the morality of the actions of the people involved.

Objective: As you read, consider the question: Are the people's actions moral? Underline phrases or sentences in the text that describe how people treat animals. Write questions you have about the animals and their treatment in the My Thoughts column. Think about how the headers help you comprehend the ideas. Use them to make predications about the text.

excerpt
Zoo Complicated: Are Captive Animals Happy?
by Kathryn Hulick

My Thoughts

1 **Why Zoos?**

We keep animals in zoos or as pets for many reasons. Sometimes the motivation is to rescue an animal or a group of animals. Hawks that fly into windows, black bears that

5 roam through human towns, and harbor seals that swim into propellers often end up in zoos. Other times a species, such as the Asian elephant, is endangered in the wild. Zoo populations help ensure that these rare animals survive. We also keep animals in captivity because we enjoy seeing them

10 and spending time with them.

But do they enjoy spending time with us? Are they happy? Animals likely don't experience emotions the same way we do. But if you have a pet dog at home, you know the difference between a tail-wagging "happy" dog, and a tail-between-the-

15 legs "sad" dog. . . .

Conversations about the way animals should be treated are ongoing. Each of the following stories raises ethical questions. Read them and decide for yourself—did the people involved do the right thing?

Lucy

20   Lucy liked drinking tea and looking in the mirror. But she wasn't human—she was a chimpanzee. Maurice and Jane Temerlin raised Lucy just like a human baby. The chimpanzee began her life with the Temerlins as the subject of research but

25   soon became a daughter. Maurice, who was a psychotherapist, wanted to know how human Lucy would become. She learned sign language and seemed to truly care for her adoptive parents. In his book, *Lucy: Growing Up Human*, he wrote: "If Jane is distressed, Lucy notices it immediately and attempts to comfort

30   her by putting an arm about her, grooming her, or kissing her."

     When Lucy grew up, though, life became difficult for the Temerlin family. An adult chimpanzee is about five times stronger than an adult human, and Lucy got into everything. What's more, she could not live a full life in a human home.

35   Eventually, the human "parents" decided to send Lucy to live with other chimps in the wild. They found a nature reserve in the Gambia, a country in western Africa. Janis Carter, a student who had been helping take care of Lucy, went along to help the chimp adjust.

40   But Lucy didn't have a clue how to live in the wild, and her health suffered during the adjustment. Carter wound up staying with Lucy for years. She ate ants and leaves to show Lucy what to do. She even lived in a cage so Lucy and the other chimpanzees couldn't reach the human objects that distracted

45   them from normal activities like seeking food and shelter.

     Eventually, Lucy did start finding her own food, and Carter moved a short distance away. One year, Lucy went missing. Carter returned from a visit to the United States to join the search. She and members of the reserve staff found Lucy's

My Thoughts

50 body. The chimp had spent half her life in a human home and half in the wild.

Do you think it's right or wrong for people to raise chimps in their homes? What could the Temerlins have done differently?

55 . . .

Katina

Katina is a female killer whale, or orca, who lived in the ocean off the coast of Iceland until she was two years old. Now, she lives at SeaWorld in Orlando, Florida, where she
60 regularly performs for huge crowds of excited onlookers. She's easy to work with, knows many tricks, and has had seven calves. Her calf Kalina was the first healthy killer whale born in captivity. "[Katina] was one of the first animals I ever got in the water with," says John Jett, currently a marine mammal
65 scientist at Stetson University. For four years in the 1990s, he was a trainer at SeaWorld. Now, John Jett feels that it is morally wrong to keep killer whales in captivity. "It doesn't work out for the animals and it's never going to work out for the animals," he says. "I think you can put all the money into
70 bigger pools that you want but never recreate the ocean."

Jett explains that killer whales in captivity tend to experience social problems and health problems. For example, captive whales often chew on the concrete edges of their pools or the steel bars that separate different areas. As a result,
75 "most of their teeth are broken, missing, ground down, or drilled out," says Jett. The whales may also float near the top of the pool for long periods. As a result, they may end up with a sunburn or a flopped-over dorsal fin—a common sight on captive male killer whales. Wild whales' fins are almost always
80 straight.

Of course, life in the wild isn't perfect, either. In fact, a whale in captivity now has about the same chance of surviving the year as a whale in the wild. "Survival of killer whales in captivity has increased over the past 30 years," says

85 Doug DeMaster, Science and Research Director of the Alaska Fisheries Science Center. In addition, research with captive whales has added to our knowledge about their physiology and life history. On several occasions, scientists have used this knowledge to aid wild killer whales in trouble.

90 Jett concedes that parks such as SeaWorld have done some good for killer whales. "We no longer fear them," he says. "People have come to appreciate the need to protect them." However, he feels that the time has come to stop keeping Katina and other whales captive.

95 What do you think? Have you been to a show at SeaWorld or a similar park? Is there any way for these parks to make life more comfortable for killer whales?

My Thoughts

FIRST RESPONSE: KEY IDEAS AND DETAILS

Based upon your first read of the article, is life in captivity better for wild animals? Support your conclusion with details from the text. Write your answer in your journal.

TECH-CONNECT

Post your response on your class website or other online site, according to your teacher's instructions.

Focus on Making Inferences

Readers constantly make inferences as they read. An inference is a conclusion not directly stated in the text. It is based on ideas in the story and your own background knowledge. As you read the text, what did you infer about the relationship between captive animals and people? Fill in the chart below.

What the text says	Inference
1. *Maurice and Jane Temerlin raised Lucy just like a human baby.*	

continued on next page

What the text says	Inference
2. *She [Lucy] learned sign language and seemed to truly care for her adoptive parents.*	
3. *What's more, she [Lucy] could not live a full life in a human home.*	
4. *Carter wound up staying with Lucy for years. She ate ants and leaves to show Lucy what to do.*	
5. *She's [Katina] easy to work with, knows many tricks, and has had seven calves.*	
6. *Wild whales' fins are almost always straight.*	

▼**Write** Write a paragraph explaining how returning captive animals to the wild is both necessary and cruel. Refer to specific examples from the article to support your answers.

REFLECT

How does having a pet differ from keeping a wild animal such as a chimp or orca captive?

Second Read: Understanding Structure and Purpose

Take turns reading the article with a partner. Partner 1 reads paragraph 1. Then partner 2 summarizes the paragraph. Switch roles for paragraph 2. Continue until you have read and summarized the entire passage.

Objective: Notice how the text is divided into three sections with headers. When you and your partner finish reading a section, work together to answer the question: What is the purpose of this section of the text? Write the purpose next to each section.

Focus on Understanding Structure and Purpose

In order to communicate ideas clearly and effectively, authors of nonfiction texts organize their ideas as logically as possible. Understanding text structure can help you be a better reader. Analyzing the structure an author uses to organize information can help you as a reader comprehend complex information. It can help you predict what an author will say next. Text structures also help you understand an author's purpose for writing.

Here are some common ways to structure text:

Description/List: lists or describes information about a topic, such as the amount of technology used in schools.

Cause and Effect: identifies a cause of something and describes its effects, such as the cause and effects of blue light from electronics on people's sleep patterns.

Problem and Solution: identifies a problem and details its solution(s), such as an endangered species and how to save it.

Compare and Contrast: compares and contrasts a topic, such as turtles versus tortoises.

Question/Answer: poses a question and then offers an answer or possible answers in response.

Sequential/Time Order: written in chronological order or a special sequence of events or steps to follow.

Claim/Reasons: makes a claim or takes a position and then explains reasons in support of the claim.

Focus on the first paragraph of the article reprinted on the next page. Underline words and transitions that help you infer the structure the author is using:

Why Zoos?

    We keep animals in zoos or as pets for many reasons.
Sometimes the motivation is to rescue an animal or a group of
animals. Hawks that fly into windows, black bears that roam
through human towns, and harbor seals that swim into propellers
often end up in zoos. Other times a species, such as the Asian
elephant, is endangered in the wild. Zoo populations help ensure
that these rare animals survive. We also keep animals in captivity
because we enjoy seeing them and spending time with them.

1. Which text structure is the author using in this paragraph?

> **CONNECT TO ESSENTIAL QUESTION**
>
> Does the same morality for how to treat people apply to the treatment of animals? Why or why not?

2. What is the purpose of the list of animals contained in the third sentence?

3. Why does the author begin her entire article with this paragraph?

Step back and consider the entire excerpt as a whole. How is the entire article structured? To answer this question think about the purpose of the first section as it relates to the rest of the article.

4. What is the purpose of the first section Why Zoos?

5. What is the purpose of the other two sections: Lucy and Katina?

REFLECT

How did domesticated animals become domesticated? Could the same process tame animals that are currently wild?

6. Overall, which text structure does the author use to present her ideas?

Speak and Listen With a partner, analyze the text structures used in the sections Lucy and Katina. Identify how each paragraph is organized and how each one relates to the purpose of that section.

Write Write a paragraph explaining the overall structure of the excerpt and how each section plays a role in the overall purpose.

TECH-CONNECT

Search online for information about Katina the orca. Post three facts about her on your class website.

Third Read: Determining Point of View

Rhetoric is the art of effective persuasive writing and speaking. To convince readers, writer use rhetorical devices including words with positive and negative connotations.

Objective: As you read the article again, consider what the author thinks about keeping animals in captivity. Underline details that suggest the author's point of view, or opinion on the topic.

CONNECT TO ESSENTIAL QUESTION

Some animal shelters have a no-kill policy. Should all shelters have this policy?

Focus on Point of View

This passage describes two stories of animals in captivity and then poses questions about the morality of the people's actions. Even though the author does not directly answer the questions about whether keeping animals captive is right or wrong, the author subtly reveals an opinion about the issue. Readers can read between the lines in order to infer whether her point of view is positive, negative, or neutral.

Infer the author's point of view by considering the following:

- the details the author includes

- the details the author leaves out

- words the author chooses to use and their connotations, or the emotions they suggest

Fill in the columns in the following chart.

Determining an Author's Point of View			
The writer mostly includes details about	The writer uses these words to describe Lucy: The writer uses these words to describe Katina:	The writer uses these words to describe life in captivity for Lucy: The writer uses these words to describe life in captivity for Katina and other orcas:	The writer doesn't say anything about

Some examples from the passage are	This makes me think that the writer believes	This makes me think that the writer believes	This makes me think that the writer believes

Based upon my answers, the author's point of view is

Speak and Listen With a partner, discuss the following:

- If Kathryn Hulick were debating the topic of keeping animals in captivity, she would be on the side of . . . .

- I think this because . . . .

Language: Sentence Structure

Sentences in English have four main structures.

Simple: A simple sentence has only one independent clause. An independent clause can stand on its own as a complete thought. In the following examples, independent clauses are underlined.

Example: We keep animals in zoos or as pets for many reasons.

Compound: A compound sentence has at least **two** independent clauses. The clauses are joined by a comma and coordinating conjunction (*and, but, for, nor, or, yet*) or by a semicolon.

Example: An adult chimpanzee is about five times stronger than an adult human, and Lucy got into everything.

Complex: A complex sentence has at least one independent clause and at least one dependent clause. A dependent clause contains a subject and verb but does not express a complete thought. It can't stand on its own. In the following examples, dependent clauses are in (parentheses).

Example: We also keep animals in captivity (because we enjoy seeing them and spending time with them.)

continued on next page

Compound-Complex: A compound-complex sentence has at least two independent clauses and at least one dependent clause.

> Example: <u>The whales may also float near the top of the pool for long periods</u>; as a result, <u>they may end up with a sunburn or a flopped-over dorsal fin</u>, (which is a common sight on captive male killer whales.)

Identify and label each of the sentences in the following paragraph. Notice how using a variety of sentence types makes the writing interesting and helps to emphasize key ideas and de-emphasize lesser ideas.

But Lucy didn't have a clue how to live in the wild, and her health suffered during the adjustment. Carter wound up staying with Lucy for years. She ate ants and leaves to show Lucy what to do. She even lived in a cage so Lucy and the other chimpanzees couldn't reach the human objects that distracted them from normal activities like seeking food and shelter.

▼**Write** Write a paragraph summarizing the article from the chapter. Use all four sentence types in your writing.

Project-Based Assessments

Digital Presentation

Conduct research and create a digital presentation about an animal rights issue. First, search online using terms such as *animal rights*. The website for the Humane Society of the United States may be helpful in finding topic ideas: www.humanesociety.org. Develop a list of issues and choose one you would like to research.

Next, find reliable sources for your information. Remember, websites that end in *.edu, .gov,* or *.org* usually have more reliable information than sites with many contributors such as Wikipedia. Check the site's About tab to find out if it is maintained by a reliable source, such as a university, government agency, research facility, or other reputable organization.

Gather the following information for your presentation:

- Name and description of the issue

- Cause of the issue

- What and how animals are affected

- Actions taken in the past to address the issue

- Potential solutions to the issue

- Three or more sources used for the project: name of article, website, date

TECH-CONNECT

Download your presentation to a flash drive or email it to yourself so that you can easily access it at school. Be sure to open your files before your presentation, especially when not using your own computer.

Finally, create an interesting and well-organized computer presentation. Each slide should have both an image or video and text. Read the rubric carefully so you know the expectations of the presentation from the beginning. Practice what you will say with each slide before presenting to the class. If working with a partner(s), decide in advance who will share which slides.

Use the following guidelines for your digital presentation.	
To receive the highest score, the project must meet all of these criteria.	Your digital presentation • uses multimedia in a professional way and is appealing both visually and aurally (i.e., to the eye and ear). • contains images or videos that clearly demonstrate understanding of the animal rights issue, its causes and effects, the animals affected, and its potential solutions. • is appropriate for the audience. • demonstrates that you clearly understand the issue. • demonstrates confidence, eye contact, and proper volume. • uses correct grammar, usage, punctuation, and spelling.

Roundtable Discussion

Participate in a roundtable discussion on the following question as posed by the author in the text:

> Did the people in the stories do the right thing by keeping Lucy and Katina in captivity? Why or why not?

In a roundtable discussion all students are equal and everyone participates. Arrange your seats in a circle so that all participants can see one another. The teacher or a discussion leader may sit in the middle. Come to the discussion with an open mind and be prepared for a challenge! You will be evaluated on the following:

Expectations for Discussion	
Listening	**Speaking**
Listen respectfully.	Speak at least two times.
Look at speaker.	Refer to the text to support conclusions.
Follow text references.	Ask questions.
Take notes on what the speaker is saying.	Offer reasons to support your point of view.
Write down follow-up questions.	Be open to other students' comments and questions.

Before the discussion, find two other sources that will help you answer the question. Make a copy or print out the sources. Highlight information that can be used as evidence to support your answer to the discussion question.

Instructions for a Roundtable Discussion

1. The discussion leader (teacher or student) begins by asking the question:

   > Did the people in the stories in the text do the right thing by keeping Lucy and Katina in captivity? Why or why not?

2. Allow each member the chance to reply to the question. Members should refer to the chapter text and other research they have conducted in their response.

3. Take notes on comments you disagree with or you have questions about. Write down what was said and who said it.

4. Go around the circle again and allow everyone to ask a follow-up question or make a comment. Questions and comments should be directed to the person who made the original comment. Try phrasing your responses in this way:

   - What did you mean by . . . . ?

   - Can you explain . . . . ?

   - I agree/disagree with . . . . because . . . .

5. Continue the discussion by having everyone respond to the following question, using steps 2–4 above.

   > Should humans ever keep wild animals in captivity? Why or why not?

On Your Own: Integrating Ideas

1. Go to Kathryn Hulick's website, kathrynhulick.com, and read the brief article about animal ethics to learn about her viewpoint.

2. In "Zoo Complicated," Hulick claims, "Animals likely don't experience emotions the same way we do." Explore how self-aware animals are by reading her article, "Do Dogs Have a Sense of Self?" Find the article at www.sciencenewsforstudents.org.

3. Watch *Blackfish* (PG-13), a documentary about killer whales in captivity. Then, read SeaWorld's response to the claims in the movie at seaworldcares.com.

4. Conduct research about Jane Goodall, a naturalist who made revolutionary discoveries about chimpanzees and their behavior.

Connect to Testing

In this chapter, you practiced the skills of making inferences, analyzing structure and purpose, and identifying point of view. When you take assessments, you will be tested on these skills. Answer the following questions.

1. **Part A:** Which inference is best supported by the text?

   A. Wild chimpanzees were confused by Lucy's behavior.

   B. The Temerlins' relationship with Lucy was that of scientist and research subject.

   C. The expectation for Lucy's return to the wild was that she would adjust naturally.

   D. The decision to send Lucy to the nature reserve was difficult for the Temerlins.

   Part B: Cite at least two details from the text to support your inference.

2. **Part A:** The author includes the stories about Lucy and Katina in order to

   A. provide illustrations of how animals have been mistreated by humans.

   B. describe two success stories about animals that were rescued from the wild.

   C. provide examples of what can happen when humans keep wild animals captive.

   D. give reasons why people keep animals in zoos.

   Part B: Which of the following lines from the text provides the best evidence to support the answer to Part A?

   A. *Sometimes the motivation is to rescue an animal or a group of animals.*

   B. *We also keep animals in captivity because we enjoy seeing them and spending time with them.*

   C. *Animals likely don't experience emotions the same way we do.*

   D. *Read them and decide for yourself—did the people involved do the right thing?*

continued on next page

3. Explain how the author's point of view about animals in captivity is expressed in the text. Include evidence from the text to support your points.

4. Read this sentence from the text. Then answer the question that follows.

> In fact, a whale in <u>captivity</u> now has about the same chance of surviving the year as a whale in the wild.

Part A: What is the meaning of *captivity* as it is used in the text?

A. The state of being held as a slave

B. The state of being denied food

C. The state of being confined

D. The state of being alive

Part B: Which of the following phrases from the text best helps the reader understand the meaning of the word *captivity*?

A. *In fact, a whale*

B. *About the same chance*

C. *Of surviving the year*

D. *As a whale in the wild*

5. Read the following paragraph and then answer the questions that follow.

Lucy liked drinking tea and looking in the mirror. But she wasn't human—she was a chimpanzee. Maurice and Jane Temerlin raised Lucy just like a human baby. The chimpanzee began her life with the Temerlins as the subject of research but soon became a daughter. Maurice, who was a psychotherapist, wanted to know how human Lucy would become. She learned sign language and seemed to truly care for her adoptive parents. In his book, *Lucy: Growing Up Human*, he wrote: "If Jane is distressed, Lucy notices it immediately and attempts to comfort her by putting an arm about her, grooming her, or kissing her."

Part A: Which of the following can be inferred from this paragraph?

A. Lucy was raised by a family with children.

B. Lucy exhibited many human behaviors.

C. Lucy became attached to her adopted parents gradually.

D. Lucy failed as a research subject.

Part B: Cite two pieces of textual evidence to support your answer.

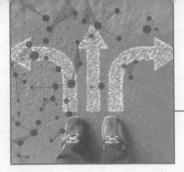

Chapter 4

Determining Characters' Points of View

Preview Concepts

Think about the last time you asked a parent or teacher for permission, and he or she said no. How did that make you feel? Did you understand the reasons for the refusal? Did you say or do anything in response? Now, put yourself in your teacher's or parent's shoes and imagine their perspective. Write a response below where you explain what happened from your parent's or teacher's point of view.

Now, write a response from your point of view.

Share your answers with a partner and decide if both points of view are reasonable.

CHAPTER GOALS

In this chapter you will

- determine central ideas in a text.
- identify figurative language.
- analyze characters' points of view.
- create a pictorial presentation or write a literary analysis.

PREVIEW ACADEMIC VOCABULARY

connotation

denotation

figurative language

metaphor

point of view

simile

Making Connections

The following excerpt is from a short story by Katherine Mansfield. You will be reading another of her stories in this chapter. As you read think about what each of the characters are most concerned about.

> "Dead!" Laura stared at Godber's man.
>
> "Dead when they picked him up," said Godber's man with relish. "They were taking the body home as I come up here." And he said to the cook, "He's left a wife and five little ones."
>
> "Jose, come here." Laura caught hold of her sister's sleeve and dragged her through the kitchen to the other side of the green baize door. There she paused and leaned against it. "Jose!" she said, horrified, "however are we going to stop everything?"
>
> "Stop everything, Laura!" cried Jose in astonishment. "What do you mean?"
>
> "Stop the garden-party, of course." Why did Jose pretend?
>
> But Jose was still more amazed. "Stop the garden-party? My dear Laura, don't be so absurd. Of course we can't do anything of the kind. Nobody expects us to. Don't be so extravagant."
>
> "But we can't possibly have a garden-party with a man dead just outside the front gate."
>
> —"The Garden Party" by Katherine Mansfield

1. What are each of the following characters concerned about?
   Godber's man—

   Laura—

   Jose—

With a partner discuss how the three characters have different points of view about the dead man. Discuss why each person might have a different perspective based on what is important to him or her. Summarize your discussion below.

First Read: Summarizing Central Ideas

In this Katherine Mansfield story, Isabel and Kezia Burnell proudly show off their new doll house to other children.

Objective: As you read, think about the conflict the narrator describes. Notice any repeated ideas. Underline details that describe the characters' feelings about the dollhouse. Write questions you have about the characters and the conflict in the My Thoughts column.

excerpt
The Doll's House
by Katherine Mansfield

	My Thoughts

1   The Burnell children could hardly walk to school fast enough the next morning. They burned to tell everybody, to describe, to—well—to boast about their doll's house before the school bell rang.

5   "I'm to tell," said Isabel, "because I'm the eldest. And you two can join in after. But I'm to tell first."

Playtime came and Isabel was surrounded. The girls of her class nearly fought to put their arms around her, to walk away with her, to beam flatteringly, to be her special friend. She

10   held quite a court under the huge pine trees at the side of the playground. Nudging, giggling together, the little girls pressed up close. And the only two who stayed outside the ring were the two who were always outside, the little Kelveys. They knew better than to come anywhere near the Burnells.

15   Lil, for instance, who was a stout, plain child, with big freckles, came to school in a dress made from a green art-**serge** table-cloth of the Burnells', with red plush sleeves from the Logans' curtains. Her hat, perched on top of her high forehead, was a grown-up woman's hat, once the property of Miss Lecky,

20   the postmistress. It was turned up at the back and trimmed with a large scarlet quill. What a little **guy** she looked! It was

serge: a strong cloth, usually made of wool
guy: a person who looks odd

impossible not to laugh. And her little sister, our Else, wore a long white dress, rather like a nightgown, and a pair of little boy's boots. But whatever our Else wore she would have looked

25   strange. She was a tiny wishbone of a child, with cropped hair and enormous solemn eyes—a little white owl. Nobody had ever seen her smile; she scarcely ever spoke. She went through life holding on to Lil, with a piece of Lil's skirt screwed up in her hand. Where Lil went our Else followed. In the playground, on

30   the road going to and from school, there was Lil marching in front and our Else holding on behind. Only when she wanted anything, or when she was out of breath, our Else gave Lil a tug, a twitch, and Lil stopped and turned round. The Kelveys never failed to understand each other. Now they hovered at

35   the edge; you couldn't stop them listening. When the little girls turned round and sneered, Lil, as usual, gave her silly, shamefaced smile, but our Else only looked.

 And Isabel's voice, so very proud, went on telling. The carpet made a great sensation, but so did the beds with real

40   **bedclothes**, and the stove with an oven door.

 When she finished Kezia broke in. "You've forgotten the lamp, Isabel."

 "Oh, yes," said Isabel, "and there's a teeny little lamp, all made of yellow glass, with a white globe that stands on the

45   dining-room table. You couldn't tell it from a real one."

 "The lamp's best of all," cried Kezia. She thought Isabel wasn't making half enough of the little lamp. But nobody paid any attention. Isabel was choosing the two who were to come back with them that afternoon and see it. She chose Emmie

50   Cole and Lena Logan. But when the others knew they were all to have a chance, they couldn't be nice enough to Isabel. One

---

bedclothes: the covering (as sheets and blankets) used on a bed

My Thoughts

by one they put their arms round Isabel's waist and walked her off. They had something to whisper to her, a secret. "Isabel's my friend."

55 Only the little Kelveys moved away forgotten; there was nothing more for them to hear.

Days passed, and as more children saw the doll's house, the fame of it spread. It became the one subject, the rage. The one question was, "Have you seen Burnells' doll's house?" "Oh,

60 ain't it lovely!" "Haven't you seen it? Oh, I say!"

Even the dinner hour was given up to talking about it. The little girls sat under the pines eating their thick **mutton** sandwiches and big slabs of johnny cake spread with butter. While always, as near as they could get, sat the Kelveys, our Else

65 holding on to Lil, listening too, while they chewed their jam sandwiches out of a newspaper soaked with large red blobs.

"Mother," said Kezia, "can't I ask the Kelveys just once?"

"Certainly not, Kezia."

"But why not?"

70 "Run away, Kezia; you know quite well why not."

At last everybody had seen it except them. On that day the subject rather flagged. It was the dinner hour. The children stood together under the pine trees, and suddenly, as they looked at the Kelveys eating out of their paper, always by

75 themselves, always listening, they wanted to be horrid to them. Emmie Cole started the whisper.

"Lil Kelvey's going to be a servant when she grows up."

"O-oh, how awful!" said Isabel Burnell, and she made eyes at Emmie.

80 Emmie swallowed in a very meaning way and nodded to Isabel as she'd seen her mother do on those occasions.

"It's true—it's true—it's true," she said.

---

mutton: lamb

My Thoughts

Then Lena Logan's little eyes snapped. "Shall I ask her?" she whispered.

85   "Bet you don't," said Jessie May.

"Pooh, I'm not frightened," said Lena. Suddenly she gave a little squeal and danced in front of the other girls. "Watch! Watch me! Watch me now!" said Lena. And sliding, gliding, dragging one foot, giggling behind her hand, Lena went over

90   to the Kelveys.

Lil looked up from her dinner. She wrapped the rest quickly away. Our Else stopped chewing. What was coming now?

"Is it true you're going to be a servant when you grow up, Lil Kelvey?" shrilled Lena.

95   Dead silence. But instead of answering, Lil only gave her silly, shame-faced smile. She didn't seem to mind the question at all. What a sell for Lena! The girls began to titter.

Lena couldn't stand that. She put her hands on her hips; she shot forward. "Yah, yer father's in prison!" she hissed, spitefully.

100   This was such a marvelous thing to have said that the little girls rushed away in a body, deeply, deeply excited, wild with joy. Someone found a long rope, and they began skipping. And never did they skip so high, run in and out so fast, or do such daring things as on that morning.

FIRST RESPONSE: KEY IDEAS AND DETAILS

How are the Kelvey girls different from the rest of the children in the story? Use evidence from the text to support your conclusions. Describe any personal connections to the text.

Focus on Summarizing Central Ideas

To determine the central ideas of a story, think about the following questions:

- What are the main events?

- How do the main characters respond to the main events?

- How do the characters change over the course of the story?

My Thoughts

TECH-CONNECT

As instructed by your teacher, send a question you had about the story to Poll Everywhere or post it on your class website.

continued on next page

Trace the characters' actions and reactions to story events by finishing the sentence starters to summarize what happens in each section.

Paragraphs 1–3 (lines 1–14): The narrator describes
Paragraphs 4–5 (lines 15–40): The narrator describes
Paragraphs 6–8 (lines 41–54): The other little girls
Paragraph 9 (lines 55–56): The Kelveys
Paragraphs 10–11 (lines 57–66): The girls   The Kelveys
Paragraphs 12–16 (lines 67–76): Kezia wonders   Her mother says

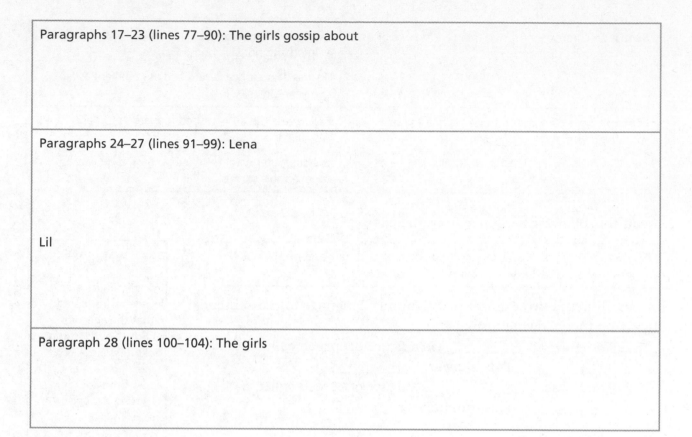

Paragraphs 17–23 (lines 77–90): The girls gossip about
Paragraphs 24–27 (lines 91–99): Lena   Lil
Paragraph 28 (lines 100–104): The girls

(**Speak and Listen** Share your answers to the sentence starters above with a partner. Then discuss these questions:

- Why do you think Kezia wants to show her dollhouse to the Kelveys?

- Has she changed her mind about them?

- What other reason might she have?

- How do the characteristics of Kezia and the Kelveys influence the events in the story?

Second Read: Understanding Figurative Language

Objective: Read the text again. Underline examples of figurative language, including similes and metaphors.

Focus on Understanding Figurative Language

Figurative language uses comparisons to help readers picture what is happening or being described. Writers use figurative language to help readers "see" the story events and characters. Two main types of figurative language are similes and metaphors.

continued on next page

> **REFLECT**
>
> In a democracy, the majority rules, but the majority is not always right. Is there a way to fix this problem when the majority is in the wrong? How have people addressed majority and minority disputes throughout history?

Simile: a comparison of two things using *like* or *as*.	Examples: Her stomach felt like a volcano had erupted and hot lava burned inside. He was as hungry as a lion and as impatient as a two-year-old.
Metaphor: a comparison that says one thing is something else.	Examples: The army rushed forward, a tornado of destruction. The computer with its unknown pass code was an impenetrable fortress.

Read the following sentence from the passage:

> She was a tiny wishbone of a child, with cropped hair and enormous solemn eyes—a little white owl.

Analyze the two examples of figurative language in the sentence by using the following formats:

1. The phrase _____ is a figure of speech called a _____. This shows _____.

2. The phrase _____ is a figure of speech called a _____. This emphasizes _____.

REFLECT

Some similes are used so frequently that they become clichés, or overused expressions. A few examples are *as blind as a bat, as easy as pie,* and *as wise as an owl.* What others have you heard or used?

Third Read: Determining Points of View

Read the passage with a partner. Take turns reading paragraphs.

Objective: Think about the following questions:

- How do the characters feel about each other?

- What makes them feel that way?

- How does the narrator feel about the Kelveys? Underline details that help you infer the narrator's attitude.

Focus on Determining Points of View

This passage has a third-person omniscient narrator. *Omniscient* means "all-knowing." This narrator relates information about all of the characters, including their interactions and some of their inner thoughts.

Point of view often refers to the perspective from which the story is told, in this case, the narrator's point of view. But point of view also describes a character's thoughts and feelings about something or someone.

In the passage, the characters are divided into two groups and two different points of view: 1) the Kelveys and 2) all of the other little girls. The narrator's description of the characters and their interactions helps you determine their points of view.

Read the quotation from the passage in the left-hand column of the chart below. Then in the right-hand column, write what the quotation reveals about the character's feelings toward the Kelveys. You may want to return to the passage to read the quotation in context. The first one is completed for you.

REFLECT

Can you think of other stories or movies where the main character is treated unfairly because of his or her social class?

Thoughts, speech, action	What it shows about how the characters feel about each other
1. *When the little girls turned round and sneered, Lil, as usual, gave her silly, shamefaced smile, but our Else only looked.*	**The little girls** They treat the Kelveys with blatant scorn. **The Kelveys** Lil and Else accept the other girls' behavior and do not seem to harbor any grudges or resentment.
2. *At last everybody had seen it except them [the Kelveys].*	**The little girls** **The Kelveys**
3. *The children stood together under the pine trees, and suddenly, as they looked at the Kelveys eating out of their paper, always by themselves, always listening, they wanted to be horrid to them.*	**The little girls** **The Kelveys**

(**Speak and Listen** Discuss how the little girls and the Kelveys feel about each other. Refer to your answers from the graphic organizer. Then discuss the following questions:

- How does the narrator feel about the Kelveys and the other girls' behavior? What details support your inference about the narrator's point of view?

Write Write a paragraph comparing and contrasting the points of view of the Kelveys, the little girls, and the narrator. Support your ideas by quoting and paraphrasing lines from the text.

Language: Connotations and Denotations

A word's denotation is its dictionary definition. A word's connotation is the implied or suggested meaning. In other words, the denotation is the literal meaning of a word, and the connotation is the emotional association people have with the word. Words can have neutral, positive, or negative connotations.

Example: *assertive, bossy*

The word *assertive* has a positive connotation, whereas *bossy* has a negative connotation.

Example: *brat, child*

Using the word *brat* to describe a child implies the child misbehaves often or is annoying. Using the word *child*, on the other hand, is neutral in that it does not imply a negative or positive connotation.

Read these sentences from the passage. Rewrite the underlined words below and label them *positive, negative,* or *neutral* based on their connotations.

1. Lil, for instance, who was a <u>stout</u>, <u>plain</u> child, with big freckles, came to school in a dress made from a green art-serge table-cloth of the Burnells', with red plush sleeves from the Logans' curtains.

2. Days passed, and as more children saw the doll's house, the <u>fame</u> of it spread.

3. Read the following two word groups and write them in order from most to least negative connotation.

curious, nosy, inquisitive, prying, snooping, questioning

group, gang, horde, bunch, team, committee

Speak and Listen Share your word ranking with a partner. Discuss the following questions:

- Which word(s) had the most negative connotation for you?
- Which word(s) had the most positive connotation for you?
- Did any of your word rankings match? Why or why not?

Project-Based Assessments

Pictorial Presentation

Create a pictorial presentation of the events in "The Doll's House."

- Create a pictorial presentation using PowerPoint, a video, or a hand-drawn storyboard of each scene.
- Use a minimum of six images, presented in order. Write captions under each image to briefly explain the scene. Include pictures that reflect what you think happens next in the story.

Use the following ideas to help you in your research for this presentation.

- Read the rubric on page 70 carefully so that you know what is expected of you.
- Plan your images before you begin so you can research more effectively.

continued on next page

- Use key words such as *school playground, children at play,* and *The Doll's House.* These words are suggestions to get you started. Even if you are hand-drawing your images, looking at ideas from the web will help you make your drawings realistic.

- Refine your search by clicking on Videos or Images.

- Once you find an image you like, save it or capture a screenshot of it. Paste that image into your presentation and crop it. If you pause a video, you can capture an image.

- If adding music, consider using "Don't Laugh at Me" by Mark Wills (1998), "The Man in the Mirror" by Michael Jackson (1987), "Coat of Many Colors" by Dolly Parton (1971), or another suitable piece.

Use the following guidelines for your pictorial presentation.	
To receive the highest score (4.0), the project must meet all of these criteria.	Your pictorial presentation • uses images or drawings in a way that captures the events of the story. • contains interesting images that tell the events in the order they happened. • includes images appropriate for the intended audience (not overly graphic or offensive). • includes short, interesting captions that are free from grammar and punctuation errors.

Literary Analysis

An analysis is a careful study of something to learn how its parts are related to the whole. Throughout this chapter, you analyzed details from "The Doll's House." Write a one-page analysis that answers the following question:

> What does "The Doll's House" communicate about how children treat each other?

First, think about the question and write a strong central idea or thesis statement that answers the question. Then think about how you can support your central idea statement using the work you did during the three reads in this chapter. How do the events of the story, the figurative language that describes the children, and the points of view of the characters support your conclusion about the behavior of children in general?

Organize your analysis into an introduction, a body, and a conclusion. Use good transitional phrases (*first, next, also*) to link ideas together. Another option is to present your analysis as an oral critique to the class. Be sure to use eye contact, a natural speaking rate, appropriate volume, and gestures that support your words.

Use the following guidelines for your literary analysis.	
To receive the highest score (4.0), the essay must meet all of these criteria.	Your literary analysis • has a clear central idea in a well-developed introduction. • clearly explains what the story communicates about how children treat each other. • has a body organized with good transitional words and phrases. • contains ideas that fit together logically to create an understandable whole. • ends with a satisfying conclusion. • maintains a formal style. • uses correct grammar, usage, punctuation and spelling.

On Your Own: Integrating Ideas

1. One commentator writes, "Katherine Mansfield respects children . . . . her attitude is not entirely new, but it is exceedingly rare." Do you agree with this assessment based on "The Doll's House?" Why or why not?

2. Read the rest of "The Doll's House" by Katherine Mansfield. Think about how the adults and children treat the Kelveys.

3. Watch *Charlie and the Chocolate Factory* (2005) or *A Little Princess* (1995) and consider what the main characters have in common with the Kelveys as well as how they differ.

4. Watch *Poor Kids*, a Frontline film focusing on the lives of three girls whose families are struggling with financial ruin. Find it at www.pbs.org on the Frontline page.

Connect to Testing

In this chapter, you practiced analyzing central ideas, figurative langauge, and point of view in a passage. When you take assessments, you will be tested on these skills. Answer the following questions.

1. **Part A:** Which statement best expresses a central idea of the text?

   A. Those who are less fortunate are often treated poorly by those from higher social classes.

   B. Children have a greater understanding of actions and their consequences than may be expected.

   C. Girls and boys have natural differences that make them interact with others in dissimilar ways.

   D. Making cruel jokes at another's expense will eventually have repercussions.

   Part B: Support the answer to Part A by explaining at least two details from the text.

2. Lena's questions to the other girls and to Lil reveal her

    A. confusion and desperation to feel superior.

    B. meanness and desire for attention.

    C. compassion and yearning to be popular.

    D. recklessness and need for control.

3. Explain how Lil and Else view their social status and their reactions to how the other girls treat them. Include evidence from the text to support your points.

4. **Part A:** Which inference is best supported by the text?

    A. The Kelveys have little interest in seeing or hearing about the dollhouse.

    B. Kezia and Isabel have a difficult relationship with each other because of jealousy.

    C. Kezia's mother worries that Kezia will show the Kelveys the dollhouse.

    D. The girls learned their behavior toward the Kelveys from their parents.

continued on next page

Part B: Cite at least two details from the text to support your inference.

5. **Part A:** What does Kezia feel toward the Kelveys?

   A. confusion

   B. pity

   C. concern

   D. dismay

Part B: Which of the following excerpts from the text best supports the answer to Part A?

   A. *"The lamp's best of all," cried Kezia. She thought Isabel wasn't making half enough of the little lamp.*

   B. *While always, as near as they could get, sat the Kelveys, our Else holding on to Lil, listening too*

   C. *"Mother," said Kezia, "can't I ask the Kelveys just once?"*

   D. *"Run away, Kezia; you know quite well why not."*

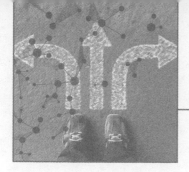

Chapter 5

Analyzing Arguments from Different Texts

Preview Concepts

A good argument supports a central claim with reasons and evidence. The following chart contains a claim and possible reasons to support the claim.

With a partner, identify which of the reasons support the claim, or are relevant to the argument the writer wants to make. Good reasons explain why a reader should agree with the claim.

Claim: Americans should put a "sin" tax on sugary drinks and junk food.	
Possible reasons	**Does it support the claim? (Is it relevant?) Yes or no?**
1. People would be forced to make healthier snack choices and thus live healthier lives.	
2. These types of "sin" taxes raise a lot of money, which could be used for better healthcare programs.	
3. "Sin" taxes are not new to America.	
4. Taxes would hurt the companies that make soft drinks and could cost people their jobs.	

Below are several statements related to the reasons above. Decide if any of them could be used as evidence to support the relevant reasons above. Write the number of the reason in the chart next to the evidence. If the evidence is not related to any reason, write none.

> 5. Denmark had a "fat tax" on junk food that raised about $200 million in one year.
> 6. Taxes on tobacco and alcohol are (and have been) highly effective in improving public health.
> 7. With the 18th Amendment in 1920, the government outlawed alcohol, but the amendment was repealed in 1933.

CHAPTER GOALS

In this chapter you will

- determine an author's purpose in a text.
- analyze the claim, reasons, evidence, and assumptions in an argument.
- evaluate the validity and effectiveness of an argument.
- compare evidence used in two texts.
- write a speech or a letter to the editor.

PREVIEW ACADEMIC VOCABULARY

argument

assumption

claim

evidence

reason

Making Connections

Read the following excerpt. Then answer the questions that follow.

Why go vegetarian? Chew on these reasons.

You'll ward off disease. Vegetarian diets are more healthful than the average American diet, particularly in preventing, treating or reversing heart disease and reducing the risk of cancer. A low-fat vegetarian diet is the single most effective way to stop the progression of coronary artery disease or prevent it entirely. Cardiovascular disease kills 1 million Americans annually and is the leading cause of death in the United States.

—"Why Go Veg?" *from vegetariantimes.com*

1. What implied claim does the author make?

2. What reason does this paragraph develop?

3. Place a a star by evidence used to support the claim. Which piece of evidence is a statistic?

4. With a partner use the following questions to evaluate the paragraph:
   - Is the argument sound? (Is it based on a logical claim and reasons?)
   - Is the evidence relevant? (Does it support the reason?)
   - Is the evidence sufficient? (Is there enough to support the reason?)

> **MAKING CONNECTIONS**
>
> In this chapter you will analyze the effectiveness of arguments related to vegetarianism.

First Read: Identifying Author's Purpose

The following is an excerpt from a nonfiction book *A Plea for the Animals* by Matthieu Ricard.

Objective: As you read this passage, think about the author's purpose. Underline one sentence that identifies this purpose. Write questions you have about Ricard's views about vegetarianism and eating meat in the My Thoughts column. Consider how the words defined in the footnotes help you comprehend this text.

from
A Plea for the Animals
"Why I Am a Vegetarian"
by Matthieu Ricard

	My Thoughts

1   My first **Buddhist** teacher, Kangyur Rinpoche, was a very strict vegetarian. I was inspired by him and also by a deep inner reasoning that suddenly became obvious to me. I never hunted in my life, but did go fishing sometimes when I was

5   a little boy in Brittany. When I was 13 years old, a thought bloomed in my mind: "How can I do something like that?" I realized that I was totally avoiding putting myself in the place of the other being. And when I was 20, I gave up eating meat. That was 50 years ago.

10   The heart of the Buddhist path is compassion. That means to value others. If you value others, you value their well-being and are concerned by their suffering.

We can find means to survive without causing suffering to others. In India for example, there are over 400 million

15   vegetarian people who survive well. They are not sacrificing their health or reducing their life span. In fact, even from a selfish standpoint, it is better to be a vegetarian. Many studies have shown that red meat increases the incidence of colon cancer and other illnesses.

Buddhist: one who practices Buddhism, a religion of eastern and central Asia that believes that suffering is inherent in life and that one can be liberated from it by cultivating wisdom, virtue, and concentration

20   However, the main reason to stop eating animals is to spare others' lives. Today, 150 billion land animals and 1.5 trillion sea animals are killed for our consumption. We treat them like rats and vermin and cockroaches to be eliminated. This would be called genocide or dehumanization if they were

25   human beings.

We even go one step further with animals: we **instrumentalize** them. They become objects. They become the pig industry, sausage or meat factories. Ethically you cannot imagine progressing toward a more altruistic or more

30   compassionate society while behaving like this. Eating meat reveals another level of selfishness in terms of fellow human beings. Rich countries consume the most meat: about 200 kilos per year per inhabitant in the USA, compared to about 3 kilos in India. The more the GDP of a country increases, usually so

35   does the amount of meat consumption.

In order to produce one kilo of meat, you need ten kilos of **vegetable protein**. This is at a cost to the poorest section of humanity. With two acres of land, you can feed fifty vegetarians or two meat eaters. The 775 million tons of soy

40   and corn that are used for industrial farming could be used to feed people in need.

The United Nations International Panel on Climate Change, a group that is not particularly fanatical about being vegetarian, recommends that we start by just eating less

45   meat. This is one of the easiest ways to reduce global warming and could make a huge difference to the rate of climate change. The main reason is that industrial farming causes the production of methane. Methane is ten times more active in

My Thoughts

---

instrumentalize: to make into an instrument for achieving a goal
vegetable protein: amino acids that are essential for life and found in vegetables

causing global warming than CO_2. It is the second main factor

50 for global warming before transportation!

It just takes one second to decide to stop. It doesn't create any huge chaotic changes in our life. It's just that we eat something else. It's so simple. A small effort can bring a very big result for animals, for the disadvantaged, for the planet,

55 for our own health. A sensible mind can see this is not an extreme perspective. This is a most reasonable, ethical, and compassionate point of view.

_____

_____

_____

_____

_____

_____

FIRST RESPONSE: KEY IDEAS AND DETAILS

What issue is Ricard calling to people's attention? Write your answer in your journal. Be prepared to share your answer in class.

Focus on Identifying Author's Purpose

Writers have a goal when writing. They may wish to persuade, entertain, or inform their audience. The author's purpose may be clear and easy to identify—even directly stated. Or it may be difficult to determine, so the audience must infer it from the details in the text.

Use the following graphic organizer to analyze Ricard's overall purpose and how each paragraph contributes. Three of the cells have been completed for you.

Paragraph 1 (lines 1–9)	Ricard explains his own experience with Buddhism and how this led to his becoming a vegetarian.	It describes his journey to becoming a vegetarian due to his religious beliefs.
Paragraph 2 (lines 10–12)	Buddhism believes in being compassionate to "others" and concerned by their suffering.	

continued on next page

Section of the Text	Key Idea	Purpose
Paragraph 3 (lines 13–19)		
Paragraph 4 (lines 20–25)		
Paragraphs 5–6 (lines 26–41)		
Paragraph 7 (lines 42–50)		
Paragraph 8 (lines 51–57)		

Ricard's purpose for writing is to _____.

TECH-CONNECT

Search online for two of the statistics or facts cited in the passage. Check if the information is derived from reliable sources.

Second Read: Evaluating an Argument

Objective: Read the article a second time. As you read, mark the following in the text:

- Underline the sentence that most clearly reveals the central claim of the article. Label it *claim*.

- Underline sentences that give reasons in support of the central claim. Write *reason* next to them.

- Underline the sentence in the final paragraph that summarizes the four reasons outlined in the rest of the essay.

Focus on Evaluating an Argument

When a writer's purpose is to persuade his audience to think or act a certain way, he builds an argument. An argument usually contains the following elements:

- Claim or position statement: This is what the author wants the reader to believe or to do.

- Reasons: Logical statements that support the claim. Reasons explain why the reader should accept the author's claim.

- Evidence: Facts, data, statistics, and expert opinions that support the reasons.

- Counterargument/alternative explanation: Explains an opposing viewpoint and explains why this viewpoint is not valid.

Analyze Ricard's argument in "Why I Am a Vegetarian" by identifying his reasons and evidence. If Ricard doesn't offer evidence, write *none*.

Claim: Humans should be vegetarians.

Reason 1:

Evidence:

Reason 2:

continued on next page

REFLECT

How much meat do you eat in a day? If you are not already a vegetarian, how difficult would it be for you to forgo eating meat?

TECH-CONNECT

This passage is excerpted from *A Plea for the Animals,* which was published in 2016. However, the idea of vegetarianism has existed for centuries. Conduct an Internet search using the phrase *American Vegetarian Society 1850* to discover three facts about vegetarianism in the United States. Post your facts on your class website, according to your teacher's instructions.

Evidence:

Reason 3:

Evidence:

REFLECT

Some claims are based on statistics, but the source of the statistics must be considered before accepting them as accurate and unbiased. One reliable source is a government document. What are some other reliable sources?

Reason 4:

Evidence:

▼ **Write** Write one or two paragraphs answering the following questions:

1. Which reasons are most convincing? Why?
2. Is enough evidence provided to support each reason?
3. Can you think of additional evidence that might weaken or lend support to the reasons?
4. In general, does the argument make sense logically?

Third Read: Comparing and Contrasting Arguments

Read the passage a third time. Then read the following article on the same topic.

Objective: Mark the following as you read.

- Write *claim* next to the author's claim.

- Put a star by any reasons that are similar to ones used by Ricard in the previous text.

- Put a plus sign (+) by new reasons introduced by this text.

CONNECT TO ESSENTIAL QUESTION

People believe in many things from justice to love to equality. What do you believe in? What makes you believe in it?

Vegetarianism
by Judy Krizmanic

My Thoughts

Lots of kids today are becoming vegetarians.

1   What's a vegetarian? Someone who's decided to stop eating meat. Kids do this for a lot of reasons, but the most common is that they think it's wrong to kill animals and eat them.

5   People have been arguing about vegetarianism for centuries. Most of the arguments have stayed the same: killing a living creature that feels pleasure and pain is wrong, especially since we don't need to eat meat to be healthy. Other people say that plants and animals are only here so that

10   humans can use them. Or they say it's just the way the world is—that since animals eat other animals, humans should be able to kill animals for food.

   Kids argue about the same things today. Ilana Kaplan-Shain, age 13, says, "I don't want to kill something to eat it.

15   My friends say it's a stupid reason not to eat meat. Or they say, it's stupid, you kill the plants. But I say, it's my decision. Live with it."

   "Most kids who are vegetarian are doing it for ethical reasons," says Danny Seo, age 19, a vegetarian who started

20   his own animal rights and environmental group. Danny gets

hundreds of letters from kids and teens who, as they put it, don't want to eat anything with a face.

Some people don't think about where their neatly plastic-wrapped meat comes from. It's just something to be cooked and eaten. "If pork were called pig and steak were called cow, I think more of the world would be vegetarian," says Matthew McDonough, age 12. Johanna Gidseg is a 10-year-old vegetarian. When she was 6, she went to McDonald's with her dad and sister. "I looked down at my food and said, 'Dad, what's hamburger?' And he said, 'It's beef.' I said, 'What's beef?' He said, 'It's cow.' I said, 'Dad, do I have to eat my hamburger?'" Johanna's been a vegetarian ever since.

But some kids do know where meat comes from, and it doesn't really bother them. Charley Goss, age 9, eats meat: "When I was little, I couldn't imagine meat coming from an animal. I thought it was gross. But I just grew out of it. I don't really pay much attention to it anymore." . . .

Why Aren't There More Vegetarians?

Even with all the reasons that people give for not eating meat (and we haven't gone into all of them), the question still comes up, why aren't there more vegetarians? Julie Kostynick thinks that most people "think meat tastes good and they're just not thinking about the animal and its life." Most people grow up eating meat—it's what their families have been eating for generations. We're used to it. It's tradition. Some people can't imagine Thanksgiving without a turkey. Andrew Mabey, age 15, acknowledges vegetarian arguments against meat eating, but he says he's not going to change his diet. "Humans have been eating meat for so many years, and they've been doing OK. Life is too short to worry about it."

My Thoughts

Some kids just like the taste of meat. Charley Goss says, "I don't want to eat just vegetables." Some people end up eating meat just because it's more convenient—it's offered just about everywhere. If you're a vegetarian, you'll have a tougher time

55   finding things to eat at Burger King. You also might have to bring your own lunch to school if your cafeteria doesn't serve vegetarian food. On the other hand, it is getting easier to find vegetarian food—just about any restaurant has at least one vegetarian entrée on the menu. . . .

60   But the number of people, including kids, becoming vegetarians is on the rise. There are a lot more vegetarians today than there were 10 years ago. And some kids find being a vegetarian isn't that hard at all. So what if they have to ask whether their soup is made with beef broth? They

65   say it's worth it. They enjoy creating new traditions—like Thanksgiving without the turkey. Being vegetarian opens up a whole new world of food for them. "I'm taking part in something I believe in," says Julie Gerk, a vegetarian. "It feels great to be eating with awareness."

My Thoughts

Focus on Comparing and Contrasting Arguments

Both passages advocate vegetarianism, but they do it in different ways. In order to compare and contrast the two texts, you must bring together, or synthesize, the ideas found in both. Which ideas are similar? Which are different?

Answer the following questions to compare and contrast the claims and evidence used in the two texts. Use textual evidence to support your answers.

1. What is the main claim in Ricard's text?

continued on next page

2. What is the main claim in Krizmanic's text?

TECH-CONNECT

Use an online polling site to compare which argument your classmates believe has more convincing evidence: Ricard's or Krizmanic's. Post your results on your class website.

3. How is Ricard's purpose different from Krizmanic's purpose?

4. What type of evidence does Ricard use to support his points?

5. What type of evidence does Krizmanic use to support her points? Does she include any counterarguments and evidence against the counterarguments? Is this effective? Why or why not?

6. What similar evidence is used in the two texts?

CONNECT TO ESSENTIAL QUESTION

What do you feel strongly enough about to change your life?

Write Synthesize the ideas from both texts to write a few paragraphs analyzing the arguments presented by the two authors.

Language: Consistent Verb Tenses

Verb tense indicates when an action takes place. The three main verb tenses are present, past, and past perfect.

- Present tense examples: *is, have, eat, make*

- Past tense examples: *was, had, ate, made*

- Past perfect examples: *had been, had had, had eaten, had made* (had/has + past tense of verb)

When writing an essay, a story, or an exam answer, keep your verbs in the same tense. For example, use past tense verbs when writing about historical events for social studies class. Use present tense verbs when summarizing the events in a story and when writing an argument. Only switch to past tense to describe events that actually happened in the past.

Read the following paragraph. Notice how Matthieu Ricard uses present and past tense verbs correctly in the excerpt. Present tense verbs are underlined. Past tense verbs are bold.

My first Buddhist teacher, Kangyur Rinpoche, **was** a very strict vegetarian. I **was inspired** by him and also by a deep inner reasoning that suddenly became obvious to me. I never **hunted** in my life, but **did** go fishing sometimes when I **was** a little boy in Brittany. When I **was** 13 years old, a thought **bloomed** in my mind: "How can I do something like that?" I **realized** that I **was** totally **avoiding** putting myself in the place of the other being. And when I **was** 20, I **gave** up eating meat. That **was** 50 years ago.

The heart of the Buddhist path <u>is</u> compassion. That <u>means</u> to value others. If you <u>value</u> others, you <u>value</u> their well-being and <u>are</u> concerned by their suffering.

Matthieu Ricard begins in the past tense because he is talking about how he was inspired by his first Buddhist teacher to become a vegetarian. This was 50 years ago. He correctly switches to present tense in the second paragraph when he explains the principles of Buddhism, which exist today.

Read the following paragraph. Think about what is happening now and what happened in the past. Consider the underlined verbs. Circle those that are incorrect, and write the correct form in the margin to the right.

But some kids do know where meat <u>comes</u> from, and it <u>didn't</u> really bother them. Charley Goss, age 9, <u>eats</u> meat: "When I <u>am</u> little, I couldn't imagine meat coming from an animal. I <u>think</u> it <u>was</u> gross. We <u>would visit</u> a meat packing plant and <u>see</u> the cattle, the sides of beef hanging in the freezer, and then they <u>would give</u> us a slice of beef lunchmeat to eat. I <u>didn't eat</u> meat for a couple of years. But I just grew out of it. I <u>didn't pay</u> much attention to it anymore."

Project-Based Assessments

Awareness Speech

REFLECT

Why do people sometimes do the wrong thing even when they know it is wrong?

Write a 3-5 minute speech to raise awareness of an issue. Follow these steps to write your speech:

1. Identify a problem or issue at your school that should be addressed or could be changed. Possible ideas might include the following:
   - Availability of junk food
   - Cell phone policy
   - Volunteer opportunities at your school
   - Sports participation policies
   - Mandatory class requirements

2. Plan your speech by introducing the problem, providing facts and information about it, and offering a solution.

3. Conduct research about your topic so that you can add facts to your speech. You may need to interview school administrators, teachers, and other students to gather firsthand information. Use the Internet to learn about policies at other schools.

4. Practice your speech by reading it aloud several times. Make sure you are not tied to your notes. Make eye contact often with your audience. Avoid speaking too quickly. Make your voice interesting by using inflections and pauses effectively.

Use the following guidelines for your speech.	
To receive the highest score, the speech must meet all of these criteria.	Your speech • clearly and creatively explains the problem using facts and/or personal examples. • offers a reasonable solution to the problem. • shows evidence of research and demonstrates knowledge of the topic. • is three to five minutes in length. • is free from grammar, spelling, and punctuation errors. • is presented in a professional manner with good vocal variety to communicate ideas.

Letter to the Editor

A letter to the editor is a response to an article that is usually published in the editorial section of a newspaper. Most letters to the editor share an opposing viewpoint of a previously published article. They reference the content of the letter with which the writer disagrees, state why they disagree, and offer evidence to support an alternative point of view. For this project, you will write your own letter to the editor in response to "Why I Am a Vegetarian" or "Vegetarianism."

Follow these steps:

- Read some examples of letters to the editor in your local newspaper or an online newspaper. Think about the evidence the writer uses to support his or her claims.

- Before writing, think about your point of view toward vegetarianism. Provide evidence to support your position or that contradicts evidence presented in the text to which you are responding.

- Use business letter format in a block style and include the following: date, recipient's address (use information for your local newspaper's editor), salutation, body, closing, and signature.

Use the following guidelines for your letter to the editor.	
To receive the highest score, the letter must meet all of these criteria.	Your letter • references points made in the passage in this chapter. • clearly explains your point of view. • strongly supports your opinion by presenting reasons and evidence. • contains convincing and effective language and style. • is in business letter format with a header, salutation, body, and closing. • uses correct grammar, usage, punctuation, and spelling.

On Your Own: Integrating Ideas

1. Listen to one of Matthieu Ricard's TED talks, "The Habits of Happiness" or "How to Let Altruism Be Your Guide." Both can be found at www.ted.com.
2. Search online to discover the differences between vegetarians, vegans, and pescetarians. Also find out about the Paleolithic diet and how it compares to a vegan diet.
3. Learn more about teens and vegetarianism by reading Judy Krizmanic's *A Teen's Guide to Going Vegetarian.*
4. Go to www.matthieuricard.org to read an interview with Matthieu Ricard by the Garrison Institute, view some of his photographs, or learn more about his life.
5. Two of the chapters in this unit deal with the human treatment of animals. How has society's attitude toward animals changed in the last century? Why do you think this change has occurred?

Connect to Testing

In this chapter, you determined an author's purpose and analyzed evidence used in different arguments. When you take assessments, you will be tested on these skills. Answer the following questions.

1. Which of the following facts does Ricard use to support a selfish reason to eat only vegetables?

   A. *We can find means to survive without causing suffering to others.*

   B. *In India for example, there are over 400 million vegetarian people who survive well.*

   C. *They are not sacrificing their health or reducing their life span.*

   D. *Many studies have shown that red meat increases the incidence of colon cancer and other illnesses.*

2. Ricard's central claim is based on the assumption that the lives of animals and people are equally valuable. Which of the following quotations best support Ricard's assumption? (Choose all that apply.)

   A. *If you value others, you value their well-being and are concerned by their suffering.*

   B. *We can find means to survive without causing suffering to others.*

   C. *In India for example, there are over 400 million vegetarian people who survive well.*

   D. *In fact, even from a selfish standpoint, it is better to be a vegetarian.*

   E. *This would be called genocide or dehumanization if they were human beings.*

   F. *The main reason is that industrial farming causes the production of methane.*

3. Which sentence from "Vegetarianism" **most clearly** explains a central reason in support of vegetarianism?

   A. *killing a living creature that feels pleasure and pain is wrong, especially since we don't need to eat meat to be healthy.*

   B. *If pork were called pig and steak were called cow, I think more of the world would be vegetarian*

   C. *Humans have been eating meat for so many years, and they've been doing OK.*

   D. *Being vegetarian opens up a whole new world of food for them.*

4. **Part A:** Which claim is best supported by "Vegetarianism"?

   A. Many kids become vegetarians because they dislike the taste of meat.

   B. Many kids become vegetarians because they now have more options available outside of their homes.

   C. Many kids become vegetarians because they are concerned for their health.

   D. Many kids become vegetarians because they don't want to kill animals for food.

   Part B: Explain your reasoning for your answer in Part A above. Use textual evidence in your answer.

5. **Part A:** What does Krizmanic convey in paragraph 7 (lines 40–51)?

   A. Most people resist change, so they are unlikely to adopt vegetarianism.

   B. Most people do not question whether it is right to kill animals for meat because eating meat is their custom.

   C. Most people eat meat because they consider animals as lower life-forms and thus, fair game.

   D. Most people blindly follow tradition in all aspects of their lives.

continued on next page

Part B: How does Ricard address the answer to Part A in his article? Cite at least two details from the text for support.

6. **Part A:** In paragraph 4, to what does Ricard compare killing animals for food?

   A. regressing society

   B. consuming selfishly

   C. committing genocide

   D. objectifying animals

   Part B: Using your answer from Question 6, above, what does Ricard accomplish by using the comparison?

Writing an Argumentative Essay

"To educate a person in the mind but not in morals is to educate a menace to society."
— **Theodore Roosevelt**

In this unit, you read articles and stories related to the theme of right and wrong. This section will lead you step by step to use what you have learned by writing an argumentative text about an issue you believe in.

WRITING PROMPT

In chapter 5, the author of "Why I Am a Vegetarian" explains his personal reasons for choosing vegetarianism and supports these reasons with facts and statistics. What is an issue you feel strongly about and have a personal connection to? Make a claim about the issue in an argumentative essay. Support your claim with strong reasons based on research and on your own personal experience. Include a counterclaim and a response to the counterclaim. Write your essay so that it will appeal to a broad audience beyond just your teachers and classmates. Your argumentative essay should be three to five pages, typed, double-spaced, in standard Times New Roman 12-point font.

Prepare to Write

Read the prompt carefully. Underline key words that explain the requirements of the task. Break it down based on purpose, audience, content, and additional requirements by filling in the chart below.

Purpose	
Audience	
Content Requirements	
Additional Requirements	

Brainstorm

The topic of your argumentative essay should be something you feel personally connected to. Think about writing about an issue you or someone you know has experienced.

What struggles have you or someone you know faced and overcome?	What actions have you or someone you know taken to improve health or quality of life?

Complete the table to review some of the big ideas from the passages in this unit. Work independently or with a partner.

	Summary	What claim does the author make?	How could this information be used in an argumentative essay?
"Our Brains Are Wired for Morality: Evolution, Development, and Neuroscience"			

	Summary	What claim does the author make?	How could this information be used in an argumentative essay?
"Three Questions"			
"Zoo Complicated"			
"The Doll's House"			
"Why I Am a Vegetarian"			
"Vegetarianism"			

Generate Ideas

In order to help you narrow your focus and write a specific claim, explain your opinion about the following controversial topics. Then write a different opinion. This activity will help you consider counterclaims to include in your essay. Fill in the bottom two rows with your own topics.

Topic	My Opinion	A Different Opinion
cyberbullying		
the rise of social media		
teenagers working		
different standards for males versus females		
school uniforms		

In order to support your ideas about a controversial topic, gather evidence from other sources. Find and read at least four sources on your chosen topic. In your response journal, on notecards, or in a computer file, take detailed notes on your sources. As you record information, always record the source. Keep a list of your sources in the box below. Include the author's name, title of the article or book, website name, publisher, and date of publication.

Sources

1.

2.

3.

4.

Once you have enough solid information about your topic, write a strong claim. Your claim should make a statement explaining what you want to see changed about the issue you researched. In order to write a strong claim, synthesize the ideas from your research by drawing a conclusion based on the facts and evidence presented by all the sources. Make sure your claim is specific. Then think of strong reasons to support your claim. Support your reasons with evidence, such as facts and personal testimony. Study this example:

Claim: American football is dangerous to players and should be banned in high school.

Reason 1: High school football players are at a high risk of injuries, such as concussions.

Evidence: Statistics from a study by the Institute of Medicine and guidelines from the American Academy of Neurology.

Reason 2: Younger football players often feel motivated to ignore injuries to "get back in the game," and they fear letting their teammates down, so they may make unwise decisions.

Evidence: My personal testimony as a football player.

Counterclaim/Alternative evidence: Injuries happen in all sports, so it is unfair to single out injuries that occur while playing football.

Response to counterclaim/alternative evidence: Out of nine sports, football has the highest number of head injuries, which are potentially more dangerous injuries.

Now synthesize the information from your sources and write your own claim with two strong reasons below.

My claim:

Reason 1:

Reason 2:

Organize Ideas

Copy this basic outline into your response journal. Use the sentence starters to help you write a basic outline for your essay. Claim:

I. Introduction

    A. Introduce your topic, capture the reader's interest, use a quote from a text in this unit.

    B. State your claim.

II. The first reason that . . .

    A. Evidence that supports this is . . .

    B. Also, . . .

III. (Counterclaim) Some people may argue that . . .
    However, . . . (Evidence against counterclaim)

IV. Another reason is . . .

    A. Support for this includes . . .

    B. Further evidence proves that . . .

V. Conclusion

    A. In conclusion . . .

    B. Restate your claim in different words.

First Draft

Use your outline to write a draft of your essay. Here are some hints:

- Use to the outline you wrote in your response journal.
- Write quickly. You will revise and proofread later.
- Write on every other line or double-space if working on a computer. This will make it easier to make revisions.
- If you take a break and then return to drafting, reread what you have written before continuing. This will help you continue with your thoughts.
- Mark this paper Draft #1.

> **REFLECT**
>
> As you research your topic, your claim may change based on new information. This is a good thing. It means you are keeping an open mind about your topic and are willing to re-evaluate your opinion as you learn new information.

Revision

Having other students and your teacher read your essay will help you improve it. Listen carefully to their questions and comments on your writing. Applying their advice will help you refine your writing.

Here are three ways to revise your paper.

First Peer Review

This review will evaluate whether your ideas are interesting and whether they flow together in a logical order. With a group of two or three people, complete the following steps.

Steps for Peer Review

1. Select a timekeeper. Each writer gets 15 minutes. Respect the time limit.

2. One person begins by reading aloud his or her first paragraph while other members listen.

3. Pause. The same writer reads the first paragraph aloud a second time.

4. The writer asks, "Does the introduction clearly explain my claim and make you want to know more? " Each member responds, as the writer takes notes on his or her draft.

5. The writer reads the entire essay, pauses, and then reads it again.

6. As the writer reads, members take notes.

7. The writer asks, "Did I use strong reasons to support my claim? Did I include effective evidence? Do my key ideas fit together clearly and logically? The writer jots down replies.

8. Repeat Steps 1-7 with the next member of the group who becomes the writer.

REFLECT

The introduction usually has a "hook" to get readers' attention. This hook may be a quote, story, or startling statistic.

©Perfection Learning® • No Reproduction Permitted

Using Transitions

Transitional words and phrases help readers make connections among ideas. As you revise your paper, make sure you have used appropriate transitions between and within paragraphs.

Transitions			
Point to a reason	**Identify a conclusion**	**Show a contrast**	**Show sequence**
because	as a result	although	first, second, third
if	thus	even though	then
since	so	however	next
for this reason	consequently	but	finally
the first reason, another reason	then	on the other hand	before, after, later
	therefore	in contrast	soon
	in conclusion	instead	when

As soon as possible after peer review, revise your draft based on your peers' questions and comments. Mark this paper Draft #2.

Second Peer Review

With a partner, trade essays and use the following checklist to evaluate your partner's essay.

Think big. Look at the draft as a whole.

☐ Has the writer covered everything required by the prompt?
☐ Is the flow between paragraphs smooth or choppy?
☐ Is the point of view consistent throughout?

Think medium. Look at the draft paragraph by paragraph.

☐ Does the introduction hook the reader and make him or her want to read more?
☐ Does each paragraph support the claim with various types of valid evidence?
☐ Are the ideas supported by research?
☐ Did the writer include a valid counterclaim or alternative explanations?

Think small. Look at your draft sentence by sentence.

☐ Which sentences are long and confusing? Short and choppy?
☐ Are any sentences unclear?
☐ Are there errors in spelling, grammar, or usage?

When you finish the steps, mark the version Draft #3.

> **REFLECT**
>
> Reading and revising the same paper over and over again may become tiresome and make you start skipping over words and sentences because they are so familiar. Try reading the essay in reverse to stay focused.

Final Peer Review

Ask another student to read your argumentative essay and rate it using the rubric below:

Use the following guidelines for your argumentative essay.	
To receive the highest score, the essay must meet all of these criteria.	Your argumentative essay • makes a claim about a specific topic. • supports the claim with more than one reason. • includes strong evidence that supports the reasons. • relates a personal experience in support of the claim. • includes a counterclaim, along with evidence in response to the counterclaim. • uses transitions to help the reader follow the flow of ideas. • is clearly organized with good transitions between sentences and paragraphs. • uses correct grammar, usage, punctuation, and spelling.

Proofread

As you prepare a final draft, make sure you have included correct grammar and punctuation. Proofread carefully for omitted words and punctuation marks, especially when using direct quotations. If you used a word processing program, run spell-check, but know that it won't catch every error. Proofread again to detect the kinds of errors the computer can't catch.

Final Essay

Share your completed essay with audiences beyond your classroom. Read it to your family and friends. Upload your finished digital copy to your class website. If you have a school or personal blog or website, share it with your readers.

Practice Performance Task

A performance task evaluates your ability to comprehend selections of literature and informational text and then demonstrate your knowledge in writing. The task may begin with several multiple-choice or short-answer questions on key vocabulary and the key ideas of the passage(s). The task culminates with a writing assignment. Complete the following performance task based upon selections from Unit 1.

Source #1

Read the following excerpt from "Our Brains Are Wired for Morality: Evolution, Development, and Neuroscience" by J. Decety and J. Cowell. Then answer the questions that follow.

Humans are an extremely <u>social</u> species. We are dependent on each other and cannot survive and flourish without interacting with others. Newborns only survive to adulthood if given enough care, and societies succeed through cooperation. Almost all of our actions and thoughts are about others or are in response to others. We cooperate with and help people who are not related to us at a level that is unmatched in the animal kingdom [1]. Since humans are, by nature, both helpful and selfish, we think that morality evolved to support our helpful social interactions with others and control our somewhat selfish tendencies.

However, it would be misleading to see morality as only a result of evolution. Although some human traits, like skin color, are determined by our genes alone, morality is quite different in that it is also determined both by our nature and the society in which we live. Many moral rules and values vary between different <u>cultures</u> and also change over time. For instance, bull fighting is seen as a cruel form of entertainment or even as animal torture in North America and most European countries, but it is still very popular in Spain and Colombia where it is considered a form of expression, despite the obvious suffering of the animals. An example of a shift in morality over time is our attitude toward slavery. Most people in the world today think that it is immoral to own slaves but that was not the case a century ago.

continued on next page

Thus, our morality has been formed over thousands of years from the combination of both our genes and our culture, rather than just one or the other. This genetic and cultural evolution has shaped our brains to care for others, react to those who try to harm us, and to create moral rules that help us to live together successfully [2].

1. **Part A:** According to the passage, the word *social* most nearly means
   A. having to do with evolution.
   B. related to relationships.
   C. knowing right and wrong.
   D. fighting for survival.

   Part B: Which of the following lines from the text provide the strongest evidence for your answer to Part A? Choose all that apply.
   A. *dependent on each other*
   B. *without interacting with others*
   C. *only survive to adulthood*
   D. *societies succeed through cooperation*
   E. *Almost all of our actions*

2. The word *cultures* is best explained by which phrase from the passage?
   A. *our nature*
   B. *the society in which we live*
   C. *moral rules and values*
   D. *change over time*

3. **Part A:** Which of the following best summarizes the **key idea** of the passage?
   A. Concepts of right and wrong have been formed through evolutionary changes in our biological makeup and through the communities in which we live.
   B. An understanding of right is wrong is unique to humans and not found in the animal kingdom.
   C. Morality is often based on culture and thus changes depending on where you live.
   D. Morality has to do with caring for others within our own society, protecting ourselves from enemies, and creating standards by which to live.

Part B: Which sentence from the text best supports the answer to Part A?

A. *Newborns only survive to adulthood if given enough care, and societies succeed through cooperation.*

B. *morality evolved to support our helpful social interactions with others and control our somewhat selfish tendencies.*

C. *Most people in the world today think that it is immoral to own slaves but that was not the case a century ago.*

D. *Thus, our morality has been formed over thousands of years from the combination of both our genes and our culture*

Source #2

Read the following passage from the short story "Three Questions" by Leo Tolstoy.

The King approached him, and said:

"For the last time, I pray you to answer my questions, wise man."

"You have already been answered!" said the hermit, still crouching on his thin legs, and looking up at the King, who stood before him.

"How answered? What do you mean?" asked the King.

"Do you not see," replied the hermit. "If you had not pitied my weakness yesterday, and had not dug those beds for me, but had gone your way, that man would have attacked you, and you would have repented of not having stayed with me. So the most important time was when you were digging the beds; and I was the most important man; and to do me good was your most important business. Afterwards when that man ran to us, the most important time was when you were attending to him, for if you had not bound up his wounds he would have died without having made peace with you. So he was the most important man, and what you did for him was your most important business. Remember then: there is only one time that is important—Now! It is the most important time because it is the only time when we have any power. The most necessary man is he with whom you are, for no man knows whether he will ever have dealings with anyone else: and the most important affair is, to do him good, because for that purpose alone was man sent into this life!"

continued on next page

4. **Part A:** The hermit's response to the King reveals that his point of view of morality is based on

A. respect for others.

B. helping the weak and the needy.

C. paying back those who've wronged you.

D. living a simple life of poverty.

Part B: Identify two lines from the text that support the answer to Part A. Explain how these lines provide evidence for the answer.

Your Assignment

WRITING PROMPT

In this unit you read a variety of texts related to the Essential Question: *How do you know right from wrong?* You read informational articles that discussed people's desire to know right and wrong, stories in which characters made good and bad choices, and arguments in which authors developed their point of view on the issues of keeping wild animals in captivity and vegetarianism.

Write an essay in which you bring together ideas about morality from the texts in this chapter as you answer the question: How do you know right and wrong? In your answer, refer to at least three different texts in the unit as support for your conclusions about morality.

To gather ideas for your essay, fill in the following graphic organizer with details from the texts in this unit.

	What does the text say about how we (or the author) know right from wrong?	What does the text say (or imply) about specific actions that are right or wrong?
"Our Brains Are Wired for Morality: Evolution, Development, and Neuroscience"		
"Three Questions"	The hermit tells the King that the current time is the most important time because it is only now in the current moment that we have any power.	

continued on next page

	What does the text say about how we (or the author) know right from wrong?	What does the text say (or imply) about specific actions that are right or wrong?
"Zoo Complicated"		Keeping wild animals in captivity just for human enjoyment is wrong.
"The Doll's House"		
"Why I Am a Vegetarian"	The author's beliefs about vegetarianism come from his practice of Buddhism, which believes in showing compassion and valuing all creatures.	
"Vegetarianism"		

Your Assignment (continued)

Read the prompt carefully. Underline words that indicate how to write your essay. The rubric on page 116 features the qualities on which your writing will be evaluated. Study the rubric before you begin to write.

Use the organizer below and your answers to the chart on pages 113 and 114 to plan your essay. Make sure your thesis statement is a response to the unit Essential Question. Use evidence from at least three texts in the unit.

Introduction: Main idea statement (answer to Essential Question):
One way I know right from wrong:
Another way I know right from wrong:
Conclusion:

Your writing will be evaluated on the following. Think about each of these points in relation to your writing. Fill in notes about whether you have met the standard or if you need to make revisions.

Reading Comprehension

- How well did you understand the texts?

- Does your essay reflect a correct understanding of the sources?

Writing Expression

- Does your writing address the requirements of the prompt?

- Does your informative essay include a clear thesis statement?

- Is your essay clearly organized with points that fit together logically?

- Does your writing style contain precise, accurate language and content appropriate to the purpose, task, and audience?

Writing Conventions

- Does your writing follow the rules of standard English with few or no errors in grammar, usage, and spelling?

Use the list above to help you revise your essay.

Unit 2

Essential Question
Can you trust what you see, hear, and read?

Sometimes it's hard to know what to trust. Can that shocking headline you just saw online be true? Or is it just "fake news"? Will that alternative medicine really make you healthier, or is that "one weird trick" just a scam? Sometimes you can't even trust your own senses.

When the world seems like it is out to fool you, what can you do? It might be tempting to give up on the idea of truth altogether. If it's impossible to know what is real, then why bother trying? A more powerful way to respond is to become a more critical consumer. Instead of giving in to the lies, you can develop mental habits to help you tell facts from falsehoods and strike back against dishonesty.

Unit 2 will explore issues of trust, truth, and fact-finding. You'll read about the ultimate con man, your tricky brain and eyes, fake news, sketchy medicine, and a society that is not as perfect as it seems. As you read these texts, remember that the truth is out there, even if it's not always easy to find. Sometimes you have to hunt for it.

GOALS

- To determine central ideas and analyze how they develop
- To analyze the interactions between individuals, events, and ideas
- To explore how the structure of a text contributes to its meaning
- To determine point of view and author's purpose
- To research how one scientific explanation replaced another
- To write an explanatory essay comparing two texts

Chapter 6

Understanding Different Points of View

Preview Concepts

Name someone you trust. Why do you trust this person? Write your response below. Include two details from your interactions with him or her.

Share your answers with a partner. Based on your discussion, form a definition of *trustworthy* you both agree on. Write your definition in the space below.

Making Connections

Read the following excerpts. They express strong points of view about honesty and lying.

> Uncompromising integrity of character is invaluable. It secures to its possessor a peace and joy which cannot be attained without it—which no amount of money, or houses and lands can purchase. A man who is known to be strictly honest, may be ever so poor, but he has the purses of all the community at his disposal . . . .
>
> —from *The Art of Money Getting* by P. T. Barnum

> People have a careless way of talking about a 'born liar,' just as they talk about a 'born poet.' But in both cases they are wrong. Lying and poetry are arts . . . .Many a young man starts in life with a natural gift for exaggeration which, if nurtured . . . might grow into something really great and wonderful.
>
> —from "The Decay of Lying: An Observation" by Oscar Wilde

What is P. T. Barnum's point of view about honesty? Include evidence from the text to support your response.

What point of view about lying is expressed in the second excerpt? Include evidence from the text to support your response.

MAKING
CONNECTIONS

The main text in this chapter was written by a man famous for tricking people. Think about the points of view people have of him as well as how he sees himself.

First Read: Making an Inference

Frank Abagnale Jr., the coauthor of the excerpt below, spent the late 1960s and early 1970s pretending to be people he was not, including a doctor, a lawyer, and a government agent. He also stole a great deal of money through many schemes. In this excerpt from the first chapter of his book *Catch Me If You Can*, Frank describes tricking people into thinking he is an airplane pilot. At the time, he was only seventeen years old.

Objective: As you read, underline sentences that suggest whether people trust Frank Abagnale. Record any questions you have about the passage in the My Thoughts column.

from
Catch Me If You Can
by Frank Abagnale Jr. with Stan Redding

	My Thoughts

1   A man's alter ego is nothing more than his favorite image of himself. The mirror in my room in the Windsor Hotel in Paris reflected my favorite image of me—a darkly handsome young airline pilot, smooth-skinned, bull-shouldered and

5   immaculately groomed. Modesty is not one of my virtues. At the time, virtue was not one of my virtues.

Satisfied with my appearance, I picked up my bag, left the room and two minutes later was standing in front of the cashier's cage.

10   "Good morning, Captain," said the cashier in warm tones. The markings on my uniform identified me as a first officer, a co-pilot, but the French are like that. They tend to overestimate everything save their women, wine and art.

I signed the hotel bill she slid across the counter, started to

15   turn away, then wheeled back, taking a payroll check from the inside pocket of my jacket. "Oh, can you cash this for me? Your Paris night life nearly wiped me out and it'll be another week before I'm home." I smiled ruefully.

She picked up the Pan American World Airways check and
20 looked at the amount. "I'm sure we can, Captain, but I must
get the manager to approve a check this large," she said. She
stepped into an office behind her and was back in a moment,
displaying a pleased smile. She handed me the check to
endorse.

25   "I assume you want American dollars?" she asked, and
without waiting for my reply counted out $786.73 in Yankee
currency and coin. I pushed back two $50 bills. "I would
appreciate it if you would take care of the necessary people,
since I was so careless," I said, smiling.

30   She beamed. "Of course, Captain. You are very kind," she
said. "Have a safe flight and please come back to see us."

    I took a cab to Orly, instructing the driver to let me off at
the TWA entrance. I bypassed the TWA ticket counter in the
lobby and presented my FAA license and Pan Am ID card to
35 the TWA operations officer. He checked his manifest. "Okay,
First Officer Frank Williams, **deadheading** to Rome. Gotcha.
Fill this out, please." He handed me the familiar pink form for
nonrevenue passengers and I penned in the pertinent data.
I picked up my bag and walked to the customs gate marked
40 "CREW MEMBERS ONLY." I started to heft my bag to the
counter top but the inspector, a wizened old man with a wispy
mustache, recognized me and waved me through.

    A young boy fell in beside me as I walked to the plane,
gazing with unabashed admiration at my uniform with its
45 burnished gold stripes and other adornments.

    "You the pilot?" he asked. He was English from his accent.

    "Nah, just a passenger like you," I replied. "I fly for Pan Am."

My Thoughts

---

deadheading: riding without buying a ticket

"You fly 707s?"

I shook my head. "Used to," I said. "Right now I'm on DC-
50 8s." I like kids. This one reminded me of myself a few years
past.

An attractive blond stewardess met me as I stepped aboard
and helped me to stow my gear in the crew's luggage bin.
"We've got a full load this trip, Mr. Williams," she said. "You
55 beat out two other guys for the jump seat. I'll be serving the
cabin."

"Just milk for me," I said. "And don't worry about that
if you get busy. Hitchhikers aren't entitled to anything more
than the ride."

60 I ducked into the cabin. The pilot, co-pilot and flight
engineer were making their pre-takeoff equipment and
instrument check but they paused courteously at my entrance.
"Hi, Frank Williams, Pan Am, and don't let me interrupt you," I
said.

65 "Gary Giles," said the pilot, sticking out his hand. He
nodded toward the other two men. "Bill Austin, number two,
and Jim Wright. Good to have you with us." I shook hands
with the other two airmen and dropped into the jump seat,
leaving them to their work.

70 We were airborne within twenty minutes. Giles took the
707 up to 30,000 feet, checked his instruments, cleared with
the Orly tower and then uncoiled himself from his seat. He
appraised me with casual thoroughness and then indicated his
chair. "Why don't you fly this bird for a while, Frank," he said.
75 "I'll go back and mingle with the paying passengers."

His offer was a courtesy gesture sometimes accorded a
deadheading pilot from a competing airline. I dropped my

cap on the cabin floor and slid into the command seat, very

much aware that I had been handed custody of 140 lives,

80 my own included. Austin, who had taken the controls when

Giles vacated his seat, surrendered them to me. "You got it,

Captain," he said, grinning.

    I promptly put the giant jet on automatic pilot and hoped

to [heck] the gadget worked, because I couldn't fly a kite.

85   I wasn't a Pan Am pilot or any other kind of pilot. I was

an impostor, one of the most wanted criminals on four

continents, and at the moment I was doing my thing, putting a

super hype on some nice people. . . .

    Oddly enough, I never felt like a criminal. I was one, of

90 course, and I was aware of the fact. I've been described by

authorities and news reporters as one of this century's cleverest

bum-check passers, flimflam artists and crooks, a con man

of Academy Award caliber. I was a swindler and poseur of

astonishing ability. I sometimes astonished myself with some

95 of my impersonations and shenanigans, but I never at any time

deluded myself. I was always aware that I was Frank Abagnale, Jr.,

that I was a check swindler and a faker, and if and when I were

caught I wasn't going to win any Oscars. I was going to jail.

FIRST RESPONSE: KEY IDEAS AND DETAILS

Return to the sentences you underlined. How do other people
feel about Frank? How do you know? Write your answers to
these questions in your reading journal. Use details from the
text in your response.

My Thoughts

TECH-CONNECT

Post your First
Response answers
on your class web
page. Compare your
answers to those
posted by other
students.

Focus on Making an Inference

After reading the passage, what do you think? Do people trust Frank Abagnale? Analyze the text to find out.

The word *analyze* means "to discover or reveal something through close examination." When you analyze a text, you are reading closely to figure out what the text says and how it says it.

Complete the chart below. In the column on the right, provide the evidence that answers each question. Then at the bottom of the chart, write your conclusion to this question: Do people seem to trust Frank Abagnale?

Question	Evidence
Does the cashier trust Frank?	
Does the "wizened old man" at the gate trust Frank?	
Does Gary Giles, the pilot, trust Frank?	
Your conclusion: Do people seem to trust Frank?	

You might not realize it, but you just made an inference. An *inference* is "a conclusion based on textual evidence and your prior knowledge." In the chart on the previous page

- your conclusion is about whether people trust Frank.

- the evidence consists of details from the text that support your conclusion.

- your prior knowledge is what you already know. In this case, you already know how people usually act toward someone they trust.

It might seem obvious that the people in the story trust Frank. But Frank never actually says, "These people trusted me." No character openly says, "I trust you, Frank." You as the reader came to the conclusion that people trust Frank, and you supported that conclusion with evidence.

Write Frank Abagnale was eventually caught by police. Do you think he wrote this book *before* or *after* his capture? Why do you think this? Support your inference with at least two details from the text.

Second Read: Analyzing Point of View

In literature, the term *point of view* refers to a narrator's or character's thoughts and feelings about something. That "something" can be a person, a place, an action, a series of events, or anything else that a person can have an opinion about.

Objective: Read the passage again. As you read, think about Frank's point of view about his skills as a pilot and Gary Giles's point of view about Frank's skills. Draw boxes around evidence showing each man's point of view.

Focus on Analyzing Point of View

As a narrator, Frank has a point of view about himself and his actions. The details he presents as the author are evidence of that point of view. But it's not just *Frank* who has a point of view about himself. Other characters do too. For example, Gary Giles has a point of view about Frank and his piloting skills.

REFLECT

Think about the first sentence: "A man's alter ego is nothing more than his favorite image of himself." What does Frank mean here by *image?* Do you have a favorite image of yourself? Do you consider that image an *alter ego*, which means "another self"?

CONNECT TO ESSENTIAL QUESTION

In the excerpt, Frank the character is obviously trying to fool people. But what about Frank the narrator, who is telling the story? Do you think he is trustworthy? What evidence do you have for your opinion?

continued on next page

You can analyze Frank's and Gary's points of view about Frank's skills as a pilot. Use the chart below to perform your analysis.

Two Points of View About Frank's Skills as a Pilot	
Frank's point of view about his skills as a pilot:	Gary's point of view about Frank's skills as a pilot:
Two pieces of evidence showing Frank's point of view:	Two pieces of evidence showing Gary's point of view:

The point of view of a narrator or character is not always explicit. For example, Gary's point of view might seem obvious through his actions, but nowhere does he explicitly say, "Frank, I know that you have great piloting skills." You as the reader had to infer his point of view.

Third Read: Comparing and Contrasting Presentations

People tell stories through different media, such as books and films. Each medium has different techniques, or methods, for telling that story.

- When a story or a book tells a narrative, its techniques are textual. These techniques can include rambling sentences, brief fragments, interesting similes, odd metaphors, punchy dialogue, long paragraphs—the list goes on and on.

- When a film tells a story, it uses different techniques: lighting, sound, color, camera focus, camera angles, and so on. In a film, everything you see and hear has been carefully chosen to make the audience feel a certain way.

Whether you're reading a text or watching a film, you can analyze how the techniques of each medium work together to tell a story. And if you read a story and watch a film based on it, you can compare how the two media tell their tales.

Watch a scene from the film version of *Catch Me If You Can*. Analyze the techniques the film uses to present events. You should watch it at least three times to gather enough details to complete the chart.

Film Analysis Worksheet of *Catch Me If You Can*
During Viewing
Color Describe the colors in the scene. Are they gray, dark, or washed out? Are they bright, full, or strong? Why do you think the director chose to film the scene this way?
Point of View Sometimes we see Frank interacting with characters. Other times we see the world from Frank's point of view. How does switching the camera's point of view help to tell the story?

continued on next page

Music As the plane takes off, music begins. What does the music communicate to the viewer? Is it meant to express something about Frank's feelings or situation? Does it try to make the audience feel a certain way? (If it helps, try imagining that same scene without the music.)

Lighting As the plane takes off, sunlight moves over Frank's face. This shows the plane is moving. But could the light have any other purposes? (If it helps, try imagining that moment without the light moving.)

After Viewing

Overall Impressions What did you like and dislike about the scene? What emotions did you experience? Do you think the film made you feel what the director wanted you to feel?

Objective: Read the text a third time. Write Similar in the My Thoughts column next to details that are similar and Different if the details are different.

Focus on Comparing and Contrasting Presentations

Think about the scene from the film and the text. You're ready to compare and contrast the two presentations of these events in Frank's story.

What scene from the text does the clip show?

Use the chart below to gather information so you can compare and contrast the text and the scene from the film. The first row and the first column in the second row have been completed for you.

Question	Text	Film
How is Frank presented physically?	Frank describes himself as "bull-shouldered" (large) and "darkly handsome." He sounds like a grown man.	Frank looks slender and brunette. He seems more boyish than adult.
What are Frank's words and reactions as he checks in at the gate?	The passage doesn't describe them, but all interactions prior to that point suggest Frank has been talking and reacting confidently.	

continued on next page

Question	Text	Film
What does Frank know about the "jump seat"? How do you know?		
What kinds of things does Frank say to the pilots before takeoff?		
How does Frank feel as the plane takes off? What is the evidence?		
Are there other important similarities or differences you noticed? What are they?		

Speak and Listen Form a small group with three or four classmates and compare charts. Discuss how the text and the film clip are similar and different. Refer to specific sentences and paragraphs in the text. When discussing the film, refer to the information you recorded in your chart.

Write Write a paragraph comparing and contrasting the differences and similarities between the text and the movie. Consider events, characterization, and style of writing/film. Be specific as possible, referring to at least two details in the book and two techniques (such as lighting or music) in the film.

Language: Understanding Context Clues

The excerpt uses some words you might not know. Using context clues, or nearby words or sentences, is one way to determine the meaning of unknown words.

The following chart has words from *Catch Me If You Can*. Use context clues to make an inference about the meaning of each word. Then check the dictionary definition to determine whether your inference is accurate. The first row has been completed for you.

Word	My Inference About the Word's Meaning	Context Clues Supporting My Inference	Dictionary Definition
immaculately (line 5)	"perfectly" or "wonderfully"	He looks at himself in a mirror. He says he is not modest. He is satisfied with his appearance. This suggests he groomed himself perfectly.	*Immaculately* means "free from flaws or mistakes."
manifest (line 35)			

continued on next page

Word	My Inference About the Word's Meaning	Context Clues Supporting My Inference	Dictionary Definition
adornments (line 45)			
appraised (line 73)			

Project-Based Assessments

Introducing Frank Abagnale

In the 1970s, law enforcement captured and jailed Frank Abagnale. After several years in prison, Abagnale was released and went on to live a very different kind of life. What did Abagnale do after prison? Does his life offer any lessons?

Imagine you're introducing Frank Abagnale to an audience of people who know nothing about his life. What was Frank like as a young man? What is he doing now? What lesson can we draw from his life?

TECH-CONNECT

Watch other scenes from *Catch Me If You Can* on YouTube. Think about how the movie uses lighting, music, and dialogue to shape the audience's attitude toward Frank Abagnale and his adventures.

Write a paragraph introducing Frank Abagnale. Follow these steps.

1. Reread the excerpt from *Catch Me If You Can*. Describe the kind of person Abagnale used to be. Use at least two details from the excerpt.

2. Using the Internet or information provided by your teacher, find out what Abagnale has done since leaving prison. Provide at least two details about his life.

3. Explain to your audience what lesson, if any, you think Abagnale's life teaches.

Use the following guidelines for your introduction.	
To receive the highest score (4.0), the introduction must meet all of these criteria.	Your introduction • describes and gives details about who Frank Abagnale used to be. • describes and gives details about what Abagnale is doing now. • makes a claim for a lesson people can draw from Abagnale's life. • contains correct grammar, usage, punctuation, and spelling.

Character Analysis

Frank Abagnale's story is real, but *Catch Me If You Can* is not strictly true. As Abagnale later wrote, "I was interviewed by the co-writer only about four times. I believe he did a great job of telling the story, but he also over-dramatized and exaggerated some of the story."

Because the book tells events in story form, you can write about the character Frank Abagnale just as you would any other character. A character analysis describes what a character is like based on what he or she thinks, says, and does.

Write a paragraph in response to the following task.

> In the film, the character Frank Abagnale shows he is unsure of himself. For example, he doesn't know what *deadheading* means. He also doesn't know what or where the jump seat is; the stewardess has to open it for him.

In contrast, the book excerpt presents Frank differently. Write a paragraph responding to these questions:

- In the book, does Frank seem unsure to you? If not, what does he seem to be?

- What does Frank think, say, and do in the book that makes you think this?

continued on next page

Use specific details from the excerpt to support your ideas.

Use the following guidelines for your character analysis.	
To receive the highest score (4.0), the character analysis must meet all of these criteria.	Your character analysis • clearly states what the character Frank is like. • gives examples of what Frank thinks, says, and does that support your statements. • uses linking words and phrases such as *for example*, *also*, or *in addition*. • is free from grammar, spelling, and punctuation errors.

On Your Own: Integrating Ideas

1. Frank Abagnale has spent several decades teaching both individuals and institutions how to combat fraud. Visit his website Abagnale.com to learn how he turned his life of crime into a business that helps other people. You can also see Frank answer many questions about his life of crime at forum-network.org/lectures/catch-me-if-you-can-frank-abagnales-story/.

2. Frank Abagnale actually has advice for *you* about how to avoid scams. Visit the site news.bbc.co.uk/2/hi/business/4754733.stm to read an interview in which Frank tells how to avoid getting tricked by people like him.

3. In traditional literature, a trickster is a character who cheats or deceives people. Famous tricksters include Coyote in Native American folktales, Anansi the Spider in African folktales, and Loki in Norse mythology. Do some research on the qualities of tricksters, whom they typically come into conflict with, and what often happens to the characters in their stories. Then discuss with a partner: Even though Frank Abagnale is a real person, can you also consider him a literary trickster? Why or why not?

> **REFLECT**
>
> What is the relationship between truth and trust? Is there ever a time when it is okay to lie to a person who trusts you?

Connect to Testing

In this chapter, you supported ideas with text evidence, analyzed different points of view, and compared two presentations of a story. When you take assessments, you will be asked questions related to these skills. Answer the following questions over these skills. Try to answer the first question on your own before reading the explanation below.

1. Read this statement about Frank Abagnale, the narrator and main character of *Catch Me If You Can*.

   > Frank feels pride in his skills at fooling people.

   Which of the following choices from the excerpt is the **best** evidence supporting this statement?

   A. *A man's alter ego is nothing more than his favorite image of himself.*

   B. *I like kids. This one reminded me of myself a few years past.*

   C. *I promptly put the giant jet on automatic pilot and hoped to [heck] the gadget worked, because I couldn't fly a kite.*

   D. *I sometimes astonished myself with some of my impersonations and shenanigans, but I never at any time deluded myself.*

EXPLANATION

- The question asks you to find evidence that Frank Abagnale is at least a little proud of his abilities.

- Choice A is a claim that Frank makes about people generally, and one he believes about himself. But it does not suggest pride in his ability to fool others.

- Choice B is evidence that Frank likes not just kids but also the kid he used to be, but the statements are unrelated to Frank's feelings about his ability to fool people.

- Choice C is evidence that Frank is fooling people, but it does not indicate how he feels about his skills.

- Choice D is the correct answer. The fact that Frank could "astonish" himself suggests he feels at least a little pride in his skills in fooling people.

continued on next page

2. Which excerpt from *Catch Me If You Can* suggests that Frank feels guilty about how he used to fool people?

   A. *The mirror in my room in the Windsor Hotel in Paris reflected my favorite image of me—a darkly handsome young airline pilot. . . .*

   B. *A young boy fell in beside me as I walked to the plane, gazing with unabashed admiration at my uniform. . . .*

   C. *I was an imposter, one of the most wanted criminals on four continents, and at the moment I was doing my thing, putting a super hype on some nice people. . . .*

   D. *I've been described by authorities and news reports as one of this century's cleverest bum-check passers. . . .*

3. **Part A:** Which word **best** describes how the character of Frank behaves around other people?

   A. quiet

   B. humble

   C. nervous

   D. boastful

   Part B: Which of the following best supports your answer to Part A?

   A. *The mirror in my room in the Windsor Hotel in Paris reflected my favorite image of me—a darkly handsome young airline pilot, smooth-skinned, bull-shouldered and immaculately groomed.*

   B. *The markings on my uniform identified me as a first officer, a co-pilot, but the French are like that. They tend to overestimate everything save their women, wine and art.*

   C. *"Oh, can you cash this for me? Your Paris nightlife nearly wiped me out and it'll be another week before I'm home." I smiled ruefully.*

   D. *"Just milk for me," I said. "And don't worry about that if you get busy. Hitchhikers aren't entitled to anything more than the ride."*

4. **Part A:** How does Frank the narrator view his younger self?

   A. Frank sees himself as a better person than he was as a young man.

   B. Frank believes he is exactly the same person he used to be.

   C. Frank feels he is a worse person now than when he was young.

   D. Frank believes he has nothing in common with the person he was.

Part B: In the paragraph below, underline one sentence that supports the answer to Part A.

A man's alter ego is nothing more than his favorite image of himself. The mirror in my room in the Windsor Hotel in Paris reflected my favorite image of me—a darkly handsome young airline pilot, smooth-skinned, bull-shouldered and immaculately groomed. Modesty is not one of my virtues. At the time, virtue was not one of my virtues.

5. Which of these correctly describes a difference between the written and filmed versions of *Catch Me If You Can*?

A. The written version uses dialogue showing how people react to Frank. The filmed version does not.

B. The written version shows Frank tricking his way onto a plane. The filmed version does not.

C. The filmed version reveals Frank's thoughts as he fools people. The written version does not.

D. The filmed version shows how Frank feels as the plane takes off. The written version does not.

Chapter 7

Analyzing Central Ideas

Preview Concepts

You've probably heard the phrase "Seeing is believing." But what does it actually mean? Explain below what you think the phrase means, using at least one example from your own life.

Making Connections

Read the following excerpt from a book by a scientist who lived more than one hundred years ago. He talks about the difference between seeing and looking.

> What we do see depends mainly on what we look for. When we turn our eyes to the sky, it is in most cases merely to see whether it is likely to rain. In the same field the farmer will notice the crop, geologists the fossils, botanists the flowers, artists the colouring, sportsmen the cover for game. Though we may all look at the same things, it does not at all follow that we should see them.
>
> —*The Beauties of Nature and the Wonders of the World We Live In* by John Lubbock (1892)

According to Lubbock, how are *seeing* and *looking* related? Why do people *look* at the same thing and *see* something different? Quote a detail from the text that supports your answer.

MAKING CONNECTIONS

In this chapter you will analyze a book excerpt that discusses whether the phrase "seeing is believing" is entirely accurate.

First Read: Analyzing Central Ideas

If you see it with your own eyes, it must be true. Right? Not according to Guy Harrison, an American writer, journalist, and photographer.

Objective: As you read the excerpt, underline the most important idea of each paragraph. Record any questions you have in the My Thoughts column.

excerpt
Think: Why You Should Question Everything
by Guy Harrison

	My Thoughts

1   Have you heard the old saying, "seeing is believing"?
Well, it's often a case of *believing is seeing*. It is well known
by researchers that what we think we see can be strongly
influenced by images and ideas we have been exposed to
5   previously as well as our own thoughts and imagination. This
probably explains why it's the people who already believe
in ghosts or UFOs who keep seeing ghosts or UFOs, and why
so few nonbelievers do. Seeing things that are not there can
happen to anyone because the human brain *constructs* and
10   *interprets* the visual reality that is around it. What we see
is something the brain has produced for us *based on* input
it received via the eyes. It's never a 100 percent true and
complete reflection of what our eyes are pointed at. For this
reason, we can't always be sure about what we think we see.
15   Yes, that might be an angel that you see up ahead. Or your
brain could be showing you an angel that it has mistakenly
constructed out of a bush or some other object.

   Construct and interpret reality? It sounds crazy when
you think about it. We don't really "see" the things we look
20   at? How can this be? Most people probably assume that the
brain simply shows us or somehow faithfully relays whatever

©Perfection Learning® • No Reproduction Permitted

images come in through the eyes, but that's just not how it
works. What actually happens is that light patterns enter the
eyes and electrical impulses are sent along optic nerves to
25 the brain. Then the brain *translates* these impulses into visual
information that you "see" in your head. Your brain doesn't
reflect or replay the scenery around you like a mirror or a
camera and monitor would. It provides you with its own highly
edited and customized *sketch* of the scene. Your brain gives
30 you a *version* of what you look at. It's as if your brain comes
up with something like a Hollywood movie production that is
loosely based on what is really going on around you. You are
not watching a video feed; you are watching a docudrama.
The brain takes the liberty of leaving out what it assumes are
35 unimportant details in the scene before your eyes. Just like
memory, this is not necessarily bad most of the time. In fact,
it's necessary in order to avoid information overload. You don't
need to see every leaf in every tree and every blade of grass in
full detail when you look around a park. That would be way
40 too much data. It would clutter your thoughts and make you
less efficient, if not incapacitate you. What you need in order
to walk through a park and function well is to have a general
picture of your surroundings, so that's what your brain gives
you. If you need more detail, then your eyes and brain zoom in
45 and focus on a single leaf or an individual blade of grass.

It gets weirder. Not only do our brains leave out a
tremendous amount of detail, they also routinely fill in gaps
in our vision with images that you can't possibly "see" or that
maybe don't even exist in reality at all. Your eyes might not
50 be able to track a fast-moving object, for example, so your
brain will sometimes conjure it up and show it to you anyway,

figuring that it might be useful to you to see a projected

version of reality. The brain also fills in missing elements that

"should be there" in static scenes because, again, it can help

55 us to navigate our way through the environment. Magicians

have known about this for many years. Even if they don't

understand or care about the science behind it, they take full

advantage of the way our vision works when they do their

sleight-of-hand coin tricks, for example. Again, our brains

60 don't do any of this for a gag or to make fools of us. They do it

because it is the most effective and efficient way to function in

life most of the time.

In addition to filling in missing images, our brains also find

patterns or connect the dots when we look around. They do

65 this automatically and do it very well. It helps us to see things

that otherwise might be difficult or impossible to recognize.

It's probably one of the main reasons you and I are alive right

now. Like many other animals, our prehistoric ancestors relied

on this ability to eat and to avoid being eaten. When they

70 needed to spot well-camouflaged birds and rabbits hiding

in the bushes in order to avoid starvation, this ability to see

things through clutter was crucial. It was no less important, of

course, for them to identify the vague outline of a predator

hiding in ambush in order to avoid becoming dinner in the

75 short term and avoid extinction in the long term. . . .

On one hand, it makes sense for us to see some patterns

of things that aren't really there in order to be very good

at seeing real ones that matter. On the other hand, we

need to be aware of this phenomenon because it can lead

80 to a confident belief in things that are not real or true. . . .

Good skeptics understand how the brain often creates false

patterns, so we know to be very cautious when considering claims of UFO sightings, for example, or anything else that is unusual. It only makes sense to be skeptical and ask for

85 additional evidence when people claim to have seen or heard extraordinary things. Maybe they did, maybe they didn't. Given what we now know about the brain, however, are you going to believe someone who tells you she saw a flying saucer or Bigfoot last week? She doesn't have to be lying to be wrong.

90 Anyone with perfect vision can see poorly.

My Thoughts

FIRST RESPONSE: KEY IDEAS AND DETAILS

Based on your first reading of the text, what do you think the author *most* wants you to understand about how you see the world? Record your first response in your journal.

TECH-CONNECT

Post your answer to the First Response question to your class web page or online site as per your teacher's instructions.

Focus on Analyzing Central Ideas

In an informational text, an author can develop one or more central ideas. A central idea is an idea an author wants readers to understand fully and which the author develops throughout a text. In Guy Harrison's *Think*, the first paragraph clearly states one of the text's central ideas: "The human brain *constructs* and *interprets* the visual reality that is around it." Harrison then develops this idea with key ideas.

CONNECT TO
ESSENTIAL QUESTION

Is Harrison suggesting we can't trust *anything* we perceive? Or is his argument subtler than that?

The diagram below restates one of *Think*'s central ideas and one of its key ideas. Complete the diagram with key ideas from the third and fourth paragraphs.

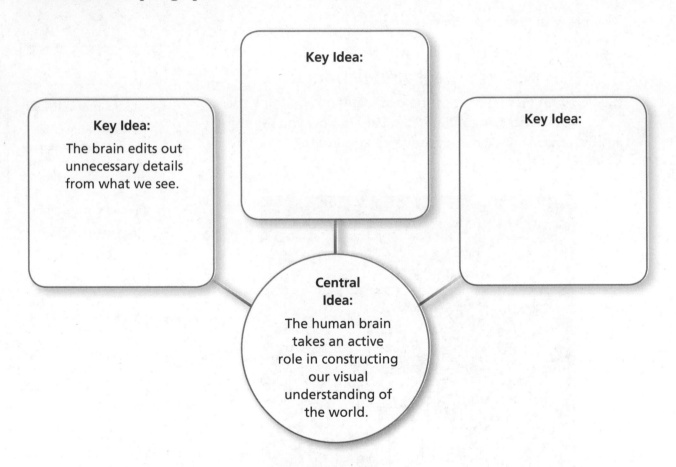

Key Idea:

Key Idea:
The brain edits out unnecessary details from what we see.

Key Idea:

Central Idea:
The human brain takes an active role in constructing our visual understanding of the world.

An author further develops central and key ideas with details such as facts, examples, comparisons, and any other information that will help readers understand what the ideas mean.

Consider this key idea: "The brain edits out unnecessary details from what we see." Read the fact. Then find an example and a comparison Harrison uses to develop this idea. These are supporting details. Write your answers in the blank boxes.

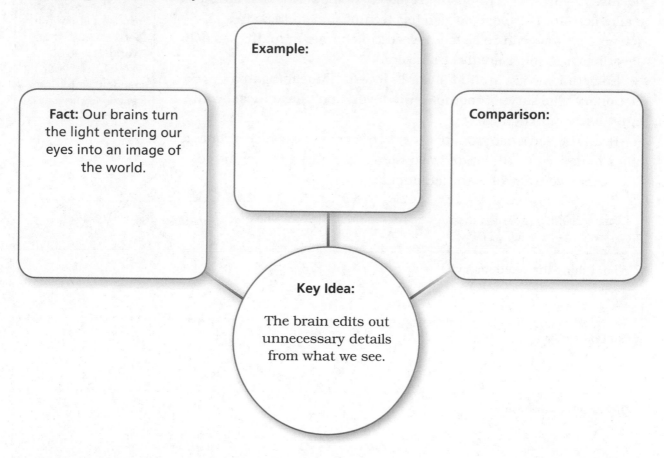

Example:

Fact: Our brains turn the light entering our eyes into an image of the world.

Comparison:

Key Idea:

The brain edits out unnecessary details from what we see.

🌙**Speak and Listen** With a partner, find a second central idea in *Think*. Discuss how Harrison develops the second central idea with key ideas, facts, examples, and so on.

📖**Second Read:** Determining Word Meanings

When people talk about the meaning of a word or phrase, they usually mean its dictionary definition. But words and phrases can also have technical, connotative, and figurative meanings.

Objective: Reread the text. As you read, circle words or phrases that express ideas in unusual or creative ways.

TECH-CONNECT

We're always glad when our eyes work well, but fooling them can be fun. If you have an interest in optical illusions, check out the site Optics4Kids.org and click on the Optical Illusions box.

Focus on Determining Word Meanings

A word or phrase can have a technical meaning, one used largely in subjects such as math or science. Think about the word *positive*. If you say, "I'm positive I did my homework," this means you're certain. But *positive* also has technical meanings. In science, *positive* can refer to an electrical charge. In math, *positive* describes a number greater than zero.

Sometimes you can find a word's technical meaning in a dictionary, glossary, or footnote. But if you don't have these, you must use context clues.

Read the sentence from the text in the chart below. Use context clues to figure out the underlined word. Then use a dictionary to check the accuracy of your definition.

REFLECT

Harrison discusses some of the basic ways that we make mistakes about our perception of the world. Have you ever noticed your mind playing tricks on you in this way?

What actually happens is that light patterns enter the eyes and electrical impulses are sent along <u>optic</u> nerves to the brain.
What I think the word means:
Context clues:
Dictionary definition:

A word or phrase might have a connotative meaning, which is the feeling it produces. Connotations range from strongly negative (bad) to strongly positive (good). If a word doesn't evoke much of a feeling, its connotation is neutral.

In the chart on the next page, read the sentence from *Think*. On the line beneath the sentence, say whether *influenced* feels positive, negative, or neutral to you. Then state whether each word that could replace *influenced* has a positive, negative, or neutral connotation.

Sentence from *Think*	Replacement for *Influenced*	Positive, Negative, or Neutral?
It is well known by researchers that what we think we see can be strongly <u>*influenced*</u> *by images and ideas we have been exposed to previously as well as our own thoughts and imagination.*	shaped	
	warped	
	informed	
	twisted	
	guided	
Connotation of *influenced*:		

Texts, including nonfiction texts, use figurative language to express ideas in creative ways. Some types of figurative language include the following:

- simile—a comparison that uses the word *like* or *as*

- metaphor—a comparison that says one thing is something else; does not use the word *like* or *as*

- personification—a comparison that gives human qualities to an animal or object

When you encounter figurative language in a text, ask, What does the author really mean by this?

In the table below, identify whether the example is a simile, metaphor, or personification. Then state what the author is actually saying.

Sentence from *Think*	Type of Figurative Language	What the Author Means
Again, our brains don't do any of this for a gag or to make fools of us.		
You are not watching a video feed; you are watching a docudrama.		
It's as if your brain comes up with something like a Hollywood movie production that is loosely based on what is really going around you.		

continued on next page

Skilled authors choose words to give their text a certain tone. Tone is like the personality of a text. Texts can have all sorts of tones: friendly, distant, formal, funny, mean, helpful, angry, and so on. Connotative and figurative meanings play a large role in producing a text's tone.

Speak and Listen Discuss with a partner: What is the overall tone of *Think*? What specific words, phrases, or sentences in the text are evidence of this tone?

Write Based on your discussion, write a paragraph describing the tone of *Think*. Refer to specific words, phrases, or sentences from the text to support your claim about the tone.

Third Read: Evaluating an Argument

Because *Think* describes how the brain constructs and interprets what we see, you might think it is an informative text. This isn't entirely true. The excerpt provides information, but that information is part of an argument.

An argument tries to convince readers that an author's viewpoint about a topic is correct. Parts of an argument include claims, reasons, and evidence.

- A claim is a statement the author tries to prove is true. (*Vanilla is better than chocolate.*)

- A reason explains why the readers should agree with the claim. (*Vanilla is more popular than chocolate.*)

- Evidence supports the reason. Evidence comes in many forms: data, details, examples, definitions, quotations, and so on. (*Surveys conducted by the International Ice Cream Association found vanilla to be the most popular flavor.*)

Writers also use rhetorical devices to use emotion to convince their audience. Here are two examples:

- Direct address is when the writer speaks directly to the audience in a familiar or friendly way. The writer does this to establish trust.

- Rhetorical questions are used to make the audience or reader think about an idea. Often rhetorical questions don't have answers but instead are used to make a point.

Objective: Read the text again. In the first paragraph, write a C by the claim and an R by a reason. In paragraphs 2, 3, and 4, write an E by three examples of evidence supporting the claim. Identify an example of direct address and of a rhetorical question.

Focus on Evaluating an Argument

The subtitle for *Think* is *Why You Should Question Everything.* As you can tell from the subtitle, the entire book is an argument. Harrison wants to convince readers to question *everything*—or at least a lot of things.

The excerpt you read makes a more focused argument than "question everything." Complete the chart below. Locate the reason in the text that supports the given claim, and write that reason in your own words. Read the supporting evidence provided for paragraph 2. Then locate supporting evidence in paragraphs 3 and 4 and restate that evidence.

Claim (Paragraph 1): We can't always be sure about what we think we see.
Reason (Paragraph 1):
Evidence (Paragraph 2, lines 18–46): Our brains don't capture every piece of information, such as every blade of grass or leaf in a park.
Evidence (Paragraph 3, lines 47–63):
Evidence (Paragraph 4, lines 64–76):

Harrison wants people to "question everything." That includes questioning his argument. Focus on one aspect of his argument: the relevance of his evidence, or how well the evidence actually supports the claim.

The chart on the next page restates Harrison's claim, one example of evidence for it, and the relevance of that evidence. Complete the chart by restating a second example of evidence and its relevance.

continued on next page

Claim	Evidence	How Relevant Is the Evidence?
We can't always trust what we think we see.	Our brains don't capture every piece of information, such as every blade of grass or leaf in a park.	The evidence is relevant. If our brains don't capture every piece of information, then it's possible they might miss something important. And if we miss something important, then it's possible that we are wrong about what we think we see.

Speak and Listen At some point, you've probably heard the phrase "question everything." But what does that even mean? In a group of four or five classmates, discuss these questions:

- What are some real-world examples of "everythings" that could be questioned?

- What sorts of questions should be asked about the examples you mentioned?

- To whom would you ask those questions, and why?

> **CONNECT TO ESSENTIAL QUESTION**
>
> Have you ever been asked to believe something you thought was false? How did you react?

Language: Using Commas with Coordinate Adjectives

Adjectives are words that describe nouns. When two or more adjectives are used to describe one noun, they are called coordinate adjectives. Coordinate adjectives must be separated either by a comma or the word *and*. Read these examples:

He read a fun, lively book.
He read a fun and lively book.

These adjectives both modify the noun *book* in the same way. Neither word carries more weight than the other. *Fun* and *lively* make sense in either order, so a comma is required. (No comma is needed after the final adjective.)

He read a lively, fun book.

If the adjectives are not equally important, they are not considered coordinate. If you reorder the adjectives and the sentence no longer makes sense, then you should *not* put a comma between them.

> She loved <u>exciting horror</u> movies.
> She loved <u>horror exciting</u> movies. (*incorrect*)
> She loved <u>exciting and horror</u> movies. (*incorrect*)

Only the first version of the sentence makes sense. This means that *exciting* and *horror* are not coordinate adjectives, so they should not have a comma between them.

Read the following sentences. If the adjectives in the underlined phrases are coordinate, add a comma where necessary. If the adjectives are not coordinate, write "correct" above the phrase.

1. I went to a <u>small private museum</u> yesterday.

2. The museum was founded by a <u>quirky rich man</u>.

3. The man claims to own <u>many important objects</u> proving that aliens visited Earth.

4. The exhibit included <u>blurry gray photographs</u> of flying saucers.

5. I also saw <u>special plaster casts</u> with shapes labeled "alien footprints."

6. Computer screens showed videos of <u>numerous eyewitness accounts</u>.

7. Finally, there were several <u>large smooth flat rocks</u> with <u>countless odd drawings</u> on them.

8. The museum proved that we still don't have <u>much convincing evidence</u> of alien life.

Project-Based Assessments

Response Essay

The excerpt from *Think* begins this way: "Have you heard the old saying, 'seeing is believing'? Well, it's often a case of *believing is seeing*." But what's your opinion? Do you agree that what we believe affects how we understand events? Do you disagree? Or is your response more complex than just "agree" or "disagree"?

Write an essay responding to the idea that "believing is seeing." Use these steps to develop your essay:

1. Brainstorm:

   - Write "believing is seeing" in the center of a blank sheet of paper. Circle the phrase.

   - Record memories from your life that seem relevant to the idea "believing is seeing." These memories could be experiences you've had, conversations with friends and family, song lyrics, Internet videos or memes, and so on.

   - You may also want to speak with classmates or family members about their reactions to the idea that "believing is seeing."

2. Write an opinion sentence declaring what you think about the idea that "believing is seeing." The goal of your essay is to develop your opinion.

3. Think about the best way to develop your opinion. Use the ideas from your brainstorming session. Choose the two most interesting ideas you came up with—ideas you can develop with details, examples, and so on.

4. Write your essay. Try to write at least one full page.

5. Get feedback from a friend. Ask your friend to say which of your two ideas could be improved, and how.

6. Revise your essay based on your friend's feedback.

Use the following guidelines for your response essay.	
To receive the highest score (4.0), the response essay must meet all of these criteria.	Your essay should • clearly state an opinion regarding the idea that "believing is seeing." • contain details that develop and support your opinion about the idea. • be clearly organized, using good transitional words and varying sentence structure. • use correct grammar, usage, and punctuation.

Draw a Diagram

Guy Harrison describes the connection between the eyes and the brain in this way: "Light patterns enter the eyes and electrical impulses are sent along optic nerves to the brain." But how the eye works is a little more complicated than that.

In your classroom library, your school library, or on the Internet, research the human eye and what its parts do. Based on your research, draw a diagram of the human eye on an 8.5″ × 11″ sheet of paper. Use markers or colored pencils (if available) to clearly show each part.

Make your diagram large enough to fill the page. Show, label, and describe the functions of these parts:

- the cornea
- the pupil
- the uvea (which includes the iris)
- the lens
- the sclera
- the vitreous humor
- the retina, including a description of its rods and cones cells
- the optic nerve

When finished, show your diagram to a family member or friend outside the class. Use it to educate him or her about the human eye.

	Use the following guidelines for your diagram.
To receive the highest score (4.0), the diagram must meet all of these criteria.	Your diagram • is large enough to fill the entire page. • clearly shows each part of the human eye. • accurately labels each part. • clearly describes the function of each part.

On Your Own: Integrating Ideas

1. The book *Think: Why You Should Question Everything* includes a section titled "A Thinker's Guide to Unusual Claims and Weird Beliefs." That section includes chapters such as "UFOs," "Conspiracy Theories," and "Ancient Alien Astronauts." If these topics interest you, visit your library and see if they have the book. If your library doesn't have it, ask your librarian if he or she can get you a copy.

2. Guy Harrison is clearly fascinated with how the human brain works. If you have a similar interest, watch the *Nova* documentary titled "How Does the Brain Work?" Go to the website www.pbs.org/wgbh/nova and search for the documentary.

Connect to Testing

In this chapter, you analyzed central ideas, determined the meanings of words and phrases, and evaluated part of an argument. When you take assessments, you will be asked questions related to these skills and tested over your ability to support your ideas with textual evidence. Below is an example of this type of question. Try to answer the question on your own before reading the explanation below.

1. Which sentence states two central ideas developed in *Think*?

    A. *Have you heard the old saying, "seeing is believing"?*

    B. *It is well known by researchers that what we think we see can be strongly influenced by images and ideas we have been exposed to. . . .*

    C. *Seeing things that are not there can happen to anyone because the human brain constructs and interprets the visual reality that is around it.*

    D. *This probably explains why it's the people who already believe in ghosts or UFOs who keep seeing ghosts or UFOs, and why so few nonbelievers do.*

EXPLANATION

- Think about what you know about central ideas. A central idea of a passage is an idea the author wants readers to understand fully and which the author develops throughout a text. This question wants to identify two central ideas expressed in one sentence.

- Choice A is wrong. The sentence poses a question, but it is actually the opposite idea—that believing can affect what we see—that the author develops in the passage.

- Choice B is incorrect because it states just one idea developed in the passage, that what we think we see can be influenced by other factors.

- Choice D is incorrect because it is an example of how people with different belief systems might perceive events differently.

- Only choice C states two central ideas of the passage. The author develops two ideas in the passage: The human brain constructs and interprets visual reality, and anyone can see things that aren't really there. The rest of the passage develops these ideas.

continued on next page

2. Which of the following sentences is correctly punctuated?

   A. We saw many unusual puzzling rocks from space.

   B. We saw many, unusual puzzling rocks from space.

   C. We saw many unusual, puzzling rocks from space.

   D. We saw many, unusual, puzzling rocks from space.

3. **Part A:** Read these sentences from the second paragraph of *Think*.

> We don't really "see" the things we look at? How can this be?

What tone do these sentences convey?

   A. worried

   B. doubtful

   C. paranoid

   D. confused

Part B: Which sentence from the passage indicates a tone similar to the one identified in Part A?

   A. *Seeing things that are not there can happen to anyone because the human brain constructs and interprets the visual reality that is around it.*

   B. *What you need in order to walk through a park and function well is to have a general picture of your surroundings, so that's what your brain gives you.*

   C. *Like many other animals, our prehistoric ancestors relied on this ability to eat and to avoid being eaten.*

   D. *Given what we now know about the brain, however, are you going to believe someone who tells you she saw a flying saucer or Bigfoot last week?*

4. Read this sentence from *Think*.

> Or your brain could be showing you an angel that it has mistakenly constructed out of a bush or some other object.

Which of the following is closest in meaning to the phrase *mistakenly constructed*?

   A. accidentally made

   B. poorly built

   C. carelessly seen

   D. foolishly thought

Chapter 8

Determining Author's Purpose

Preview Concepts

In September 2016, only 32% of Americans said they trusted the news media to be accurate and fair. Compare this with 1976, when 72% of Americans felt confident that the news media were doing a good job.

Why do you think trust in the news media has fallen so far since 1976? Did Americans change? Did the media? Or did both change? Write your response below.

Making Connections

Read the following excerpt.

> No experiment can be more interesting than that we are now trying, and which we trust will end in establishing the fact, that man may be governed by reason and truth. Our first object should therefore be, to leave open to him all the avenues to truth. The most effectual hitherto found, is the freedom of the press.
>
> —President Thomas Jefferson

This letter was written in 1804, just twenty-eight years after the signing of the Declaration of Independence. In the first sentence, to what "experiment" is Thomas Jefferson likely referring?

What is this experiment trying to prove?

Jefferson feels the experiment depends on "avenues to truth." What, for him, is the most effective avenue to truth?

> **MAKING CONNECTIONS**
>
> As you read the passage in this chapter, pay attention to how each section of text develops the author's central idea.

First Read: Making an Inference

During the 2016 presidential election, people began talking about "fake news." Fake news refers to stories that look like they come from reliable news outlets but are actually packed with misleading or false information. Readers, assuming the stories are accurate, may share them with friends and family on social media sites such as Facebook and Twitter.

Glenn Kessler is a reporter who works at the *Washington Post*. In this article, he discusses ways to figure out whether a story is "fake news" or not.

Objective: As you read, underline any sentences that suggest what Kessler assumes about his readers. Record any questions you have in the My Thoughts column.

excerpt
The Fact Checker's Guide for Detecting Fake News
by Glenn Kessler
from *The Washington Post*

	My Thoughts

1   Anyone active on social media has probably done this at least once: shared something based on the headline without actually reading the link.

Let's face it, you've probably done this many times.

5   According to a study released in June by computer scientists at Columbia University and the French National Institute, 59 percent of links shared on social media have never actually been clicked.

So the first thing you can do to combat the rise of "fake
10   news" is to actually read articles before sharing them. And when you read them, pay attention to the following signs that the article may be fake. There are fake news stories generated by both left-leaning and right-leaning websites, and the same rules apply to both.

15 Determine whether the article is from a legitimate website

There's ABC News, the television network, with the Web address of abcnews.go.com. And there's ABC News, the fake news website, with the Web address of abcnews.com.co.

20   The use of ".co" at the end of the URL is a strong clue you are looking at a fake news website. (It signifies the Internet country code domain assigned to the country of Colombia.) But there are other signs as well.

Check the 'contact us' page

25   Some fake news sites don't have any contact information, which easily demonstrates it's phony. The fake "ABC News" does have a "contact us" page—but it shows a picture of the controversial Westboro Baptist Church in Topeka, Kan. (An inside joke?) The real television network is based in New York

30 City, housed in a 13-story building on 66th Street.

Examine the byline of the reporter and see whether it makes sense

On the fake ABC News site there is an article claiming a protester was paid $3,500 to protest [Donald] Trump. It's

35 supposedly written by Jimmy Rustling. "Dr. Jimmy Rustling has won many awards for excellence in writing including fourteen Peabody awards and a handful of Pulitzer Prizes," the author biography claims. If that doesn't seem absurd, then how about the fact that he claims to have a Russian mail order bride of

40 almost two months and "also spends 12-15 hours each day teaching their adopted 8-year-old Syrian refugee daughter how to read and write."

All of the details are signs that "Dr. Rustling" is not a real person.

My Thoughts

Read the article closely

Many fake articles have made-up quotes that do not pass the laugh test. About midway through the article on the protest, the founder of Snopes.com—which debunks fake news on the Internet—is suddenly "quoted," saying he approves of the article. It also goes on to describe Snopes as "a website known for its biased opinions and inaccurate information they write about stories on the internet." It's like a weird inside joke, and in the readers' minds it should raise immediate red flags.

Scrutinize the sources

Sometimes fake articles are based on merely a tweet. *The New York Times* documented how the fake news that anti-Trump protesters were bused in started with a single, ill-informed tweet by a man with just 40 followers. Another apparently fake story, that Trump fed police officers working protests in Chicago, also started with a tweet—by a man who wasn't even there but was passing along a claim made by "friends." The tweeter also has a locked account, making the "news" highly dubious. Few real news stories are based on a single tweet, with no additional confirmation.

If the article has no links to legitimate sources—or links at all—that's another telltale sign that you are reading fake news.

Look at the ads

A profusion of pop-up ads or other advertising indicates you should handle the story with care. Another sign is a bunch of questionable ads or links, designed to be clicked— . . . "Naughty Walmart Shoppers Who have no Shame at All"— which you generally do not find on legitimate news sites.

My Thoughts

Use search engines to double-check

75   A simple Google search often will quickly tell you if the news you are reading is fake. Our friends at Snopes have also compiled a Field Guide to Fake News Sites, allowing you to check whether the article comes from a fraudster. There is also a website called RealorSatire.com that allows you to post

80   the URL of any article and it will quickly tell you if the article comes from a fake or biased news website.

Combating the spread of fake news begins with you, the reader. If it seems too fantastic, it probably is. Please think before you share.

FIRST RESPONSE: KEY IDEAS AND DETAILS

Glenn Kessler assumes that most readers have accidentally shared a "fake news" story on social media. Have you accidentally shared one? How do you know it was fake news? Was it really an accidental sharing, or did you share it for another reason? Record your response in your journal.

TECH-CONNECT

Post your First Response answers on your class web page. Compare your answers to those posted by other students.

Focus on Making an Inference

Glenn Kessler's "Fact Checker's Guide" describes actions that you, the reader, can take to figure out whether an article is "fake news." But what does Kessler assume about his readers? The article says *you* a lot, so it's fair to think he has assumptions about who *you* are. But he doesn't explicitly say what he thinks about his readers. Is there any textual evidence that can help you figure this out?

Complete the activity below. Respond to each quotation by completing each sentence that begins, "This quote assumes that the readers . . . ." The first row has been completed for you.

Quotations from "Fact Checker's Guide"	Assumption About Readers
Anyone active on social media has probably done this at least once: shared something based on the headline without actually reading the link.	This quote assumes that the readers . . . know what social media are; are social media users and possibly active; have possibly shared a link based on the headline alone.
So the first thing you can do to combat the rise of "fake news" is to actually read articles before sharing them.	This statement assumes that the readers . . .
And when you read them, pay attention to the following signs that the article may be fake.	This statement assumes that the readers . . .
Combating the spread of fake news begins with you, the reader. If it seems too fantastic, it probably is. Please think before you share.	These statements assume that the readers . . .

▼ **Write** Based on your analysis of the quotes, write a paragraph describing what Kessler assumes about his readers. Specifically, describe his assumptions about the following:

- readers' experience with social media
- readers' background knowledge about fake news
- readers' belief about whether spreading fake news is good or bad
- what readers want to do about fake news

Speak and Listen With a partner, share your description of Kessler's assumptions. If your descriptions differ significantly, figure out why. Are you interpreting the evidence differently? Are you responding to the article from different points of view, and if so, what are they?

Second Read: Analyzing Text Structure

The central idea of Kessler's article can be summed up this way: Readers must identify fake news and stop it from spreading. But how does the article develop this idea?

After the introduction, the article has seven sections, each introduced with a heading. These sections work together to develop the central idea. But what does *work together* mean for a text? And how do these sections work together?

Objective: Read the article a second time. As you finish each major section, answer this question in the My Thoughts box: How does this section help develop the central idea?

Focus on Analyzing Text Structure

Think about the phrase *work together*. Imagine a team of house builders, each with different skills. The plumber gets the water working. The electrician makes sure the lights work. The roofer makes sure rainfall doesn't ruin the walls and floors. Each worker has a job, and they work together to build a house that functions well.

The major sections of Kessler's article are like those workers. Each section has its own job, and they all work together to develop the central idea.

Use the chart below to analyze how each major section relates to the central idea. Use words such as *example*, *describe*, *explain*, and *convince*. The first two have been done for you.

Article Section	Purpose of Section
Determine whether the article is from a legitimate website	provides the first step in identifying fake news; explains one way fakers try to deceive readers
Check the 'contact us' page	provides the second step; gives an example of what a fake news source looks like

Article Section	Purpose of Section
Examine the byline of the reporter and see whether it makes sense	
Read the article closely	
Scrutinize the sources	
Look at the ads	
Use search engines to double-check	

Speak and Listen Kessler's article uses subheads to introduce the sections. With a partner, discuss the purpose of these subheads and how each section contributes to the author's central idea.

Write This article was shared on social media platforms such as Facebook and Twitter. Could *this* article be "fake news"? Why or why not? Write a paragraph explaining your reasons in your reading journal.

Third Read: Determining Point of View and Purpose

When discussing nonfiction texts, you should distinguish between authors' point of view and their purpose.

- Point of view is the author's opinion about the ideas or events being described. Authors may hold a point of view about an issue because of the way it affects them, in a good way or a bad way. How does the issue of fake news affect a journalist like Glenn Kessler?

- Purpose is the goal the author wants the text to accomplish. Purposes include entertaining or informing readers, convincing readers to take action, and so on. What does Glenn Kessler hope to do by writing this article?

Objective: As you read the article a third time, think about Kessler's point of view and his purpose. Write POV next to a paragraph that most clearly states his point of view. Then write AP next to a paragraph that most clearly states his purpose.

Focus on Determining Point of View and Purpose

Sometimes an author's point of view and purpose are explicit, or clearly stated. Other times, the point of view and purpose are not explicit, and you must infer them.

What is Kessler's point of view regarding fake news? How can you tell? Write your response in the space below. Support your response with details from the text.

TECH-CONNECT

Find an example of a fake news article on social media. Using Kessler's article, identify at least three factors that show the article is fake. Post your findings on your class website.

REFLECT

Why is accurate news important in a democracy? What would happen to a democracy if accurate news disappeared?

What is Kessler's main purpose in writing his article? How can you tell? Write your response in the space below. Support your response with details from the text.

CONNECT TO ESSENTIAL QUESTION

We tend to trust people or groups we know and like. We also tend to distrust people or groups we do not know well or disagree with. Is this always a good instinct?

Language: Correcting Misplaced Modifiers

In sentences, a phrase or clause can modify (describe) words, phrases, or clauses. Look at the example sentence below.

> The problem of fake news, <u>which came to prominence in 2016,</u> has existed for as long as journalism itself.

Notice that the phrase "which came to prominence in 2016" modifies the phrase "The problem of fake news." It is important for a modifier to be placed near the words it describes. Otherwise, the sentence might be confusing or make no sense at all. To fix a sentence with a misplaced modifier, just move the modifier closest to the word or phrase it should actually modify.

Study the sentence below.

> We stood and talked about all the fake news <u>in the living room.</u>

The phrase "in the living room" is meant to modify "stood." As written, the sentence suggests "all the fake news" is somehow in the living room. Rewrite the sentence so it is correct.

continued on next page

Now read this sentence, which also has a misplaced modifier.

I made the mistake of sharing fake news stories on social media sites, <u>which are harmful to good decision-making</u>.

Explain why the sentence is confusing. Then fix it by rewriting it.

The following sentences contain misplaced modifiers. Rewrite each one, placing the modifier correctly.

1. Dana told us how Laura had shared fake news stories in the car.

2. Laura shared stories with her friends that were completely false.

3. One story claimed a politician wanted to make his dog a senator because he had gone insane.

4. Dana used her phone to show evidence that the stories were fake to Laura.

5. Laura got grumpy at Dana because she does not like being wrong.

6. Dana told Laura, which is useful, to read Glenn Kessler's article.

Project-Based Assessments

Investigative Report

Write a five-paragraph newspaper report explaining why fake news is a problem.

Make a list of questions the public would want answered. Examples might include the following:

- What is fake news?

- Why do people make it?

- What are its harmful effects?

Then conduct online research using terms such as *fake news*, *effects*, and *society*. Websites that end in *.edu*, *.gov*, or *.org* usually have more reliable information than sites ending in *.com*. Keep track of your source information as you do your research.

Newspaper reports follow an inverted-pyramid structure. The most important ideas come first (the wide part of the pyramid) and lead into less important ideas (the point of the pyramid). Your report will need a catchy headline. Headlines are usually incomplete sentences, such as "How Fake News Harms Our Democracy."

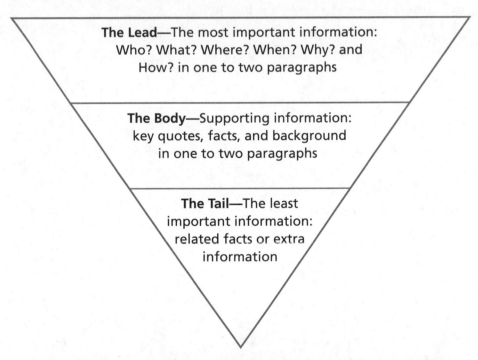

The Lead—The most important information: Who? What? Where? When? Why? and How? in one to two paragraphs

The Body—Supporting information: key quotes, facts, and background in one to two paragraphs

The Tail—The least important information: related facts or extra information

Use a word processing or design program to type your article using newspaper format. Follow these guidelines:

- one-inch margins

- three columns (go to Format/Columns to set up)

- single-spacing, indented first lines of paragraphs, 12-point font (Times)

- headline and your byline (example: by Jackie Smith) at the top of the article.
- a picture or image that supports your writing along with a caption; make the text wrap around the picture

Use the following guidelines for your investigative report.	
To receive the highest score (4.0), the investigative report must meet all of these criteria.	Your newspaper report should • have an interesting headline that reveals the main point. • answer important questions in the first two paragraphs. • provide supporting information in the rest of the report. • use correct grammar, usage, punctuation, and spelling.

Compare and Contrast Essay

People show bias when they favor one thing, person, or group over another. Even news articles from reliable sources can show bias. It is important to read news stories from a few sources about any important event. You will get a more complete picture or at least understand why people have different views about the same event. For this project, you will write a four-paragraph essay comparing and contrasting how two news sources report the same event.

In the chart below, the left column lists news sources considered to have a liberal bias. This means the sources generally favor policies that increase the role of the federal government. The right column lists outlets considered to have a conservative bias. In general, these sources favor policies that reduce the role of the federal government.

News Sources with a Liberal Bias	News Sources with a Conservative Bias
The Atlantic (www.theatlantic.com)	*The Economist* (www.economist.com)
The Guardian (www.theguardian.com/us)	The Hill (www.thehill.com)
MSNBC (www.msnbc.com)	*The Fiscal Times* (www.thefiscaltimes.com)
The New York Times (www.nytimes.com)	Fox News (www.foxnews.com)

Follow these steps:
- Visit one site listed in the chart. Find an article on a recent, important event that interests you. Be sure to find an article instead of an editorial. Bookmark the article.

continued on next page

- Visit a site listed in the other column. Find an article on the same event. Again, make sure to find an article, not an editorial. Bookmark the article.

- Print each article. You'll be marking them to identify information for your essay.

As you read each article, do the following:

- Underline at least one sentence that clearly states what each article is reporting on.

- Place a star next to any important information appearing in both articles.

- Draw a box around important information that appears in one article but not the other. (Note: If you find yourself drawing too many boxes, your articles might be reporting on different events. If so, dig back into the sites and look for new articles.)

- Circle words or phrases that suggest some kind of bias. Pay attention to connotations, or words and phrases meant to stir positive or negative feelings in readers.

- In the margins, jot down other thoughts that occur to you as you read.

Now, write your compare and contrast essay. You will write four paragraphs.

- **First paragraph:** Describe the event, identify the sources, and tell your opinion of whether the articles covered the event similarly, differently, or somewhere in-between.

- **Second paragraph:** Describe important similarities. Do the articles present events in the same order? Place the same emphasis on events? Use the same or similar quotations?

- **Third paragraph:** Describe important differences. Do they emphasize different aspects of the event? Does one article have important information the other does not? Do they use words with different connotations to describe the same events?

- **Fourth paragraph:** Restate your opinion regarding the two sources. Then draw a conclusion. If two sources report events similarly, is that always good? Or, if they report events differently, is that necessarily bad? Explain what you think and why.

CONNECT TO ESSENTIAL QUESTION

It's become common for people to say, "The media never tell you the truth." What do you think of this claim? Do you think it's possible to find the truth?

Use the following guidelines for your compare and contrast essay.	
To receive the highest score (4.0), the compare and contrast essay must meet all of these criteria.	Your compare and contrast essay should • introduce the news event and the sources you chose. • state your opinion about whether the sources differ. • describe important similarities and differences between the articles. • use details from each article to illustrate the similarities and differences you describe. • restate your opinion and draw a conclusion based on your analysis. • use correct grammar, usage, punctuation, and spelling.

On Your Own: Integrating Ideas

- "Fake news" is a problem as old as news itself. To read about famous examples of fake news—some of them more outrageous than others—visit the following site: http://hoaxes.org/archive/display/category/newspapers_and_magazines.

REFLECT

Is the news important in your life? Will it become more important to you as you age? Why or why not?

- With the rise of fake news has come the rise of websites that try to debunk fake news. Two sites are broadly respected: FactCheck.org and PolitiFact.com. Glenn Kessler also mentions Snopes.com and RealorSatire.com. Check out one or all of those sites; chances are good you will be using them in the future.

- In Washington, D.C., the Newseum is a museum devoted to the history of journalism. Many of its exhibits appear on its website, newseum.org. There you can learn why accurate news is vital to the "experiment" Thomas Jefferson wrote about at the beginning of this chapter.

Connect to Testing

In this chapter, you made inferences, analyzed text structure, and determined the author's point of view and purpose. The following questions are examples of how these skills may be tested on standardized tests.

1. **Part A:** What is the central idea of "The Fact Checker's Guide"?

   A. People should read more news articles from reliable sources.

   B. People should understand the consequences of spreading fake news stories.

   C. People should evaluate news stories using the methods the author describes.

   D. People should realize that members of all political parties spread fake news stories.

   Part B: Select two sentences from the passage that best support the answer in Part A.

   A. *Anyone active on social media has probably done this at least once: shared something based on the headline without actually reading the link.*

   B. *So the first thing you can do to combat the rise of "fake news" is to actually read articles before sharing them.*

   C. *And when you read them, pay attention to the following signs that the article may be fake.*

   D. *There are fake news stories generated by both left-leaning and right-leaning websites, and the same rules apply to both.*

   E. *There's ABC News, the television network, with the Web address of abcnews.go.com.*

   F. *If it seems too fantastic, it probably is.*

2. How does the author structure the passage to develop the central idea?

   A. by identifying the most common types of fake news stories

   B. by explaining how fake news stories mislead people

   C. by ordering fake news stories from least to most believable

   D. by describing ways to determine whether a story is fake news

3. Read the sentence below. It has a misplaced modifier.

> Eric told us he had read a fake news story in the morning after lunch.

Choose the answer that best corrects the misplaced modifier in the sentence.

A. After lunch, Eric told us he had read a fake news in the morning.

B. Eric told us he had read a fake news story after lunch in the morning.

C. In the morning after lunch, Eric told us he had read a fake news story.

D. Eric told us, in the morning, he had read a fake news story after lunch.

4. **Part A:** What is the author's main purpose in writing the passage?

A. to slow the spread of fake news

B. to show how fake news is a growing problem

C. to explain that all political parties spread fake news

D. to identify the sources of fake news

Part B: Which sentence from the passage best supports the answer in Part A?

A. *Anyone active on social media has probably done this at least once: shared something based on the headline without actually reading the link.*

B. *So the first thing you can do to combat the rise of "fake news" is to actually read articles before sharing them.*

C. *There are fake news stories generated by both left-leaning and right-leaning websites, and the same rules apply to both.*

D. *There's ABC News, the television network, with the Web address of abcnews.go.com.*

5. In the passage, the author refers to a website named Snopes. Which sentence from the passage most clearly shows the author's actual point of view about Snopes?

A. *About midway through the article on the protest, the founder of Snopes. com—which debunks fake news on the Internet—is suddenly "quoted," saying he approves of the article.*

B. *It also goes on to describe Snopes as "a website known for its biased opinions and inaccurate information they write about stories on the internet."*

C. *It's like a weird inside joke, and in the readers' minds it should raise immediate red flags.*

D. *Our friends at Snopes have also compiled a Field Guide to Fake News Sites, allowing you to check whether the article comes from a fraudster.*

Chapter 9

Evaluating Reasons and Evidence

Preview Concepts

The following poster was made in 1936 by the United States government. It tells readers how to detect a fake doctor called a "cancer quack."

According to the poster, what is evidence that a doctor is a "cancer quack"?

Why is evidence important when you make an important decision?

©Perfection Learning® • No Reproduction Permitted

Making Connections

Read the following excerpt from a government website.

MAKING CONNECTIONS

As you read the excerpt in this chapter, you'll identify how the author supports a claim.

> Homeopathy, also known as homeopathic medicine, is an alternative medical system that was developed in Germany more than 200 years ago. . . .
>
> Supporters of homeopathy point to two unconventional theories: "like cures like"—the notion that a disease can be cured by a substance that produces similar symptoms in healthy people; and "law of minimum dose"—the notion that the lower the dose of the medication, the greater its effectiveness. . . .
>
> Most rigorous clinical trials and systematic analyses of the research on homeopathy have concluded that there is little evidence to support homeopathy as an effective treatment for any specific condition.
>
> —National Center for Complementary and Integrative Health

The excerpt uses the phrases "rigorous clinical trials" and "systematic analyses." Using either a dictionary or your own knowledge, define each word.

Word	What Does It Mean?
rigorous	
clinical	
systematic	
analyses	

What is the purpose of performing "rigorous clinical trials" and "systematic analyses" on medical treatments? Use the word "evidence" in your response.

First Read: Analyzing Interactions of Ideas, People, and Events

John Grant is a writer of fiction and nonfiction. In *Debunk It! How to Stay Sane in a World of Misinformation*, Grant argues against "woo." "Woo" consists of ideas that seem science-like but aren't supported by scientific evidence.

Objective: As you read, pay attention to how ideas can influence people's actions and lead to events. Underline ideas that seem to directly affect people. Then draw an arrow connecting the idea to the people it affects.

Record any questions you have in the My Thoughts column.

excerpt
Debunk It!
How to Stay Sane in a World of Misinformation
by John Grant

	My Thoughts

1   What's often difficult for us to realize is quite how recent of a science medicine is. For example, while the idea that some diseases are infectious seems obvious to us, it wasn't as obvious to our ancestors: One reason epidemics spread so swiftly

5   through ancient Rome was that the Roman doctors often prescribed sick people a trip (or a series of trips) to the public baths—where, of course, they mixed intimately with everyone else. Again, the notion that illness—especially mental illness— was a consequence of people being invaded by demons lasted

10   for many centuries (and can still be found in some communities today). . . .

The word *homeopathy* refers to a form of medicine in which you try to treat a symptom by applying something that would cause the *same* symptom. It was the brainchild

15   of a German physician called Christian Friedrich Samuel Hahnemann, who was active in the late eighteenth century and the first part of the nineteenth. He saw that the failure rate of contemporary medicine was astonishingly high and

concluded this was because physicians misunderstood what

20 symptoms were. They thought symptoms were a product
of the illness, whereas Hahnemann suggested they were
manifestations of the body *coping with* the disease. In many
instances he was absolutely correct. If you have a fever, for
example, that's because your body's immune system is fighting

25 the infection.

So Hahnemann's big idea was that the way to cure illness
was not to counter the symptoms but to help them. Instead
of applying something that would have the opposite effect
to the symptom (throwing iced water over someone with a

30 fever, for example), he suggested using medicines that would
have the same effect as the symptom. However, Hahnemann
was conscious that increasing a symptom could be dangerous
in itself, so he said the dosages in his medicines should be very
small.

35 Extremely small.

Um, smaller even than that.

Hahnemann decreed that his medicines should be diluted
several times, the mixture being given a **prescribed** number
of shakes between each dilution. The overall result is that most

40 homeopathic medicines are so dilute that there's *not a single*
molecule of the supposed active ingredient left in the dose. In
some cases the dose could be the size of all the world's oceans
and there *still* wouldn't be a relevant molecule in it.

Even if somehow you managed to beat the impossible odds

45 and be so lucky as to have that single molecule of the active
ingredient in your dose, what effect can a single molecule have

manifestations: signs
prescribed: recommended
molecule: a piece of matter made of two or more atoms

on your body? Just in the same way that a single molecule of **strychnine** can't do you any harm, a single molecule of medicine can't do you any good.

50   Of course, Hahnemann couldn't have been aware of this as a problem, since no one knew about molecules at the time. Modern fans of homeopathy, however, obviously *are* aware of the dilution **conundrum**. They've therefore proposed the idea that the active agent, even though completely absent because

55   of the dilution, might have "imprinted" itself upon the water in such a way that its one-time presence is still felt. For this to be the case would require some revision of the known laws of physics. That, some homeopaths maintain, is the fault of physics, not the fault of homeopathy!

60   Other homeopaths propose that the supposed "memory" the water has of the active ingredient could be due to **quantum entanglement**. Alas, although quantum entanglement is a genuine phenomenon, it's a flimsy one: Even under laboratory conditions it's extraordinarily difficult

65   to make an entanglement last longer than a tiny fraction of a second. There's no chance at all that entanglements could survive the multiple shakings involved in a homeopathic dilution. Besides, how would changing the state of a few **subatomic** particles turn water into a medicine?

70   There's a more fundamental problem with the "water's memory" claim. Any water we drink has had a long history—a history lasting billions of years. During that time it has been recycled in all sorts of ways, and has held all manner of other

---

strychnine: a deadly poison
conundrum: problem
quantum entanglement: the theory that two or more particles smaller than atoms affect each other (are "entangled") no matter how far apart they are
subatomic: smaller than atoms

substances **in solution**, any one of which could have left

75   an "imprint." Why should water retain the "memory" of a
homeopathic molecule but not that of *everything else* with
which it has been in contact—including all the gazillions of
poops that have floated in it?

    The notion of "water's memory" takes homeopathy over

80   the conceptual border into the realm of outright woo—
especially when we read of some homeopaths claiming they
can email the "imprint" to their patients, who can supply their
own water! Even if you look just at basic homeopathy, though,
of the kind that Hahnemann invented, the dilutions mean

85   that all you get when you buy a homeopathic medicine is very
expensive water.

    On the plus side, it's pretty hard to do yourself any damage
with a homeopathic overdose.

---

in solution: dissolved in water
woo: to seek support or favor

FIRST RESPONSE: KEY IDEAS AND DETAILS
Based on your first reading, can an idea have powerful effects?
Explain your thinking. Record your first response in your journal.

My Thoughts

TECH-CONNECT

Post your response on your class web page as instructed by your teacher. Read two other students' responses and comment positively on them.

Focus on Analyzing Interactions of Ideas, People, and Events

Roughly the first half of the passage from *Debunk It!* is a history text. Typically, history texts describe the ways in which people, events, and ideas interact with each other. Through close reading, you can analyze these interactions.

Reread this section of the text. Then answer the questions that follow.

    What's often difficult for us to realize is quite how recent of a science medicine is. For example, while the idea that some diseases are infectious seems obvious to us, it wasn't as obvious to our ancestors: One reason epidemics spread so swiftly through ancient

continued on next page

Rome was that the Roman doctors often prescribed sick people a trip (or a series of trips) to the public baths—where, of course, they mixed intimately with everyone else.

What idea about curing illness did Roman doctors seem to have?

What did Roman doctors often tell sick people to do?

What event did the Roman doctors' idea about curing illness help to cause?

Use your answers from above to complete the diagram below.

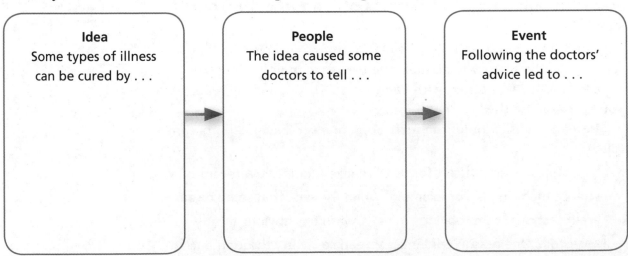

Idea	People	Event
Some types of illness can be cured by . . .	The idea caused some doctors to tell . . .	Following the doctors' advice led to . . .

Your work on the previous page illustrates something important. An idea (how to treat disease) can influence people (doctors and their patients) and lead to an event (an epidemic). People tend to underestimate the force of ideas in history, but ideas are just as important as people and events in the history of our world.

⟨ **Speak and Listen** Share your answers with a partner. Talk about how a Roman doctor's treatment for an illness could not just cause an epidemic but also make it worse.

CONNECT TO ESSENTIAL QUESTION

One definition of "science" is that it is a way to discover trustworthy evidence about the world. How could science discover trustworthy evidence about homeopathy?

Second Read: Analyzing Structure and Purpose

The excerpt is roughly composed of four major sections, each with a different purpose.

- First section: paragraph 1 (lines 1–11)

- Second section: paragraphs 2 and 3 (lines 12–34)

- Third section: paragraphs 4–7 (lines 35–49)

- Fourth section: paragraphs 8–12 (lines 50–88)

Objective: Read the text a second time. In the My Thoughts column, next to each section described above, write one sentence that sums up the central idea of the section.

Focus on Analyzing Structure and Purpose

As discussed, the first half of the excerpt from *Debunk It!* is a history text. Grant uses that history as part of a larger argument he is making. Specifically, Grant is arguing that a practice called *homeopathy* does not actually treat illness, despite what its believers say. We'll evaluate part of Grant's argument later. Right now, let's consider the author's structure of this excerpt as it relates to his purpose.

Because the excerpt is from a book, it doesn't have the structure of an argument your teacher might have you write. Specifically, the excerpt doesn't have

- an introduction with a claim.

- a body with reasons and evidence supporting the claim.

- a conclusion restating the claim.

That said, the excerpt does have a structure, and each part of that structure serves at least one purpose. One way to analyze the structure of a passage is to ask these questions:

- Why is this section here?

- What does this section accomplish (do)?

REFLECT

Have you or someone you know tried a homeopathic treatment? After reading this passage, has your opinion of homeopathy changed? Why or why not?

continued on next page

Complete the chart below.

- Under "Central Idea of Section," explain what the section is about.

- Under "Possible Purpose of Section," make a claim about the author's purpose for the section. Use words such as *inform*, *tell*, *define*, *convince*, and so on.

Part of the chart has been completed for you.

Major Section	Central Idea of Section	Possible Purpose of Section
Paragraph 1 (lines 1–11)	Before modern medicine, people's ideas about the causes and cures of diseases were often wrong.	to show that modern medical science has overcome incorrect ideas
Paragraphs 2 and 3 (lines 12–34)	Two centuries ago, a doctor wondered if using small doses of medicine to make symptoms stronger could cure a disease.	
Paragraphs 4–7 (lines 35–49)		
Paragraphs 8–12 (lines 50–88)		

▼ **Write** An author's tone is his or her attitude toward the topic. What is Grant's tone toward homeopathy and its defenders? Do you feel his tone helps or hurts his argument? In your reading response journal, write a paragraph in which you make a claim about Grant's tone. Use details from the passage to support your claim.

Third Read: Evaluating Reasons and Evidence

REFLECT

When you take medicine, how do you know whether it is working?

The excerpt from *Debunk It!* claims that homeopathy does not treat illness. But how well does Grant support his claim?

Objective: As you read the excerpt a third time, draw a star next to any evidence (facts, examples, quotations) that Grant uses to support his argument against homeopathy.

Focus on Evaluating Reasons and Evidence

To evaluate, or judge, an argument, you need to examine how well its claim is supported with reasons and evidence. A *claim* is an idea an author wants readers to agree with. Reasons explain why readers should agree with a claim. Evidence is real-world information intended to show readers that the author's claim and reasons are accurate.

Here is a simple example of an argument:

Claim: All students in the United States should get a two-year college degree. [This is what the author wants the reader to agree with.]

Reason: On average, people with two-year college degrees make more money than people with a high school diploma. [This explains why readers should agree with the claim.]

Evidence: According to the U.S. Department of Labor, the average pay for a person with a high-school degree is $678. In comparison, a person with a two-year degree makes $798 a week. That's an extra $120 per week, or $6,240 per year. [This shows readers the reasoning is based on facts, not just the author's beliefs.]

To evaluate an argument, it helps to break it into its parts. Reread the following section of *Debunk It!* Then use the chart on the next page to identify and analyze the claim, reason, and evidence.

Hahnemann decreed that his medicines should be diluted several times, the mixture being given a prescribed number of shakes between each dilution. The overall result is that most homeopathic medicines are so dilute that there's not a single molecule of the supposed active ingredient left in the dose. In some cases the dose could be the size of all the world's oceans and there still wouldn't be a relevant molecule in it.

continued on next page

Even if somehow you managed to beat the impossible odds and be so lucky as to have that single molecule of the active ingredient in your dose, what effect can a single molecule have on your body? Just in the same way that a single molecule of strychnine can't do you any harm, a single molecule of medicine can't do you any good.

Claim	
What is the central claim of the argument of *Debunk It*?	Homeopathy does not treat illness.

Reason	
What reason does this section give to support the claim?	

Evidence	
Data from scientific studies	
Quotations from experts	
Descriptions or examples that help the reader understand what Grant is saying	

Do you think Grant offers enough evidence in this section to support his claim about homeopathy? Could he offer more or better evidence, and if so, what? Explain your reasoning below.

Speak and Listen According to Grant, homeopaths claim water can "remember" being in contact with molecules it no longer holds. By answering the homeopaths' ideas, Grant is addressing counterclaims, or claims opposed to his. With a partner, discuss why a writer might want to address counterclaims in an argument.

Language: Complex Sentences with Subordinating Conjunctions and Relative Pronouns

In chapter 3, you learned the four types of sentences: simple, compound, complex, and compound-complex. Here is a quick review of the four types:

Simple: A simple sentence has only one independent clause. An independent clause can stand on its own as a complete thought. In the following examples, independent clauses are underlined.

Example: We keep animals in zoos or as pets for many reasons.

Compound: A compound sentence has at least **two** independent clauses. The clauses are joined by a comma and coordinating conjunction (*and, but, for, nor, or, yet*) or by a semicolon.

Example: An adult chimpanzee is about five times stronger than an adult human, and Lucy got into everything.

Complex: A complex sentence has at least one independent clause and at least one dependent clause. A dependent clause contains a subject and verb but does not express a complete thought. It can't stand on its own. In the following examples, dependent clauses are in (parentheses).

Example: We also keep animals in captivity (because we enjoy seeing them and spending time with them.)

continued on next page

Compound-Complex: A compound-complex sentence has at least two independent clauses and at least one dependent clause.

> Example: The whales may also float near the top of the pool for long periods; as a result, they may end up with a sunburn or a flopped-over dorsal fin, (which is a common sight on captive male killer whales.)

Well-written complex sentences clearly explain the relationship between the ideas in a sentence. In a complex sentence, a less important idea in a dependent clause is combined with a more important idea in an independent clause. Dependent clauses are often joined to independent clauses by subordinating conjunctions and relative pronouns.

Here are some commonly used subordinating conjunctions:

after	although	as	because
before	even if	if	once
since	so that	than	though
unless	until	when	while

The relative pronouns are

that	which	whichever	who
whoever	whom	whomever	

Read the following examples of sentences with subordinating clauses. The clauses are <u>underlined</u>, and the subordinating conjunctions and relative pronouns are **bold**.

> **After** I took three doses of the medicine, my fever disappeared .
>
> We will go to the beach **when** you feel better.
>
> My five-year-old brother has much more energy **than** I have.
>
> **Because** I was tired after playing soccer, I went to bed instead of going to the party.
>
> The favorite student, **who** is new to our class, is the one who answered all of the questions.

Notice that the subordinating conjunction or relative pronoun shows the relationship between the ideas by answering the questions: *When? Why? Which one?* and *To what extent?* Use a comma after a dependent clause at the beginning of a sentence. Also use a comma (or a pair of commas) to set off dependent clauses that are not essential to the meaning of the sentence.

Rewrite the sentence pairs on the next page as single complex sentences using the subordinating conjunction or relative pronoun shown in parentheses.

1. John Snow was practicing medicine in the 1850s. Doctors
   thought "foul air" caused the deadly disease cholera. (when)

2. Snow didn't know what caused the disease. He wanted to
   find out. (although)

3. He studied maps of London's water system. His study of the
   maps revealed to him the patterns of illness. (which)

4. Many people drank from wells contaminated by sewage.
   These same people became sick with cholera. (who)

5. Foul air had nothing to do with cholera. Snow discovered
   this. (that)

Project-Based Assessments

Digital Presentation

Conduct research and create a digital presentation about treating a common illness. First, search online using terms such as *common illness*. Develop a list of common illnesses and choose one to research.

Next, find three reliable sources of information. Websites that end in *.edu*, *.gov*, or *.org* usually have reliable information. Check the site's About tab to find out if it is maintained by a reputable source, such as a hospital or a medical school.

Gather the following information for your presentation:

- name of the illness

- what causes the illness

- description of its symptoms

- treatment(s) of the illness

- how long it takes to get over the illness

- three sources used for the project: name of article, website, and date

Finally, create an interesting and well-organized computer presentation. Each slide should have both an image and text. Read the rubric carefully so you know what is expected of you from the beginning. Practice your commentary with the presentation before presenting to the class. If working with a partner(s), decide in advance who will share which slides.

> **TECH-CONNECT**
>
> Download your presentation to a flash drive so that you can bring it to school. Be sure to open your files before your presentation, especially when using a computer that isn't your own.

Use the following guidelines for your presentation.	
To receive the highest score (4.0), the presentation must meet all of these criteria.	Your presentation • uses images and text in a professional, appealing way. • demonstrates understanding of the cause and symptoms of the illness. • describes the treatment(s) and duration of the illness. • demonstrates confidence, eye contact, and proper volume. • uses correct grammar, usage, punctuation, and spelling.

Brochure

Create a trifold brochure about an illness and its treatment using a word processing or design program. Follow the steps given for the digital presentation on page 74 to choose an illness and its treatment and then gather information. Design your brochure so that readers will be able to understand the illness and its treatment. Use pictures to reinforce the writing. Include your list of three sources on the back of the brochure.

Use the following guidelines for your brochure.	
To receive the highest score (4.0), the brochure must meet all of these criteria.	Your brochure • looks professional and is visually appealing. • demonstrates an understanding of the illness through details. • includes pictures that support the text. • demonstrates that you clearly understand the illness and its treatment. • uses correct grammar, usage, punctuation, and spelling.

On Your Own: Integrating Ideas

1. Doctors give children vaccines to protect them from deadly diseases such as polio and measles. Lately, however, some people have begun questioning the safety of vaccines. Watch the episode of *Frontline*, an award-winning investigative show on PBS, that discusses this controversy: www.pbs.org/video/2365449467/.

2. People sell fake medicine because they can make a lot of money. That's why it's important to investigate any medicine or treatment by consulting reliable sources, including the Food and Drug Administration's website: www.fda.gov.

3. Is quackery dead, or is it still going strong? Spend time researching whether any famous people on television or the Internet are considered "quacks" by the mainstream medical community. Quackwatch.org is a site dedicated to exposing scientifically doubtful or phony health treatments.

> **CONNECT TO ESSENTIAL QUESTION**
>
> Doctors are authority figures. In general, we are taught to trust authority figures. When is it right to question what an authority figure tells us? Is that an easy thing to do?

Connect to Testing

In this chapter, you examined how ideas, people, and events interact; considered the functions of sections of a nonfiction text; and evaluated the reasons and evidence provided in an argument. When you take assessments, you will be tested over these skills and your ability to support your ideas by using textual evidence.

1. **Part A:** How did Samuel Hahnemann influence the thinking of modern homeopaths?

   A. He argued that symptoms were produced by illnesses.

   B. He suggested that making symptoms stronger could help cure an illness.

   C. He believed that water could remember being exposed to samples of a chemical.

   D. He pointed out that any homeopathic treatment needed to have very few molecules.

   Part B: Which two details from the passage best support the answer to Part A?

   A. *The word* homeopathy *refers to a form of medicine in which you try to treat a symptom by applying something that would cause the* same *symptom.*

   B. *He saw that the failure rate of contemporary medicine was astonishingly high and concluded this was because physicians misunderstood what symptoms were.*

   C. *So Hahnemann's big idea was that the way to cure illness was not to counter the symptoms but to help them.*

   D. *The overall result is that most homeopathic medicines are so dilute that there's not a single molecule of the supposed active ingredient left in the dose.*

   E. *They've therefore proposed the idea that the active agent, even though completely absent because of the dilution, might have "imprinted" itself upon the water in such a way that its one-time presence is still felt.*

   F. *Other homeopaths propose that the supposed "memory" the water has of the active ingredient could be due to quantum entanglement.*

2. Read this sentence and answer the question that follows.

> John Snow founded epidemiology. He is famous among scientists. Epidemiology has saved many lives.

Which is the best way to combine the sentences into a compound–complex sentence?

A. John Snow founded epidemiology, he is famous among scientists, and epidemiology has saved many lives.

B. John Snow, who is famous among scientists, founded epidemiology and saved many lives.

C. John Snow founded epidemiology, which has saved many lives, and he is famous among scientists.

D. John Snow saved many lives by founding epidemiology, so he is famous among scientists.

3. **Part A:** How does paragraph 6 (lines 37–43) contribute to the structure of the passage?

A. It describes how small a molecule is.

B. It explains why a homeopathic dose is mostly water.

C. It captures the reader's interest by summarizing the dilution process.

D. It presents the reason for why Hahnemann decided homeopathy didn't work.

Part B: Which detail from paragraph 6 best supports the answer to Part A?

A. *Hahnemann decreed that his medicines should be diluted several times.* . . .

B. *. . . the mixture being given a prescribed number of shakes between each dilution.*

C. *. . . there's not a single molecule of the supposed active ingredient.* . . .

D. *. . . the dose could be the size of all the world's oceans.* . . .

4. **Part A:** Which of the following is a claim of *Debunk It!* by John Grant?

A. Hahnemann's original idea was reasonable.

B. Hahnemann's fellow doctors thought he was a quack.

C. Hahnemann misled patients on the true causes of disease.

D. Hahnemann misunderstood how molecules interact with each other.

continued on next page

Part B: Which detail from the passage best supports the answer to Part A?

A. . . . *this was because physicians misunderstood what symptoms were.*

B. *If you have a fever . . . that's because your body's immune system is fighting the infection.*

C. . . . *a single molecule of medicine can't do you any good.*

D. . . . *might have "imprinted" itself upon the water in such a way that its one-time presence is still felt.*

5. Which of the following details gives a reason for why the homeopathic idea of "imprinting" is flawed?

A. . . . *a single molecule of medicine can't do you any good.*

B. . . . *might have "imprinted" itself upon the water in such a way that its one-time presence is still felt.*

C. . . . *the supposed "memory" the water has of the active ingredient could be due to quantum entanglement.*

D. *Why should water retain the "memory" of a homeopathic molecule but not that of everything else with which it has been in contact. . . .*

Chapter 10

Analyzing Point of View

Preview Concepts

Think of a time when you changed your mind about something. The "something" could a song, a type of food, or a television show. Or it could be more important: a friendship, a subject in school, or what is best in life.

What did you originally think?

What do you think now?

What caused you to change your mind? Be specific.

Making Connections

It is good practice to preview a text before you read it. Consider the text features, the genre (type of writing), and the structure of the text. This will help you make predictions about the central ideas and the style. For example, you are about to read an excerpt from a science fiction story. Because you've read this genre before, you might predict that the story will include futuristic technology and settings that include outer space and other planets. As you read, correct and confirm your predictions to enhance your comprehension. Try this with the texts you will be reading in this chapter.

In the excerpt below, a man from the 20th century travels two hundred years into the future. Earth is now united in one society. Two members of this society, Reinhart and Sherikov, discuss what the appearance of this man means.

> Reinhart considered. "But it worries me, a man like that out in the open. Loose. A man who can't be predicted. It goes against science. We've been making statistical reports on society for two centuries. We have immense files of data. The machines are able to predict what each person and group will do at a given time, in a given situation. But this man is beyond all prediction. He's a variable. It's contrary to science."
>
> "The indeterminate particle."
>
> "What's that?"
>
> "The particle that moves in such a way that we can't predict what position it will occupy at a given second. Random. The random particle."
>
> "Exactly. It's—it's *unnatural*."
>
> Sherikov laughed sarcastically. "Don't worry about it, Commissioner. The man will be captured and things will return to their natural state. You'll be able to predict people again, like laboratory rats in a maze."
>
> —"The Variable Man" by Philip K. Dick

What can you infer about the society that Reinhart and Sherikov describe? Use details from the text to support your response.

MAKING CONNECTIONS

You will be reading an excerpt in this chapter about a future society. Pay attention to how the main character feels when he is thinking about the idea of "family."

First Read: Citing Evidence

In this science fiction novel, a boy named Jonas lives in a future society where emotions are limited and everyone is assigned a job at age twelve. Jonas has just been named the Receiver, which means he is able to absorb memories from an adult called the Giver. In this scene, Jonas has just experienced The Giver's memory of a childhood birthday party.

Objective: As you read, keep this question in mind: How much direct experience has Jonas had with older people? Underline any sentences that show Jonas's experience with older people. Record any questions you have in the My Thoughts column.

excerpt
The Giver
by Lois Lowry

	My Thoughts

1   Jonas opened his eyes and lay contentedly on the bed still luxuriating in the warm and comforting memory. It had all been there, all the things he had learned to treasure.

"What did you perceive?" The Giver asked.

5   "Warmth," Jonas replied, "and happiness. And—let me think. *Family*. That it was a celebration of some sort, a holiday. And something else—I can't quite get the word for it."

"It will come to you."

"Who were the old people? Why were they there?" It
10   had puzzled Jonas, seeing them in the room. The Old of the community did not ever leave their special place, the House of the Old, where they were so well cared for and respected.

"They were called Grandparents."

"Grand parents?"

15   "Grandparents. It meant parents-of-the-parents, long ago."

"Back and back and back?" Jonas began to laugh. "So actually, there could be parents-of-the-parents-of-the-parents-of-the parents?"

The Giver laughed, too. "That's right. It's a little like

20 looking in a mirror."

Jonas frowned. "But my parents must have had parents!

I never thought about it before. Who are my parents-of-the-

parents? *Where* are they?"

"You could go look in the Hall of Open Records. You'd

25 find the names. But think, son. If you apply for children, then

who will be their parents-of-the-parents? Who will be their

grandparents?"

"My mother and father, of course."

"And where will they be?"

30 Jonas thought. "Oh," he said slowly. "When I finish

my training and become a full adult, I'll be given my own

dwelling. And then when Lily does, a few years later, she'll get

her own dwelling, and maybe a spouse, and children if she

applies for them, and then Mother and Father—"

35 "That's right."

"As long as they're still working and contributing to the

community, they'll go and live with the other Childless Adults.

And they won't be part of my life anymore.

"And after that, when the time comes, they'll go to the

40 House of the Old," Jonas went on. He was thinking aloud.

"And they'll be well cared for, and respected, and when

they're released, there will be a celebration."

"Which you won't attend," The Giver pointed out.

"No, of course not, because I won't even know about it. By

45 then I'll be so busy with my own life. And Lily will, too. So our

children, if we have them, won't know who their parents-of-

parents are, either.

"It seems to work pretty well that way, doesn't it? The way we do it in our community?" Jonas asked. "I just didn't realize
50 there was any other way, until I received that memory."

"It works," The Giver agreed.

Jonas hesitated. "I certainly liked the memory, though. I can see why it's your favorite. I couldn't quite get the word for the whole feeling of it, the feeling that was so strong in
55 the room."

"Love," The Giver told him.

Jonas repeated it. "Love." It was a word and concept new to him.

They were both silent for a minute. Then Jonas said, "Giver?"
60 "Yes?"

"I feel very foolish saying this. Very, very foolish."

"No need. Nothing is foolish here. Trust the memories and how they make you feel."

"Well," Jonas said, looking at the floor, "I know you don't
65 have the memory anymore, because you gave it to me, so maybe you won't understand this—"

"I will. I am left with a vague wisp of that one; and I have many other memories of families, and holidays, and happiness. Of love."

70 Jonas blurted out what he was feeling. "I was thinking that . . . well, I can see that it wasn't a very practical way to live, with the Old right there in the same place, where maybe they wouldn't be well taken care of, the way they are now, and that we have a better-arranged way of doing things. But
75 anyway, I was thinking, I mean feeling, actually, that it was kind of nice, then. And that I wish we could be that way, and that you could be my grandparent. The family in the memory

My Thoughts

_____

_____

_____

_____

_____

_____

_____

_____

_____

_____

_____

_____

_____

_____

_____

_____

_____

_____

_____

_____

_____

seemed a little more—" He faltered, not able to find the word he wanted.

80   "A little more complete," The Giver suggested.

Jonas nodded. "I liked the feeling of love," he confessed.

He glanced nervously at the speaker on the wall, reassuring himself that no one was listening. "I wish we still had that," he whispered. "Of course," he added quickly, "I do understand

85   that it wouldn't work very well. And that it's much better to be organized the way we are now. I can see that it was a *dangerous* way to live."

"What do you mean?"

Jonas hesitated. He wasn't certain, really, what he had

90   meant. He could feel that there was *risk* involved, though he wasn't sure how. "Well," he said finally, grasping for an explanation, "they had *fire* right there in that room. There was a fire burning in the fireplace. And there were candles on a table. I can certainly see why those things were outlawed.

95   "Still," he said slowly, almost to himself, "I did like the light they made. And the warmth."

My Thoughts

FIRST RESPONSE: KEY IDEAS AND DETAILS

Based on your first reading of this text, how much direct experience has Jonas had with older people? Write your answer in your journal.

TECH-CONNECT

Post your answer to the First Response question to your class web page or another site as per your teacher's instructions.

Focus on Citing Evidence

When you write about a topic, it helps to imagine three things about your readers:

- They are smart enough to understand what you're writing about.

- They don't know the topic as well as you do.

- Your readers can only understand what you're telling them if you give them enough details from the text.

The details your readers need to understand your ideas is *evidence*. Evidence develops your ideas and makes them clear for your readers.

When you gather evidence, it's important to clarify why the evidence matters. Why is a certain detail important? What does it show or suggest? In the chart below, the third column is for explaining what the evidence shows.

Complete the following chart by filling in the second and third columns. The shaded cells have been completed for you.

Moment in Excerpt	Textual Evidence	What It Suggests About Jonas's Experience with Older People
When Jonas first thinks about the dream	*"Who were the old people? Why were they there?"*	Jonas doesn't understand why older people would be at a party. Maybe he's never seen old people at a celebration before.
When Jonas first thinks about the House of Old		The old people never leave the House of Old, so maybe Jonas has never . . .
When Jonas learns what grandparents are		
When Jonas thinks the old way wasn't a "practical way to live."		

Speak and Listen Share your chart with a partner. Use the following questions to help you evaluate one another's charts:

1. Are direct quotes from the text included?

2. Do the quotes provide evidence of Jonas's experience with older people?

3. Do your partner's explanations of what the evidence shows seem reasonable? Why or why not?

Add or change the information in your chart based upon your partner's evaluation.

▼ Write Now write a paragraph about how much direct experience Jonas has had with older people. Make sure that even someone who hasn't read the book will know what you're talking about.

On a separate sheet of paper:

- Write a sentence claiming how much direct experience Jonas has had with older people.

- Then support that statement with at least three pieces of evidence you gathered in the table. Use phrases such as *for example* or *for instance* to introduce your evidence.

- Finally, write at least one sentence summing up what the evidence shows. Use a sentence such as the following:

    This evidence suggests that Jonas . . . .
    The evidence proves that Jonas . . . .

CONNECT TO ESSENTIAL QUESTION

In *The Giver*, memory and truth are closely related. But are memories always trustworthy? Do they perfectly capture the world, or can they distort it?

◗ Second Read: Analyzing the Interaction of Story Elements

The excerpt from *The Giver* isn't action-packed, but something important is happening to Jonas. Analyzing the details can help you figure out what's going on.

Objective: Reread the excerpt from *The Giver*. Write "Event" next to the main event that sparks the conversation between The Giver and Jonas. Then write "Emotion" next to any emotional response the conversation brings out in Jonas.

Focus on Analyzing the Interaction of Story Elements

Stories are made of parts—events, characters, settings, and so on—and all of them affect each other. Sometimes the effects are obvious, as when a tornado (event) takes a girl and her dog (characters) from their Kansas farm (setting) to the Land of Oz (setting).

Other times, as with the excerpt from *The Giver*, the effects are not as dramatic. This is when close reading—taking the time to examine the parts of a story and how they interact—is useful.

1. According to the introduction before the story, what is the overall (main) setting of *The Giver*?

REFLECT

The character known as The Giver is important to Jonas's understanding of his society. Who in your life has been most important in helping you learn about your society? How did that person help you?

©Perfection Learning® • No Reproduction Permitted

2. Who are the characters in the excerpt?

3. What event starts the conversation between the characters?

4. What feelings does Jonas have during his conversation with
   The Giver? Write down the line numbers where you see
   evidence of these feelings.

5. Overall, how do the event and the conversation affect
   Jonas's feelings about his overall setting?

Third Read: Analyzing Points of View

The questions you answered after the second read examined how the conversation with The Giver affected Jonas's emotions. But what about Jonas's point of view?

In fiction, the phrase *point of view* has at least two meanings. Point of view can refer to the narrator's position in relation to the story being told.

- First-person point of view: This is when the narrator is a character within the story. In Chapter 6, *Catch Me If You Can* is told from a first-person point of view.

- Third-person point of view: This is when the narrator is standing outside of the events of the story. *The Giver* is told from a third-person point of view.

But point of view has a second meaning. It can refer to a character's or a narrator's attitude toward people, ideas, and events. Characters' words, thoughts, feelings, and actions are evidence of their point of view.

Objective: Read the excerpt from *The Giver* a third time. Pay attention to Jonas's point of view toward the idea of "family." Draw a box around any evidence that shows Jonas's point of view.

Focus on Analyzing Points of View

Just as a person's point of view about something can develop and change over time, so can the point of view of a narrator or character.

In the chart below, identify one positive and one negative feeling Jonas has about the family he saw in the memory. Then write down evidence from the text showing that feeling.

	Positive feeling:	Evidence from text:
Point of view toward the family in the memory		
	Negative feeling:	Evidence from text:

Now think about Jonas's point of view about how society organizes families. In the chart below, identify one positive and one negative feeling Jonas has. Then write down evidence from the text showing that feeling.

Point of view toward how society organizes families	Positive feeling:	Evidence from text:
	Negative feeling:	Evidence from text:

Before Jonas received the memory, what do you think his point of view was toward how his society organizes families? Do you think he had more than one point of view at that time?

continued on next page

Now that Jonas has the memory, what is his point of view about how his society organizes families? Does he have just one point of view?

Speak and Listen With a partner, talk about the character known as The Giver. How do you think The Giver views the way his society organizes families? Why do you think so? During your conversation, point to specific evidence from the text.

Write Based on your conversation with your partner, write a paragraph in your reading journal about The Giver's point of view regarding families in his society. Use evidence from the text in your paragraph.

Language: Expressing Ideas Precisely and Concisely

When you write and then revise your first draft, you look for ways to improve the precision and concision of your ideas.

Precision means using words that are specific or exact. You can improve your writing's precision by replacing vague words and phrases with more specific ones.

> **Vague:** *The Giver* has themes about many things.
>
> **Precise:** *The Giver* develops themes of love, family, and sacrifice in society.

Concision means describing things clearly and briefly, without extra words. You can improve your writing's concision in three ways:

- Replace phrases with single words that mean the same thing.

> **Wordy:** In order to find *The Giver*, I had a need to visit the public library.
>
> **Concise:** To find *The Giver*, I needed to visit the public library.

• Delete phrases that don't add meaning.

> **Wordy:** In the book called *The Giver*, Jonas is chosen by other people to get the memories of a Giver.
>
> **Concise:** In *The Giver*, Jonas is chosen to get the memories of a Giver.

• Avoid repeating words or ideas.

> **Wordy:** *The Giver* is set in a dystopia, and its bad society is one in which most members of a community of people feel few emotions.
>
> **Concise:** *The Giver* is set in a dystopia in which most members of a community feel few emotions.

So when you revise, focus on making your writing more precise and concise. Your ideas will be clearer, and your readers will have a better experience.

Revise each sentence below as described.

1. Replace phrases with single words.

My report is entirely focused on *The Giver,* a book that a number of people find controversial.

2. Delete phrases that add no meaning.

The Giver was written by the author named Lois Lowry and published in the year 1993.

continued on next page

3. Avoid repetition.

The book won the famous Newbery Medal, which is a famed medal awarded each and every year to the author who writes a book for children.

REFLECT

Was there ever a time when you began questioning something about your society that you had never questioned before? What brought about that questioning? What happened as a result?

4. Replace vague words.

In *The Giver,* this one character goes to another character to learn memories, and he finds out about old people.

Project-Based Assessments

Personal Essay

The Giver describes a society in which citizens have little freedom to make decisions. Your society is different. As you age, you'll make many decisions that will affect you, your loved ones, and your society.

Write a one-page personal essay in which you answer these questions:

- In your life, what do you think will be the single most important decision you ever make?

- Why will this decision be so important? Who will be affected?

- Is there just one good choice in the decision? And is there only one good outcome? Or are the decision and its possible outcomes more complicated than just "good" and "bad"?

Use the following guidelines for your personal essay.	
To receive the highest score (4.0), your essay must meet all of these criteria.	Your essay should • clearly state what you think will be the most important decision you make. • explain why that decision will be so important and who will be affected. • discuss whether the choices and outcomes involved in this decision are simple or complicated. • maintain a formal style. • contain correct grammar, spelling, and punctuation.

Roundtable Discussion

A utopia is a perfect society in which human beings are free to become their best selves. A dystopia is the opposite: a flawed, bad society in which citizens are dehumanized and treated unfairly, often by a powerful government or corporation.

Books and movies about dystopias are popular. *The Giver* is one example. Others include *The Hunger Games*, *Divergent*, and *The Ear, the Eye, and the Arm*. The final book and movie of the Harry Potter series show the magical world becoming dystopian. A dystopia even appears in the animated movie *The Lion King* when Scar takes over the hunting grounds.

Participate in a roundtable discussion on the following questions.

Why might people enjoy reading or watching movies about dystopias? What is the appeal?

continued on next page

In a roundtable discussion, all members of the group are equal and everyone participates. Arrange your seats in a circle so that everyone can see each other. The teacher or a discussion leader may sit in the middle. Come to the discussion with an open mind. You will be evaluated on the following:

Expectations for Discussion	
Listening	Speaking
Listen respectfully.	Speak at least once.
Look at the speaker.	Give reasons or examples.
Take notes on what the speaker is saying.	Ask questions.
Write down follow-up questions.	Explain and offer reasons to support your idea.
Reflect on what others say and be open to changing your mind based on new evidence.	Use appropriate tone of voice and language for an open exchange of ideas.
	Invite comments.

Instructions for a Roundtable Discussion

1. The discussion leader (teacher or student) begins by asking the following questions:

> Why might people enjoy reading or watching movies about dystopias? What is the appeal?

2. Allow each member the chance to reply to the questions.

3. Take notes on comments you disagree with or you have questions about. Record what is said and who said it.

4. Go around the circle again, and allow everyone to ask a follow-up question. Questions should be directed to the person who made the original comment. Try phrasing your questions in this way:

   - Explain what you mean by . . . .
   - Who agrees/disagrees with (name of participant)? Why?

5. Close the discussion by having everyone respond to the following questions:

> Do you think authors and filmmakers want their stories about dystopias to have important real-world effects? If so, what might they be?

Use the following guidelines for the roundtable discussion.	
To receive the highest score (4.0), the discussion must meet all of these criteria.	During the discussion, you should • listen carefully when others speak; make notes about what they said. • offer thoughtful feedback and encourage everyone to participate. • share reasonable opinions and support your opinion with examples. • speak to the question or point at hand in a clear, concise manner.

On Your Own: Integrating Ideas

1. Read *The Giver if you haven't already read it*. It is clear why it won the Newbery Medal. (Even if you have read it before, it might be worth reading again.)

2. *The Giver* was made into a 2014 movie starring Jeff Bridges and Meryl Streep. Many critics didn't like it. They thought the movie wasn't as thought-provoking as the book. If you read the book, watch the movie to see whether you agree with the critics. While watching, you can also practice analyzing how a movie communicates its content—through its choices of lighting, sound, music, color, camera angles, and so on.

3. If dystopian literature appeals to you, find some books mentioned earlier in this chapter. Two more advanced books, *1984* and *Animal Farm*, both by George Orwell, also depict dystopian societies.

> **CONNECT TO ESSENTIAL QUESTION**
>
> The Essential Question is "Can we trust what we see, hear, and read?" How do you think Jonas would answer this question after getting The Giver's memory?

Connect to Testing

In this chapter, you cited textual evidence to support your ideas, analyzed how elements of a story interact, and examined how an author develops the characters' points of view. You also practiced editing sentences for precision and concision. When you take assessments, you will be tested on such skills.

1. **Part A:** Based on the passage, which statement about *The Giver* is most likely true?

    A. Some people in the society are monitored.

    B. All young people receive the memories of old people.

    C. Children do not know who their original parents are.

    D. Parents do not get to watch their children grow up.

    Part B: Which sentence from the passage best supports the answer to Part A?

    A. *Jonas opened his eyes and lay contentedly on the bed still luxuriating in the warm and comforting memory.*

    B. *"Who are my parents-of-the-parents?"*

    C. *"I liked the feeling of love," he confessed.*

    D. *He glanced nervously at the speaker on the wall, reassuring himself that no one was listening.*

2. Read the sentence below.

    > Among other reasons, *The Giver* is a controversial book for the reason that it brings up controversial questions about older people and how society treats them.

    Which of the following best revises the sentence without changing its meaning?

    A. One reason *The Giver* is controversial is because it questions how society should treat older people.

    B. One reason why *The Giver* brings up controversial issues is to ask questions about older people.

    C. *The Giver* is a book that brings up many issues, including one that older people should not ask questions about.

    D. *The Giver* is controversial for one reason: it makes older people ask questions about society.

3. In the excerpt from *The Giver*, how does the character of The Giver most affect the resolution of this part of the story?

   A. by convincing Jonas to begin looking for his grandparents

   B. by helping Jonas to understand what love feels like

   C. by forcing Jonas to confront how horrible his society is

   D. by causing Jonas to realize how well their community works

4. **Part A:** In *The Giver*, how does the memory that Jonas receives most directly affect him?

   A. It leads him to miss his own grandparents.

   B. It leads him to recall his own birthday party.

   C. It frightens him into thinking people are listening.

   D. It makes him want to experience a loving family.

Part B: Which evidence from *The Giver* supports the answer to Part A?

   A. *"So our children, if we have them, won't know who their parents-of-parents are, either."*

   B. *"I wish we still had that," he whispered.*

   C. *He glanced nervously at the speaker on the wall, reassuring himself that no one was listening.*

   D. *"I can see that it was a dangerous way to live."*

5. **Part A:** What does the conversation between The Giver and Jonas mainly reveal about their points of view?

   A. It conveys how different their experiences of family have been.

   B. It expresses their shared, growing dislike of the community.

   C. It shows how little they know about each other's thoughts about family.

   D. It illustrates that they agree their community is better than others.

Part B: Which two choices best support the answer in Part A? Choose one choice for each character.

   A. *"And—let me think. Family. That it was a celebration of some sort, a holiday. And something else—I can't quite get the word for it."* (Jonas)

   B. *"You could go look in the Hall of Open Records."* (The Giver)

   C. *"When I finish my training and become a full adult, I'll be given my own dwelling."* (Jonas)

   D. *"It seems to work pretty well that way, doesn't it? The way we do it in our community?"* (Jonas)

   E. *"It works," The Giver agreed.* (The Giver)

   F. *"I am left with a vague wisp of that one; and I have many other memories of families, and holidays, and happiness. Of love."* (The Giver)

Writing an Informative Text

Scientific knowledge is in perpetual evolution; it finds itself changed from one day to the next.
—Jean Piaget

"Question everything," Guy Harrison writes. "Debunk it!" says John Grant. In this unit, you read about whether you can trust the evidence of your senses. Scientists have the job of testing whether ideas are accurate because even when those ideas are trustworthy, they can be proven false as people learn more. And in the last few centuries, science has overturned ideas that people held for thousands of years.

In this chapter, you will write an informative text in which you describe how a long-held belief about the natural world was proven false by modern science.

> **CONNECT TO ESSENTIAL QUESTION**
>
> Is science a way to test every idea? Or are there limits to what science can test?

WRITING PROMPT

Why does the sun rise? What is fire? Where do mountains come from? Over the centuries, humans developed ideas to explain such natural occurrences. Some of those ideas were reasonable and based on evidence, but they turned out to be wrong anyway.

In an informative text, describe one of those long-held ideas that science eventually proved wrong. Explain how science disproved that idea, and describe the idea that replaced it. Develop your descriptions and explanations with facts, details, and examples.

Because you will be writing about scientific ideas, you will likely use some domain-specific vocabulary. This means you will have to provide some definitions for your readers. And you will likely need at least one graphic, such as a photo or diagram, to illustrate the ideas you discuss. Your informative text should be two pages, typed, double-spaced, and in a standard 12-point Times New Roman font.

Prepare to Write

Read the prompt carefully. Underline key words that explain the requirements of the task. Break it down based on purpose, audience, content, and additional requirements by filling in the chart on the next page.

Purpose	to explain
Audience	classmates, teacher
Content Requirements	
Additional Requirements	

▼ The Writing Process

Brainstorm

The history of science is full of reasonable ideas, which were later overturned by modern discoveries, observations, and experiments. The chart below shows just a few of them. Don't avoid a topic just because you don't recognize a word or phrase like *phlogiston* or *luminiferous*. You're doing research, which means you'll eventually find out what it means. (A good dictionary will also tell you what each *part* of the word means, which will help you even more.)

Choose one idea below that catches your eye and get started.

Famous Ideas That Modern Science Proved Incorrect	
Physical Science	**Astronomy**
• Heavy objects fall faster than lighter ones. • The four basic elements are earth, air, fire, and water. • Objects burn if they contain a material called *phlogiston*. • Dalton's theory of the indivisible atom (Atoms cannot be destroyed.)	• The geocentric universe (Stars and planets rotate around Earth.) • The heliocentric universe (Stars and planets rotate around the Sun.) • The luminiferous ether • The steady-state universe • The nature of comets and shooting stars
Life Science	**Earth Science**
• Fossils and the history of life • Spontaneous generation • The four humors (bodily fluids that determine personality) • The miasma theory of disease ("Bad air" causes illness.) • The blank slate theory of the human mind (The brain has no rules for learning at birth.) • Lamarck's theory of evolution (Any changes to a creature are passed on.)	• The age of Earth • Neptunism (All rocks were formed from waters of an ancient ocean.) • Plutonism (All rocks were formed by volcanic activity.) • The expanding and shrinking Earth • The formation and shapes of the continents

continued on next page

Which idea on the previous page seems most interesting to you?

Why is this idea interesting to you?

What, if anything, do you know about this idea already?

What, if anything, do you know about the idea that replaced it?

Find Sources

Find sources and gather evidence to develop your text. Find two or three sources on your chosen topic. The first source should be an encyclopedia such as *World Book*, *Collier's*, *Encyclopedia Britannica*, or some other credible and respected reference. This will give you some solid facts about your topic.

Always evaluate your sources to make sure they are credible, or are written by experts who have studied the topic extensively. Identify any bias or logical fallacies, such as loaded language and overgeneralization, which writers use instead of solid facts and evidence. (See page 148 for more about fallacies.)

Record information about your sources (including the encyclopedia) in the chart below. Include the title of the article or book, the author's name, the website name, the publisher, and the date of publication.

Title of Source	Name of Journal or Website	Author Name	Publisher	Date of Publication
1:				
2:				
3:				

Gather Information

Take notes on your sources. As you record information, always write down the source the information came from.

When researching a topic, having questions in mind before you read will guide your reading and help your note-taking. Jot down the answers as you find them in the text.

Some questions related to the prompt are listed on the next page. When you find information that answers one or more of these questions, record it in your response journal or in a computer file.

Questions About the Old Idea:

- What is the old idea normally called?

- When was the old idea generally believed, or for how long?

- What aspect of the natural world did the old idea explain?

- What are the details of that explanation? For example, if the old idea explained why the Sun moves across the sky, then what was the explanation for that apparent movement?

- Are any famous people associated with the old idea? If so, who? When and where did those people live?

- Why were people convinced by the old idea? Did it seem to make sense, given what people saw and experienced? Or were there other reasons people believed it?

- Did the old idea have weaknesses, or things it couldn't explain well? If the old idea did have such holes, how did supporters of the idea respond to them?

Questions About the New Idea:

- What is the new idea normally called?

- When did the new idea begin to be accepted? Is it fully accepted, or do some people still not believe it is accurate?

- Did the new idea emerge in a short amount of time (say, less than five years), or did it take a long time to develop and be accepted?

- Are any famous people associated with the new idea? If so, who? When and where did those people live?

- What caused the old idea to be overturned? Was it new discoveries, a famous experiment, or an improved piece of equipment like a microscope or a telescope?

- How is the new idea better than the old idea? For example, does the new idea explain events or new evidence that the old idea could not?

If other useful questions occur to you, write them in the space below.

Write a Central Idea Statement

Once you have sufficient information about your topic, draft a central idea statement that will appear in your introduction. Your central idea statement explains to readers what your text will inform them about.

Study the following sentence frames. They show possible ways to draft your central idea statement.

- For many years, scientists accepted [name of old idea], but in more recent times, that idea was replaced with [name of new idea].

- Long ago, people thought [description of old idea], but now we know that [description of new idea].

- It might seem obvious today that [description of new idea], but in fact, people used to believe [name of old idea].

Now, write your central idea statement below. This is just a draft. It may change as you develop and revise your text.

My central idea statement:

Organize Ideas

You have researched, taken notes, and drafted a central idea statement. Before you begin writing, plan the order of information in your text.

Your text should have an introduction, a body, and a conclusion. You already have a draft of your central idea, which will give you some focus. Study the following sample outline.

I. Introduction

    A. Introduce the topic and capture your readers' interest. For example:

- If you're writing about phlogiston, you could ask readers if they've ever wondered what fire is and where it comes from.
- If you're writing about fossils, you could have readers imagine that they're climbing a mountain and come across fossils of ancient shark teeth.

    B. Briefly state what both the old and the new ideas explain. For example, both might explain why the sun moves, how old the Earth is, why people get sick, and so on.

    C. Provide your central idea statement.

II. Body

    A. Present the old idea.
- 1. Who developed the old idea (if known)
- 2. Where and when it was developed (if known)
- 3. How the old idea explained something about the natural world

    B. Explain what happened to the old idea.
- 1. Problems with the old idea
- 2. New evidence or discoveries the old idea could not explain

    C. Present the new idea
- 1. Who developed the new idea
- 2. Where and when it was developed
- 3. How the new idea explains something about the natural world
- 4. What the new idea does or explains better than the old idea

III. Conclusion

    A. Summarize your main points and restate your central idea statement.

B. Leave a final thought. For example:
  - Did the change force humanity to think of itself differently? If so, how?
  - Did the change lead to a new treatment of disease and thus save lives?

Provide Graphics

Because you are writing about scientific ideas, your readers will probably find it helpful to have one or more graphics. For example:

- If you're writing about the geocentric theory of the universe, you can include a diagram of what it looks like, with labels for Earth, the sun, the planets, and so on.

- If you're writing about one of Galileo's experiments regarding the motion of heavy and light objects, you can include images of that experiment. Again, include labels explaining exactly what the images are showing.

- If you're writing about the formation of the continents, your readers would benefit from seeing a map of Pangaea and another map of how Earth currently looks.

Graphics in an informational text should look professional and convey important information clearly. Make sure the graphics you include add information to the text. Provide captions for the graphics, or refer directly to them in your text.

REFLECT

Consider using headers in your paper to help your reader follow your ideas. A good header is a word or phrase that accurately summarizes the content of the section that follows it.

First Draft

Use your outline and any graphics to write a draft of your research paper. Here are some hints:

- Refer to your notes while drafting.

- Write quickly. You will revise and proofread later.

- Write on every other line or double-space if working on a computer. This will make it easier to make revisions.

- If you take a break and then return to writing, reread what you have written before continuing. This will help you resume the flow of thought.

continued on next page

- Don't copy and paste directly from other works. This is called plagiarism, and it is cheating. If you do quote directly from another work, place that text within quotation marks.

- If you are quoting a source, make sure to cite the source in your draft.

- Mark this Draft #1.

Revision

Having other students and your teacher read your text can be hugely helpful. Listen to their questions and comments on your writing. Following their advice can help improve your writing.

Three ways to revise your paper are shown.

First Peer Review

This review will help you judge whether your ideas are clear and flow logically. With a group of two to three people, complete the following steps:

Steps for Peer Review

1. Select a timekeeper. Each writer gets 10 minutes. Stick to the time.

2. One person begins by reading aloud his or her introduction while other members listen.

3. Pause. The same writer reads the introduction aloud a second time.

4. The writer asks, "Does the introduction make you want to know more?" Each member responds as the writer takes notes.

5. The writer reads the entire paper, pauses, and then reads it again.

6. As the writer reads, members take notes.

7. The writer asks, "What questions do you have about my paper? Do you understand the old and new ideas? Is anything unclear about either?" The writer jots down replies.

8. Repeat steps 1–7 with the next writer.

Use Transitions

Transitional words and phrases help your readers to follow the relationship between your ideas. As you revise, find ways to improve your transitions both between and within paragraphs.

Transitions for Showing Relationships		
Show a Sequence	Show a Contrast	Show Cause and Effect
then	but	so
next	however	then
finally	although	because
first, second, third	in contrast	therefore
before, after, later	on the other hand	as a result

Revise your draft based on your peers' questions and comments. Mark this paper Draft #2.

Second Peer Review

With a partner, trade texts and use the following checklist to evaluate:

Think big. Look at the draft as a whole.

- Is everything covered that is required by the prompt?
- Is the flow between paragraphs smooth or choppy?
- Is the tone consistent throughout?

Think medium. Look at the draft paragraph by paragraph.

- Does the introduction hook readers and make them want to read more?
- Does each paragraph develop the central idea with definitions of domain-specific words, concrete details, and relevant examples?
- Are the right kind of graphics included? Do the graphics clearly support the content of the text?
- Should headings be added between paragraphs? Will they help the readers better understand what each paragraph is about?

Think small. Look at the draft sentence by sentence.

- Which sentences are long and confusing? short and choppy?
- Are any sentences unclear?
- Are there errors in spelling, grammar, or usage?

Final Peer Review

Ask another student to read your paper and evaluate it using the rubric below.

Use the following guidelines for your informative text.	
To receive the highest score (4.0), your informative text must meet all of these criteria.	Your text should • contain a central idea statement that explains what the text is about. • be organized into an interesting introduction, body, and conclusion. • develop the central idea statement with facts and examples. • be organized logically and include good transitions. • demonstrate a clear and interesting style of writing; include a variety of sentence types. • contain correct grammar, usage, punctuation, and spelling.

Proofread

As you prepare a final draft, make sure you have included standard grammar and punctuation. Proofread carefully for omitted words and punctuation marks. If you used a word processing program, run spell-check, but be aware of its limitations. Proofread again to find the kinds of errors the computer can't catch.

Final Text

Share your completed text with audiences beyond your classroom. Read it to your family and friends. Upload your finished digital copy to your class website. If you have a school or personal blog, share your text with your readers.

Practice Performance Task

A performance task tests your ability to understand selections of literature or informational text and then demonstrate your knowledge in writing. The task may begin with several multiple-choice or short-answer questions on key vocabulary and the central ideas of the passage(s). The task ends with a writing assignment.

Complete the following performance task based upon selections from Unit 2. You will read three sources and answer questions. Finally, you will complete a longer writing task.

Source #1

Read the following excerpt from *Think: Why You Should Question Everything* by Guy Harrison from Chapter 7 of this unit.

> On one hand, it makes sense for us to see some patterns of things that aren't really there in order to be very good at seeing real ones that matter. On the other hand, we need to be aware of this phenomenon because it can lead to a confident belief in things that are not real or true. . . . Good skeptics understand how the brain often creates false patterns, so we know to be very cautious when considering claims of UFO sightings, for example, or anything else that is unusual. It only makes sense to be <u>skeptical</u> and ask for additional evidence when people claim to have seen or heard extraordinary things. Maybe they did, maybe they didn't. Given what we now know about the brain, however, are you going to believe someone who tells you she saw a flying saucer or Bigfoot last week? She doesn't have to be lying to be wrong. Anyone with perfect vision can see poorly.

1. Which of the following best states the central idea of the paragraph?

   A. A skill that helps us can also harm us.

   B. A confident belief is usually mistaken.

   C. Questioning what others tell us is wise.

   D. Our brains make patterns to help us survive.

2. **Part A:** What is the meaning of *skeptical* as it is used in this paragraph?

   A. convinced

   B. doubtful

   C. cheating

   D. curious

continued on next page

Part B: Which phrase from the paragraph supports the answer in Part A?

A. *see some patterns of things*

B. *lead to a confident belief*

C. *understand how the brain creates*

D. *we know to be very cautious*

3. According to the paragraph, why might people claim to see a flying saucer?

A. They might be trying to deceive others.

B. They might have poor vision.

C. They might want to get attention.

D. They might be seeing false patterns.

Continue the performance task by reading a second source and answering questions.

Source #2

Read the following excerpt from "The Fact Checker's Guide for Detecting Fake News" by Glenn Kessler from Chapter 8 of this unit.

> Anyone active on social media has probably done this at least once: shared something based on the headline without actually reading the link.
>
> Let's face it, you've probably done this many times. According to a study released in June by computer scientists at Columbia University and the French National Institute, 59 percent of links shared on social media have never actually been clicked.
>
> So the first thing you can do to combat the rise of "fake news" is to actually read articles before sharing them. And when you read them, pay attention to the following signs that the article may be fake. There are fake news stories generated by both left-leaning and right-leaning websites, and the same rules apply to both.

4. **Part A:** What is the central idea of this excerpt?

A. There are ways to fight the spread of fake news.

B. Fake news is spread by left- and right-leaning sources.

C. Social media are to blame for the spread of fake news.

D. Computer scientists are studying the spread of fake news.

Part B: Which sentence from the excerpt supports the answer to Part A?

A. *Anyone active on social media has probably done this at least once: shared something based on the headline without actually reading the link.*

B. *According to a study released in June by computer scientists at Columbia University and the French National Institute, 59 percent of links shared on social media have never actually been clicked.*

C. *So the first thing you can do to combat the rise of "fake news" is to actually read articles before sharing them.*

D. *And when you read them, pay attention to the following signs that the article may be fake.*

5. Which of these best describes the relationship between the first two paragraphs of the excerpt?

A. The first paragraph describes why a reader would share fake news; the second paragraph describes fake news.

B. The first paragraph makes an assumption about the reader's actions; the second paragraph links that action to larger social trends.

C. The first paragraph states that most people on social media share news stories; the second paragraph explains that nearly all those stories are fake.

D. The first paragraph explains how society has changed because of social media; the second paragraph describes ways to fight against that change.

6. Read this sentence from the first paragraph of the excerpt.

> Let's face it, you've probably done this many times.

What tone does the sentence convey?

A. annoyed

B. cheerful

C. friendly

D. pleading

Continue the performance task by reading a third source and answering questions.

Source #3

Read the following excerpt from *Debunk It!* by John Grant from Chapter 9 of this unit.

> There's a more fundamental problem with the "water's memory" claim.

> Any water we drink has had a long history—a history lasting billions of years.

> During that time it has been recycled in all sorts of ways, and has held all

continued on next page

manner of other substances in solution, any one of which could have left an "imprint." Why should water retain the "memory" of a homeopathic molecule but not that of *everything else* with which it has been in contact—including all the gazillions of poops that have floated in it?

The notion of "water's memory" takes homeopathy over the conceptual border into the realm of outright woo—especially when we read of some homeopaths claiming they can email the "imprint" to their patients, who can supply their own water! Even if you look just at basic homeopathy, though, of the kind that Hahnemann invented, the dilutions mean that all you get when you buy a homeopathic medicine is very expensive water.

On the plus side, it's pretty hard to do yourself any damage with a homeopathic overdose.

7. The following sentence appears at the end of *Debunk It!*

On the plus side, it's pretty hard to do yourself any damage with a homeopathic overdose.

Why does the author most likely include this sentence at the end of the excerpt?

A. to leave the reader with a final, funny thought

B. to warn the reader not to take too much medicine

C. to convince the reader that homeopathy is not effective

D. to encourage the reader to distrust homeopathic medicine

8. **Part A:** What is the author's tone when writing about the idea that water has a memory for molecules it touched?

A. angry

B. mocking

C. cautious

D. reasonable

Part B: Which detail from the passage best supports the answer to Part A?

A. *There's a more fundamental problem with the "water's memory" claim.*

B. *Why should water retain the "memory" of a homeopathic molecule but not . . . all the gazillions of poops that have floated in it?*

C. *The notion of "water's memory" takes homeopathy over the conceptual border into the realm of outright woo. . . .*

D. *. . . the dilutions mean that all you get when you buy a homeopathic medicine is very expensive water.*

9. What is the main claim in this excerpt?

A. People who sell homeopathic remedies are deliberately misleading others.

B. Water has been recycled many times over billions of years.

C. The idea that water remembers only certain molecules makes no sense.

D. Hahnemann's homeopathic medicines worked better than today's do.

Your Assignment

WRITING PROMPT

You have just read excerpts from three texts in Unit 2. Choose two of those passages. Find the full version of each text in its chapter. Using those full versions, write an explanatory essay comparing and contrasting the authors' purposes for writing their texts and how they addressed the Essential Question "Can you trust what you see, hear, and read?" Explain how the organization of information in each text helps the authors achieve their purposes. Cite textual evidence from each text to support your analysis.

Read the prompt carefully. Underline words that indicate ideas that should be included in your essay. Create a graphic organizer similar to the following to help you plan your ideas.

Passage One	Passage Two
Author's purpose:	Author's purpose:
Evidence of author's purpose:	Evidence of author's purpose:
Description of organization:	Description of organization:

continued on next page

Passage One	Passage Two
Evidence of organization:	Evidence of organization:

Your Assignment (continued)

Develop an outline to organize your ideas before you begin writing. Study the explanation below to understand how your writing will be evaluated.

Your compare and contrast essay will be scored using the following criteria:

Reading Comprehension:
- How well did you understand the texts?
- Does your writing reflect your understanding of the sources?

Writing Expression:
- Does your writing address the requirements of the prompt?
- Does your essay compare and contrast each author's purpose for writing?
- Does your essay compare and contrast how the organization of each passage supports that purpose?
- Does your essay include references or quotations from both sources?
- Is your essay well organized with ideas that fit together logically?
- Does the writing style contain precise, accurate language and content appropriate to the purpose, task, and audience?

Writing Conventions:
- Does your writing follow the rules of standard English with few errors in grammar, usage, and spelling?
- When you are done writing, evaluate your essay using the list above. Revise your writing as needed.

Unit 3

Essential Question
How is technology shaping society?

Not a day goes by that you do not use some type of technology. If you are reading these words in a book, you can thank the fifteenth-century invention of the printing press. If you used a subway, bus, car, or even bicycle to get to school, you can thank not just the ancient inventor of the wheel and axle but also all of the men and women who built on that simple machine. When you eat today, that food almost certainly originated in farms and factories fed by fertilizers and fossil fuels, both of which are produced by technology.

It's easy to describe relationships between individual people and technology. Less obvious, though, is how such technologies shape entire societies. The printing press, for example, led to newspapers and books. This, in turn, led to large populations sharing a common language and set of experiences. According to historians, such sharing helped produce nations—entire societies of people calling themselves German or English or French, for example. The printing press literally helped produce a type of society that hadn't existed before.

In this unit, you will explore the ways in which technology shapes modern society. You will read nonfiction texts about how digital communication affects young people and how the rise of robots influences the job market. You will read a poem on how industrial technology bent the physical world to human whims and a story of how digital technology could subject humans to the power of corporations. Finally, you will write a story regarding an interaction between a character, a technology, and the society that produced both.

GOALS
• To analyze the interactions of people, ideas, and events
• To examine the effect of repetition on meaning in a poem
• To compare differing presentations of a topic
• To determine the theme of a poem
• To analyze competing interpretations of evidence
• To write a fictional story regarding technology and society

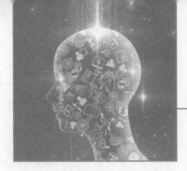

Chapter 11

Analyzing Interactions of People, Ideas, and Events

Preview Concepts

In this chapter, you will be reading a passage about the idea of "the classroom"—specifically, how classrooms are organized, and how well that organization helps them achieve their purposes.

1. What, in your opinion, is the main purpose of your classroom?

2. Describe one thing your classroom does right in achieving that purpose.

3. Describe one thing your classroom could do better in achieving that purpose. Be fair and constructive in your response. Then share your answers with a partner.

CHAPTER GOALS

In this chapter you will

- analyze the interactions between individuals, events, and ideas.
- analyze how text structure helps readers understand an idea.
- determine an author's purpose in writing a text.
- practice using dashes in sentences.

PREVIEW ACADEMIC VOCABULARY

point of view

purpose

Making Connections

Read the following quotations about education. You'll respond to one of them.

> Do not train a child to learn by force or harshness; but direct them to it by what amuses their minds, so that you may be better able to discover with accuracy the peculiar bent of the genius of each.
>
> —Plato (428–438 B.C.E.), Greek philosopher

> Plants are shaped by cultivation and men by education. . . . We are born weak, we need strength; we are born totally unprovided, we need aid; we are born stupid, we need judgment. Everything we do not have at our birth and which we need when we are grown is given us by education.
>
> —Jean Jacques Rousseau (1712–1778), French philosopher

> Let us think of education as the means of developing our greatest abilities, because in each of us there is a private hope and dream which, fulfilled, can be translated into benefit for everyone and greater strength for our nation.
>
> —John F. Kennedy (1917–1963), thirty-fifth President of the United States

Of the quotations above, which one made the strongest impression on you? Explain why it made the strongest impression.

MAKING CONNECTIONS

As you read the passage in this chapter, you'll analyze how interactions between people, events, and ideas over the last 30 years have led to a quiet revolution in how math is taught in a fifth-grade classroom.

First Read: Analyzing Interactions of People, Ideas, and Events

The author Clive Thompson studies how digital technology affects modern society. The following excerpt is from his book *Smarter Than You Think*, which was published in 2013. Because digital technology changes so quickly, some of the ideas that were new then might seem normal to you now.

Objective: As you read, look for and circle the names of people when they first appear. Record any questions you have in the My Thoughts column.

excerpt
Smarter Than You Think
by Clive Thompson

	My Thoughts

1   Matthew shouldn't be doing work remotely this advanced. He's ten years old, and this is only the fifth grade. Matthew is a student at Santa Rita Elementary, a public school in Los Altos, California, where his sun-drenched classroom is festooned with

5   a giant paper X-wing fighter, student paintings of trees, and racks of kids' books. Normally grade five math is simpler fare—basic fractions, decimals, and percentages. You don't reach **inverse trig** until high school.

But Matthew's class isn't typical. For the last year, they've

10   been using the Khan Academy, a free online site filled with thousands of instructional videos that cover subjects in math, science, and economics. The videos are lo-fi, even crude: about five to fifteen minutes long, they consist of a voice-over by Khan describing a mathematical concept or explaining how

15   to solve a problem while hand-scribbled formulas appear on-screen. The site also includes software that generates practice problems, then rewards hard work with badges—for answering a "streak" of questions right, say.

---

inverse trig: a type of math that studies angle measures in right triangles

20   How did these elementary school kids zoom ahead to high-school-level material?

In part because the site lets them learn at their own pace—allowing their teacher, Kami Thordarson, to offer much more customized instruction. The problem with traditional classroom
25   dynamics, Thordarson tells me, is that they don't easily account for the way kids learn at different rates. When she stands up at the chalkboard lecturing on a subject, there's a predictable pattern that takes hold: one quarter of the kids quickly fall behind, so they tune out. Another quarter already know the
30   material, so they tune out. At best, "you're teaching to this middle group of students," Thordarson sighs.

What works better? Personalized, one-on-one tutoring. Back in 1984, the educational scholar Benjamin Bloom compared students taught in regular classrooms—one
35   teacher lecturing to the assembled class—to students who got months of one-on-one attention or instruction in small groups. These tutored students did far better; two **standard deviations** better, in fact. To get a sense of how much of an improvement that is, think of it this way: If you took a
40   regular-classroom kid who was performing in the middle of the pack and gave her one-on-one instruction for a few months, she'd leap to the **ninety-eighth percentile**. This became known as the "Two Sigma" phenomenon, and in the decades since, public-school teachers have struggled to give
45   students more one-on-one time. This isn't easy, given that the average class in the United States has roughly twenty-five children. (Worse, after years of slightly falling, that number is

standard deviations: a number that expresses how much a subgroup differs from the average found in a large group
ninety-eighth percentile: doing better than ninety-eight percent of her peers

now rising again, due to budget cuts.) Until the government
decides it's willing to subsidize smaller classes, how can

50   teachers get more personal time?

One way is by using new-media tools to **invert** the logic
of instruction. Instead of delivering all her math lessons to the
entire class, Thordarson has them watch Khan videos and work
on the online problems. This way, the students who quickly "get

55   it" can blast ahead—and Thordarson can focus more of her class
time on helping the students who need coaching. Other teachers
are even more aggressive about inverting their classes: They
assign videos to be watched at home, then have the students do
the homework in class, flipping their instruction inside out.

60   This makes curious psychological sense. A video can often be
a better way to deliver a lecture-style lesson, because students
can pause and rewind when they get confused—impossible with
a live classroom lesson. In contrast, homework is better done in
a classroom, because that's when you're likely to need to ask the

65   teacher for extra help. (Or to ask another student: Thordarson
and her colleagues noticed students helping one another,
sharing what they'd learned, and tutoring each other.)

"Kids get to work in their place where they're most
comfortable," says Thordarson as we wander around her class.

70   "They're allowed to jump ahead. It gives kids who are above
grade level a chance to just soar! And for kids who struggle,
it gives them a chance to work through some of those issues
without everybody watching."

Still, as Thordarson quickly points out, the Khan Academy

75   isn't enough on its own. You can't just plunk kids in front of
laptops and say, "Go." The point isn't to replace teachers.

invert: turn upside-down

It's to help them reshape their classes in new ways—and spend more time directly guiding students. You can't even say it makes the teacher's job easier. If anything, it has made

80 Thordarson's job more challenging; there's more noise, more kids talking, and she's constantly darting around the room to help out. One U.S. federal study found that students learned best in classrooms with precisely this sort of "blended" learning—traditional teachers augmented with online

85 instruction. But the increase in learning wasn't because of any magic in the medium. It's just that online tools helped students and teachers spend more time on the material.

Judging by Thordarson's success, though, it works. She's seen particularly strong improvements at the low end: Only three

90 percent of her students were classified as average or lower in end-of-year tests, down from thirteen percent at midyear—and other math teachers at Santa Rita have seen similar results. The kids who need help have been getting more of it; the kids who want to push ahead are pushing ridiculously far.

95 "It's like having thirty math tutors in my room," Thordarson says.

FIRST RESPONSE: KEY IDEAS AND DETAILS
Based on your first reading of this text, what idea is leading to the changes in classrooms such as Kami Thordarson's? Record your first response in your journal.

Focus on Analyzing Interactions of People, Ideas, and Events

The excerpt from *Smarter Than You Think* is about change—specifically, a change in how teachers and students in an elementary classroom use their time. This change arose through an interaction of people, ideas, and events. Let's look at these interactions more closely.

My Thoughts

TECH-CONNECT
Post your First Response answer on your class webpage. Compare your answers to those posted by other students.

CONNECT TO ESSENTIAL QUESTION
How has a recent technology shaped your math classroom? (Or has one?)

1. Who are the people named in the passage? What are their roles or jobs?

2. How is classroom time used in Kami Thordarson's math classroom? According to the passage, how does that use of time differ from time use in most classrooms?

3. The way time is used in Kami Thordarson's classroom is partly based on an idea. What is that idea?

4. What event in the 1980s made that idea well known? Who was involved in that event?

5. What technology has been important in changing Thordarson's classroom? How has that technology interacted with the idea you discussed in the previous question?

CONNECT TO ESSENTIAL QUESTION

During your years of schooling, what new technology has come into your classroom? Has it been useful, or does it have more drawbacks than benefits?

Speak and Listen Share your answers with a partner. Did you both identify the same idea behind the use of time in Thordarson's classroom? Do you have a similar description of the event in the 1980s that made the idea well known? Use the terms *people*, *ideas*, and *events* in your discussion.

Write Using the answers to your questions and your partner discussion, write a paragraph explaining how Benjamin Bloom's actions in 1984 led to an idea that has influenced the lives of Kami Thordarson and her students. Use the terms *idea* and *event* at least once in your response.

Second Read: Analyzing Text Structure

The central idea of the excerpt is this: Using technology to increase one-on-one teaching leads to better student performance. The author develops this central idea in sections, with each section doing a specific job. What are these sections?

- First section: Paragraphs 1–3 (lines 1–20)
- Second section: Paragraphs 4–5 (lines 21–49)
- Third section: Paragraphs 6–8 (lines 50–72)
- Fourth section: Paragraphs 9–11 (lines 73–95)

How does each section help develop the central idea so the reader understands it? To determine this, identify the main idea of each section.

Objective: Draw lines dividing the sections from each other. Then read the passage aloud with a partner, taking turns reading every other section. When you get to the end of each section, discuss with your partner what you think the main idea of the section is. Write the main idea of the section in the "My Thoughts" column.

Focus on Analyzing Text Structure

Any text is made of parts: sentences, paragraphs, sections, and so on. Skilled authors know how to make those parts work together to develop a central idea. Clive Thompson is a skilled author. Each section of this excerpt has a purpose.

As sections develop a central idea, they also help you, the reader. When thinking about the purpose of a section, ask yourself: How does this section help me? What is it trying to do for me? For example, does the section:

- raise the reader's interest?

- clearly introduce an idea for the reader?

- help the reader understand through details or examples?

- make a claim about why the idea and its effects are important?

Through structure, a skilled author both develops an idea *and* guides the reader through it.

Finish the chart below. Part of the chart has already been completed for you.

- Under "Main Idea of Section," state what the section is about.

- Under "Possible Purpose(s) of Section," make a claim about the purpose of the section for readers. Use words such as "inform," "explain," "point out," and so on.

Major Section	Main Idea of Section	Possible Purpose(s) of Section
Paragraphs 1–3 (lines 1–21)	A classroom is using technology to help fifth-grade students learn how to do tenth-grade math.	to inform readers of something incredible and get them wondering how it happened
Paragraphs 4–5 (lines 22–50)	Classroom time is organized to provide one-on-one tutoring, which research shows gets better results.	
Paragraphs 6–8 (lines 51–73)		
Paragraphs 9–11 (lines 74–96)		

Speak and Listen Share your answers from the chart in a class discussion. Use hand signals to indicate when you want to talk.

- Thumbs up means you want to share something new.

- A peace sign means you have something to add to the last person's statement.

Finish by discussing these questions:
- Why do you think Clive Thompson used eleven paragraphs to develop his central idea?

- Could he have just stated it, given several sentences of evidence, and left it at that?

- What are the pros and cons of both approaches?

Write Although the activity divided the passage into four sections, it's also true that each paragraph plays a unique role in developing the central idea. In your response journal, write the central idea. Then write eleven bullet points stating the purpose of each paragraph. Share your answers with a partner.

Third Read: Analyzing Point of View and Purpose

In nonfiction, an author's point of view is the attitude or opinion the author has toward the topic he or she is writing about. An author's purpose is the reason the author is writing a text—what the author hopes the text will accomplish.

Objective: Read the text a third time. Draw boxes around at least five words or phrases that suggest the author's point of view toward the topic.

Focus on Analyzing Point of View and Purpose

An author's point of view and purpose are different, but related. For example, an author with negative feelings about a topic writes to get readers to share those feelings. In other words, one of the author's purposes is to get readers to develop negative feelings too.

The relationship between point of view and purpose is most obvious in argumentative texts. Such texts are written with strong points of view that authors hope readers will accept.

continued on next page

> **TECH-CONNECT**
>
> Send a private e-mail to your teacher explaining how the all-class discussion went. Describe one thing that went well and one thing that could go better next time. Be polite and constructive in your e-mail.

> **REFLECT**
>
> Does your math classroom use video technology in the way Clive Thompson describes? If it does, what are its good and bad points? If it doesn't, would you want it to? Why?

Explanatory texts present information on a topic without necessarily taking a strong position. However, explanatory texts are also written with a definite point of view and purpose. The excerpt from *Smarter Than You Think* is such an explanatory text. There's a definite a point of view and purpose, but it's not as clearly or powerfully stated as an argumentative text would be.

1. In the space below, describe Clive Thompson's point of view on using videos in math classrooms. Use the words and phrases you boxed as evidence to support your answer.

2. In the space below, describe Thompson's purpose in writing the text. Say more than just "to explain" or "to convince." Describe what you think Thompson might want to happen in the real world because of his writing.

Language: Using Dashes

Clive Thompson uses dashes skillfully and in several ways.

- To introduce a list:

> Normally grade five math is simpler fare—basic fractions, decimals, and percentages.

- To set off a parenthetical element:

> Back in 1984, the educational scholar Benjamin Bloom compared students taught in regular classrooms—one teacher lecturing to the assembled class—to students who got months of one-on-one attention or instruction in small groups.

- To emphasize set-off text:

> A video can often be a better way to deliver a lecture-style lesson, because students can pause and rewind when they get confused— impossible with a live classroom lesson.

- To indicate a change in thought:

> This way, the students who quickly "get it" can blast ahead—and Thordarson can focus more of her class time on helping the students who need coaching.

Read the following sentences. Then rewrite each so it uses at least one dash.

1. If you need help with math, and many students do, you can visit online tutors.

2. Students can work with online tutors on many platforms, such as desktop computers, laptops, and phones.

3. You can work with tutors at most times of day. This is giving you more flexibility.

4. Some of the best universities host MOOCs, which is short for Massive Open Online Courses, and which let you watch college-level math lectures.

5. You get to watch the world's best teachers teaching some of the world's trickiest math, and you get to do so for free!

Project-Based Assessments

Letter to the Principal

Imagine your school is thinking about changing your math class to be exactly like Kami Thordarson's. It would rely heavily on videos, working with your peers, and one-on-one tutoring. Do you like that idea? Or do you want your math class to remain as it is?

For this project, you will write a letter to your principal that politely expresses your opinion about the possible change to your math class. Fairly and accurately describe how your math class currently runs. Then explain if and how it should change. Provide at least two reasons to support your explanation.

Write a formal letter, not an email. Use business letter format in a block style and include the following: date, recipient's address, salutation, body, closing, and signature. Visit Purdue Online Writing Lab to view an example: owl.english.purdue.edu. In the search box, type business letter.

Use the following guidelines for your letter to the principal.	
To receive the highest score (4.0), the letter must meet all of these criteria.	Your letter to the principal • expresses your opinion about the possible change. • fairly and accurately describes your current math class. • explains why one type of classroom is better than the other. • gives at least two reasons supporting your explanation. • is in business letter format with a header, salutation, body, and closing. • uses correct grammar, usage, mechanics, and spelling.

Write a Narrative

Imagine it is the year 2099. You are in your favorite class. It could be art, math, science, even some future subject that hasn't been invented yet—whatever you like best. Your teacher announces, "Students, our school just got an exciting new technology that will make your learning experience in this class even better." What could it be? A shrinking ray? A time machine? A device that lets you talk to animals, plants, or minerals? Because it's the year 2099, that technology could be pretty wild.

Write a narrative (a story) about the day in 2099 that your favorite class gets this new technology. Your narrative must:

- describe the "exciting new technology" your teacher mentioned.

- show the new technology in action.

- present at least one outcome of using the technology.

- paint a picture of the setting (your futuristic classroom, for instance).

- depict characters (yourself, your teacher, and anyone else important to the story).

- use realistic dialogue, which can also have futuristic slang.

TECH-CONNECT

Share your story on your class website. Read other students' stories as well.

continued on next page

Writers, take note: Although Clive Thompson is positive about using new technologies in the classroom, your story does not have to be so upbeat. What if the new technology seems great at first but has unintended, bad consequences? What if something goes drastically wrong? What if it accidentally ruins your favorite subject—or does something even worse? This is your story to tell, and not all stories end happily.

Use the following guidelines for your narrative.	
To receive the highest score (4.0), the narrative must meet all of these criteria.	Your narrative • describes the new technology, how it works, and at least one outcome from using it. • includes a setting, characters, and dialogue. • uses correct grammar, usage, mechanics, and spelling.

On Your Own: Integrating Ideas

1. Clive Thompson mentions that Kami Thordarson's classroom uses something called "Khan Academy." Guess what? It's still around, and it's bigger and better than ever. You can visit it at khanacademy.org. Search for the type of math you have the hardest time understanding. Preview the videos and see if they help you better understand the topic.

2. Does your school mostly use textbooks? Has it switched (or will it soon switch) to using tablets? An ongoing debate exists regarding the pros and cons of each. You can learn about different points in the debate at tablets-textbooks.procon.org. Where do you stand after reading about it?

3. Your school organizes people, space, and time in specific and purposeful ways: Students are divided into grades, for example, and teachers into departments. The space may be defined by classrooms, hallways, gymnasiums, the library, and so on. Each day comprises class periods, lunch schedules, passing time, and more.
   Whether you're in a private school, a public school, a home school, or in some other model, the way you learn resulted from interactions of people, ideas, and events. So, where did your model of schooling come from? Who or what is responsible for it? What are its goals? And is it really the best way for humans to learn? Conduct research to answer these questions. Start by interviewing your teacher.

Connect to Testing

In this chapter, you analyzed how people, ideas, and events interact; how the structure of a text develops ideas and guides readers; and how an author conveys point of view. You'll be tested over such reading skills during assessments. Answer the question below before reading the Explanation.

1. Read the following sentence from the passage.

   > How did these elementary school kids zoom ahead to high-school-level material?

   What role does this sentence play in developing the central idea of the text?

   A. It poses a rhetorical question that has no answer but prompts readers to think.

   B. It introduces an explanation of how the students are performing so well.

   C. It leads to a description of how digital technology has affected one student.

   D. It begins a comparison between past and present ways of learning math skills.

EXPLANATION

- Choice A is incorrect because the question is answered. The remaining paragraphs all describe how the elementary students became proficient in high-school-level material.

- Choice C is incorrect because the previous paragraphs (one and two) describe the effects of digital technologies on one student, Matthew.

- Choice D is incorrect because the passage does not draw explicit comparisons between how students used to learn with how they learn now.

- Paragraphs 1 and 2 describe how well students in Kami Thordarson's class were performing. Paragraph 3 marks a shift in the focus of the passage, from a description of classroom performance to what has caused that performance. The correct choice is B.

continued on next page

2. Which sentence from the passage best expresses the author's point of view concerning how Kami Thordarson runs her math classroom?

   A. *Matthew shouldn't be doing work remotely this advanced.*

   B. *Instead of delivering all her math lessons to the entire class, Thordarson has them watch Khan videos and work on the online problems.*

   C. *Still, as Thordarson quickly points out, the Khan Academy isn't enough on its own.*

   D. *Judging by Thordarson's success, though, it works.*

3. **Part A:** According to the passage, what word best describes the learning and teaching in the new classroom structure?

   A. stressful

   B. lively

   C. confusing

   D. impersonal

   Part B: Which sentence from the passage best supports the answer to Part A?

   A. *When she stands up at the chalkboard lecturing on a subject, there's a predictable pattern that takes hold: one quarter of the kids quickly fall behind, so they tune out.*

   B. *Instead of delivering all her math lessons to the entire class, Thordarson has them watch Khan videos and work on the online problems.*

   C. *In contrast, homework is better done in a classroom, because that's when you're likely to need to ask the teacher for extra help.*

   D. *If anything, it has made Thordarson's job more challenging; there's more noise, more kids talking, and she's constantly darting around the room to help out.*

4. Read the following sentences.

   Public education is often underfunded. It needs more economic support.

   Which of the following correctly revises the sentences into a single sentence?

   A. Public education—often underfunded—needs more economic support.

   B. Public education—often underfunded, needs more economic support.

   C. Public education, often underfunded—needs more public support.

   D. Public education—often underfunded, needs more—public support.

Chapter 12

Analyzing Repetition and Structure in Poetry

Preview Concepts

At this point in your life, you have probably read many nonfiction texts about machines. In your science books, you've read about simple machines such as the wedge, inclined plane, or pulley, for example. Perhaps you have read a history article about the Wright brothers and their invention of the airplane. And you have likely read or watched a science fiction movie or novel that involved machines.

But what about poetry? Are machines an appropriate subject for poetry? Why or why not?

Share your answers with a partner. Summarize your conclusions from your discussion.

Making Connections

Listen as your teacher reads aloud the following poem. As you listen, think about what the central idea of the poem could be.

All Watched Over by Machines of Loving Grace
by Richard Brautigan

I like to think (and
the sooner the better!)
of a cybernetic meadow
where mammals and computers
live together in mutually
programming harmony
like pure water
touching clear sky.

I like to think
(right now, please!)
of a cybernetic forest
filled with pines and electronics
where deer stroll peacefully
past computers
as if they were flowers
with spinning blossoms.

I like to think
(it has to be!)
of a cybernetic ecology
where we are free of our labors
and joined back to nature,
returned to our mammal
brothers and sisters,
and all watched over
by machines of loving grace.

A central idea of this poem is that plants, animals, and computers should be combined to create a paradise. In each stanza, underline one line that develops this central idea.

The first two stanzas speak of mammals and machines living side-by-side. With a partner, talk about how the third stanza is different. Refer to details in that stanza to support your ideas. Record your observations in your response journal and be prepared to discuss.

> **MAKING CONNECTIONS**
>
> As you read the poem in this chapter, try to determine its central idea and how the lines develop it.

---

cybernetic: computerized

©Perfection Learning® • No Reproduction Permitted

First Read: Determining a Central Idea

Rudyard Kipling published "The Secret of the Machines" in 1911. Many of the machines he describes had existed for only a few years. Nonetheless, machines had already changed the world profoundly.

Objective: Based on the title, the poem is likely about a hidden or forgotten truth about machines. As you read the poem, underline lines that seem to reveal what the secret is.

The Secret of the Machines
by Rudyard Kipling

My Thoughts

1   We were taken from the **ore-bed and the mine**,

We were melted in the furnace and the pit—

We were cast and wrought and hammered to design,

We were cut and filed and tooled and gauged to fit.

5   Some water, coal, and oil is all we ask,

And a thousandth of an inch to give us play:

And now, if you will set us to our task,

We will serve you four and twenty hours a day!

We can pull and haul and push and lift and drive,

10   We can print and plough and weave and heat and light,

We can run and race and swim and fly and dive,

We can see and hear and count and read and write!

Would you call a friend from half across the world?

If you'll let us have his name and town and state,

15   You shall see and hear your crackling question hurled

Across the arch of heaven while you wait.

Has he answered? Does he need you at his side?

You can start this very evening if you choose,

And take the Western Ocean in the stride

20   Of **seventy thousand horses and some screws!**

---

ore-bed and the mine: where metals are found

seventy thousand horses and some screws: the horsepower of a passenger ship's propellers

The **boat-express** is waiting your command!

You will find the *Mauretania* at the quay,

Till her captain turns the lever 'neath his hand,

And the monstrous nine-decked city goes to sea.

25   Do you wish to make the mountains bare their head

And lay their new-cut forests at your feet?

Do you want to turn a river in its bed,

Or plant a barren wilderness with wheat?

Shall we pipe aloft and bring you water down

30   From the never-failing **cisterns** of the snows,

To work the mills and **tramways** in your town,

And irrigate your orchards as it flows?

It is easy! Give us dynamite and drills!

Watch the iron-shouldered rocks lie down and quake

35   As the thirsty desert-level floods and fills,

And the valley we have dammed becomes a lake.

But remember, please, the Law by which we live,

We are not built to comprehend a lie,

We can neither love nor pity nor forgive.

40   If you make a slip in handling us you die!

We are greater than the Peoples or the Kings—

Be humble, as you crawl beneath our rods!—

Our touch can alter all created things,

We are everything on earth—except The Gods!

boat-express: a train that takes passengers to their ships
cisterns: water tanks
tramways: electric trains used in public transportation

45   *Though our smoke may hide the Heavens from your*

        eyes,

        It will vanish and the stars will shine again

        Because, for all our power and weight and size

50   *We are nothing more than children of your brain!*

My Thoughts

_____

_____

_____

FIRST RESPONSE: KEY IDEAS AND DETAILS

In your response journal, write a single sentence to sum up what "The Secret of the Machines" is about.

> **REFLECT**
>
> Read the last stanza again. What lesson or message do those lines present to the reader?

Focus on Determining a Central Idea

We are used to finding central ideas in informational texts and even stories. But poems also have central ideas. As with all genres, a poem's central idea is what it says about its subject, including what the subject does. The subject of a poem can be anything from the poet's own life to the universe itself. We can state the central idea of a poem in the form of a sentence about the subject. For example, the central idea of "All Watched Over by Machines of Loving Grace" might look like this:

The speaker looks forward to a time when technology and nature are joined together to meet all human needs.

Complete the chart below to determine the central idea of "The Secret of the Machines." Describe how each machine helps society, according to Kipling. Then write lines from the poem supporting your description.

Machine	How the Machine Helps Society	Supporting Lines
The telephone (lines 13–19)		"You shall see and hear your crackling question hurled / Across the arch of heaven while you wait."

continued on next page

Machine	How the Machine Helps Society	Supporting Lines
The passenger ship (lines 20–24)		
Dams and water pipelines (lines 25–32)		
Dynamite and drills (lines 33–36)		

Refer to the sentences and supporting lines in the chart you just completed and ask yourself: What single important idea could all of these lines be developing?

Sometimes, you have to draft a few ideas until you find what you believe is the right one. In the space below, write three different sentences in which you "try out" different possible central ideas.

Speak and Listen With a partner, share the central idea sentence you believe is the most accurate. Talk to your partner about why that central idea is likely the best one. Refer to details from the poem in your answer.

CONNECT TO
ESSENTIAL QUESTION

"The Secret of the Machines" describes how humans use machines to transform nature. How can transforming nature also transform human society?

Second Read: Examining the Impact of Repeated Sounds

Many poems rhyme, or use similar sounding words at the ends of lines. But poems can use sound repetition in many other ways. Consider this short poem:

> I love the springtime blooms in pink and white.
> I love the summer surge of humid heat.
> I love the autumn leaves in colors bright.
> I love the winter snow, a linen sheet.

This poem uses a few kinds of repetition.

- It repeats sounds at the start of nearby words—for example, "summer surge" and "humid heat." This type of repetition is called *alliteration*.

- It repeats phrases at the beginning of lines—in this case, "I love the . . . ." This type of repetition is called *anaphora*.

- It uses meter, or repeats patterns of stressed and unstressed syllables. In the poem, each line has 10 syllables grouped into 5 feet made up of one unstressed and one stressed syllable. Note that some lines open with two unstressed syllables.

Some sections of "The Secret of the Machines" use similar sound patterns.

Objective: Your teacher will read aloud "The Secret of the Machines." Listen for the types of repetition described above. Draw a star next to any stanza that seems rich with such repetition.

Focus on Examining the Impact of Repeated Sounds

As mentioned, sections of "The Secret of the Machines" uses the sound devices described above. Consider the sounds of the second stanza (lines 9–12):

> We can pull and haul and push and lift and drive,
> We can print and plough and weave and heat and light,
> We can run and race and swim and fly and dive,
> We can see and hear and count and read and write!

Why does Kipling use so many different types of repetition in

continued on next page

this stanza? What impact does such repetition have on the poem's meaning?

In the space below, describe what the second stanza is about.

Describe three different sound patterns, including rhyme and meter, that are found in this stanza. Give one example of each.

Sound Pattern in Stanza	Example from Stanza

Speak and Listen Form groups of three or four. Have one partner read the second stanza aloud. Then discuss how the repetition of sounds you described above might help express what the stanza is all about.

Write Based on the results of your discussion, write a paragraph that analyzes how the repetition of sounds in the second stanza helps express its main idea. Give at least two quotes from the poem in your response.

©Perfection Learning® • No Reproduction Permitted

Third Read: Analyzing How Structure Helps Develop an Idea

Objective: Read "The Secret of the Machines" a third time. After each stanza, write one sentence in the "My Thoughts" column stating the purpose of the stanza. You will write eight sentences. Consider how the visual arrangement of the lines and their indentations communicate meaning.

Focus on Analyzing How Structure Helps Develop an Idea

In informational texts, paragraphs are typically used to develop the central idea with examples, facts, definitions, and so on. Literary texts, especially poetry, have a broader range of structures to develop ideas. That said, "The Secret of the Machines" is organized much like an informational text.

How are the stanzas in "The Secret of the Machines" like paragraphs? Why are the lines of some stanzas staggered and others are lined up together on the right?

In the chart below, collect your sentences stating the purpose of each stanza. You may edit or replace your sentences to make them more accurate.

Stanza	What the stanza is mainly about
1 (lines 1–8)	
2 (lines 9–12)	

continued on next page

Stanza	What the stanza is mainly about
3 (lines 13–20)	
4 (lines 21–24)	
5 (lines 25–32)	
6 (lines 33–36)	
7 (lines 37–44)	
8 (lines 45–50)	

Speak and Listen Discuss your answers to the chart with a partner. If you decide to change your answers based on your discussion, use a different color pen or pencil to cross out or add information.

Write Based on your chart and your conversation, write a paragraph explaining how "The Secret of the Machines" uses stanzas to develop its central idea. Begin with a sentence restating the central idea. Then write at least three sentences telling how stanzas develop that central idea.

Language: Interpreting Figures of Speech

Figures of speech convey feelings and ideas beyond the simple meanings of words and are used in literary and informational text. One type of figure of speech is allusion.

An *allusion* is a reference to characters, settings, or events from myths, the Bible, or literature. Allusions bring with them ideas and feelings, but only if a reader is familiar with the source.

The tables below list some common mythological, Biblical, and literary allusions and their meanings.

Allusions to Greek Myths	
Allusion	**Description**
Achilles' heel	The warrior Achilles cannot be harmed except on one of his heels. He is killed by an injury to that heel.
Gordian knot	The leader Alexander, faced with a knot that cannot be untied, draws his sword and cuts it in half.
Hercules	A strong and courageous Greek god uses his enormous strength to accomplish great feats.
Prometheus	A Titan takes fire from the gods and gives it to humanity, who live and thrive because of it. The gods punish Prometheus by chaining him to a mountain and having an eagle attack him each day.

Allusions to the Bible	
Allusion	**Description**
the garden of Eden	The garden of Eden is a perfect land where the first humans live, with rivers and fruit trees providing water and food. The people must leave Eden after they disobey God.
Job	Job is a wealthy man who experiences great misfortune and tragedy. Despite his suffering, Job patiently believes in the justice and goodness of God.

continued on next page

Allusions to the Bible	
Allusion	**Description**
Leviathan	Leviathan is an enormous, fire-breathing sea monster larger than any sea creature.
the good Samaritan	A man generously helps a stranger who has been beaten and robbed, when others have ignored the stranger.

Allusions from Famous Literature	
Allusion	**Description**
albatross	In the poem "The Rime of the Ancient Mariner," a sailor kills an albatross (a large seabird), bringing a curse on the ship and its crew. The crew then hangs the albatross around the sailor's neck as punishment.
Frankenstein's monster	In *Frankenstein; or, the Modern Prometheus*, scientist Victor Frankenstein builds a creature from the bodies of dead people. The creature escapes Frankenstein's control and goes on to harm others.
Jekyll and Hyde	In *The Strange Case of Doctor Jekyll and Mister Hyde*, a kind, decent scientist (Jekyll) takes a formula that transforms him into a cruel, cunning villain (Hyde).
Scrooge	In *A Christmas Carol*, Ebenezer Scrooge is a bitter and greedy person who learns to share his wealth and treat others kindly.

Each sentence below contains an allusion. Rewrite the sentence so it no longer uses the allusion but keeps its meaning.

1. My brother Mike was being a real Scrooge about sharing his candy.

2. For my part, I responded to my brother's greediness better than even Job could.

3. But my irritation toward him was practically of Leviathan-like proportions.

4. When it came to getting Mike to share his candy, however, I knew his Achilles' heel.

5. I pretended to cry. Mike couldn't stand it when anyone cried—he always had to be the good Samaritan.

6. Most of the time I don't use such dirty tricks, but I'll admit it: I have a bit of a Jekyll and Hyde personality.

REFLECT

Reread "All Watched Over by Machines of Loving Grace." What allusion is present throughout this poem?

Project-Based Assessments

Poem About Modern Technology

Kipling's "The Secret of the Machines" was first published in 1911. Since then, many more machines and technologies have transformed our world. The chart below lists some of these technologies in categories.

continued on next page

Transportation	Communication	Computer-Related	Other
electric car	the Internet	calculator	artificial limb, organ
helicopter	portable music player	digital camera	lasers
jet airplane	radio	personal computer	radar
rocket	satellite	robotics	space probes
self-driving car	smartphone	video game console	space station
submarine	television	voice recognition	X-ray machine

Write a poem similar to "The Secret of the Machines," using a first-person speaker with the perspective of a machine. Include at least three machines in your poem. Your poem should have a minimum of three stanzas, with at least four lines per stanza and a clear rhyme scheme. Use alliteration in one line. Use anaphora in two consecutive lines.

Use the following guidelines for your poem.	
To receive the highest score (4.0), your poem must meet all of these criteria.	Your poem • is about three or more machines. • is written from a machine's first-person perspective. • has a minimum of three stanzas, with at least four lines per stanza and a clear rhyme scheme. • uses alliteration in one line and anaphora in two consecutive lines.

Digital Presentation

Conduct research and create a digital presentation about the history of one of the technologies listed in the table above.

Remember to use only reliable sources for your information. Websites that end in *.edu*, *.gov*, or *.org* usually have more reliable information than sites with many contributors such as Wikipedia. When it comes to the history of technology, some of the best sources include large public universities, science museums, history museums, and government organizations.

TECH-CONNECT

Save your presentation to a flash drive so you can bring it to school. Be sure to open your file before your presentation to make sure it will work on the school computer.

Gather the following information for your presentation:

- the primary inventor or inventors of the technology

- important dates related to the technology, including when it was invented, when it became popular or commonly used, and when it was replaced by a newer technology

- significant changes to the technology over time, for example, how computers became smaller, or when private companies began launching rockets

- at least one important effect the technology has had on human society

- three sources used for the project: name of article, website, and date

Finally, create an interesting and well-organized computer presentation. Each slide should have both an image and text. Read the rubric carefully so you know what is expected of you from the beginning. Practice your presentation. If working with a partner, decide in advance who will share which slides.

Use the following guidelines for your presentation.	
To receive the highest score (4.0), the presentation must meet all of these criteria.	Your presentation • uses images and text in a professional, appealing way. • clearly identifies the invention and names its inventor(s). • explains important ways the invention has changed over time. • describes at least one important effect the technology has had on modern society. • demonstrates confidence, eye contact, and proper volume. • uses correct grammar, usage, punctuation, and spelling.

On Your Own: Integrating Ideas

1. Some fans of Rudyard Kipling's poetry have made "The Secret of the Machines" the basis of YouTube videos. One such video uses a recording of Kipling reading his poem and pairs it with a photo of the poet. Just go to YouTube and type in "The Secret of the Machines." If you watch two or more videos, think about why the producers of the videos might have made the choices they did.

2. Compare the two poems about machines in this chapter. (See pages 250 and 251-253.) Analyze the effect of rhyme scheme, meter, and graphical elements (punctuation, capitalization, line arrangement).

> **CONNECT TO ESSENTIAL QUESTION**
>
> In the year 600, the planet held about 200 million people. By 1800, that number had grown to 1 billion people. Now, Earth holds 7.5 billion people. What part has technology played in this change?

continued on next page

3. "The Secret of the Machines" is written from a first-person point of view of the machines that humans have built. Of course, machines don't yet think in the ways that human beings do. But many people who study technology believe that machines will one day become as smart as humans—and probably smarter. But what happens then? Are we, as a society, ready for it? The philosopher Sam Harris thinks a lot about these issues, and he is more than a little concerned. You can watch him give a fascinating 15-minute talk on this issue. Go to TED.com, search for "Sam Harris," and watch his talk "Can we build AI without losing control over it?"

4. Rudyard Kipling wrote about more than machines, of course. He was the author of *Just-So Stories* and *The Jungle Book*, and he won the Nobel Prize for Literature in 1907. His most famous poem is probably "If—." As with "The Secret of the Machines," it features anaphora and alliteration. It also has a clear theme. You can find and download any of his work for free at Project Gutenberg. Just go to Gutenberg.org and search for Rudyard Kipling.

Rudyard Kipling

Connect to Testing

In this chapter, you identified a central idea, considered the effects of repetition, analyzed how structure affects meaning, and learned about several common allusions. When you take assessments, you will be tested over such skills and your ability to support your ideas by using textual evidence. Here is an example of this type of question. Try to answer the question before reading the Explanation.

1. Read the following stanza from "The Secret of the Machines."

> *Though our smoke may hide the Heavens from your eyes,*
>
> *It will vanish and the stars will shine again*
>
> *Because, for all our power and weight and size*
>
> *We are nothing more than children of your brain!*

What is the main idea of this stanza?

A. Machines will eventually take over the world and control humanity.

B. Machines are powerful, but without humans they would not exist.

C. Machines will one day be able to produce their own "children."

D. Machines dirty the air, which humans are working to clean up.

EXPLANATION

- Choice A is incorrect because the poem mentions the power of the machines but does not suggest it will be turned against humanity.

- Choice C is incorrect because the poem states that machines are children of the human brain, not that machines will make more machines.

- Choice D is incorrect because the poem does not state that humans will clean up the air.

- The correct answer is Choice B. In this stanza, line 3 states that the machines have great power, but line 4 says that machines are "nothing more" than products of the human mind. It stands to reason, then, that machines would not exist without humans.

continued on next page

2. The following sentence contains an allusion.

> For some people, carrying a smartphone feels like lugging around an albatross.

Which of these best restates the meaning of the sentence?

A. For some people, carrying a smartphone is a burden.

B. For some people, carrying a smartphone is birdlike.

C. For some people, carrying a smartphone is useful.

D. For some people, carrying a smartphone is heavy.

3. Read the first four lines of "The Secret of the Machines."

> We were taken from the ore-bed and the mine,
>> We were melted in the furnace and the pit—
> We were cast and wrought and hammered to design,
>> We were cut and filed and tooled and gauged to fit.

What is the impact of the repetition of "we were" at the beginning of each line?

A. It reminds readers that only humans can produce machines.

B. It stresses that each machine was created in a different way.

C. It makes readers believe that the machines are coming to life.

D. It emphasizes that all the machines share similar beginnings.

4. **Part A:** Which of these best describes the relationship between stanza 3 and stanza 4 (lines 13–24)?

A. Stanza 3 describes a task; stanza 4 describes how a machine can do that task.

B. Stanza 3 describes a region of the world; stanza 4 describes a city far from that region.

C. Stanza 3 describes a person; stanza 4 describes how a machine can replace that person.

D. Stanza 3 describes a type of communication; stanza 4 describes how that communication works.

Part B: Which two stanzas have a relationship that most closely resembles the relationship between stanzas 3 and 4?

A. stanzas 1 and 8

B. stanzas 2 and 6

C. stanzas 5 and 6

D. stanzas 6 and 7

5. **Part A:** What is the central idea of "The Secret of the Machines"?

   A. Machines can destroy as much as they build.

   B. Humans are using machines to produce a paradise.

   C. Humans have made machines that can transform the world.

   D. Machines view themselves as slaves that do dangerous jobs.

Part B: Which line from the poem best restates its central idea?

   A. *And now, if you will set us to our task,* (line 7)

   B. *Do you wish to make the mountains bare their head* (line 25)

   C. *We are not built to comprehend a lie* (line 38)

   D. *Our touch can alter all created things* (line 43)

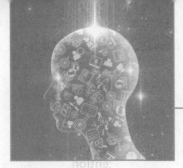

Chapter 13

Comparing Presentations of a Topic

Preview Concepts

Robots occupy an important place in our popular culture. They show up in movies, television shows, books, comic books, and so on. And our feelings about robots aren't consistent. Sometimes we love them, and sometimes we don't.

1. What is a common positive idea in popular culture about the relationship between robots and humans?

2. What is a common negative idea in popular culture about the relationship between robots and humans?

Robots aren't just the stuff of science fiction, of course. They've been part of the real world for the last century, and they're only getting more important. In this chapter, you'll be considering some of the real-world consequences of the rise of robots in human lives.

Making Connections

Read the following excerpt from the 1920 play *R.U.R.* (*Rossum's Universal Robots*) by Czech playwright Karel Čapek. The word *robot* comes from a Czech word meaning "forced labor" and first appeared in the play. In this excerpt, a woman named Helena Glory meets with two executives of a robot manufacturing company.

MAKING CONNECTIONS

As you read the articles in this chapter, pay attention to how they develop their central ideas.

Helena: Why do you make them?

Busman: Hahaha, that's a good one! Why do we make robots!

Fabry: So that they can work for us, Miss Glory. One robot can take the place of two and a half workers. The human body is very imperfect; one day it had to be replaced with a machine that would work better.

Busman: People cost too much.

Fabry: They were very unproductive. They weren't good enough for modern technology. And besides, . . . besides . . . this is wonderful progress that . . . I beg your pardon.

Helena: What?

Fabry: Please forgive me, but to give birth to a machine is wonderful progress. It's more convenient and it's quicker, and everything that's quicker means progress. Nature had no notion of the modern rate of work. From a technical point of view, the whole of childhood is quite pointless. Simply a waste of time.

1. What central idea is presented in this part of the play?

2. Does the idea in the play seem relevant today? Why or why not?

First Read: Analyzing the Development of Central Ideas

One long-term trend in the world of work is automation, or the replacement of human workers with machines. Over the decades, robots have replaced humans in jobs that required repetitive or easily programmable actions. But what happens as machines grow more sophisticated? What other jobs could they take? And how should societies help workers prepare for that future?

Objective: The passage below has two important ideas regarding automation. The first important idea appears in the first half of the passage; the second one appears in the second half. Underline each idea. Then draw boxes around two sentences with details related to each idea. Record any questions you have in the My Thoughts column.

excerpt
Robots will eliminate 6% of all US jobs by 2021, report says
by Olivia Solon, *The Guardian*

My Thoughts

1   By 2021, robots will have eliminated 6% of all jobs in the US, starting with customer service representatives and eventually truck and taxi drivers. That's just one cheery takeaway from a report released by market research company

5   Forrester this week.

These robots, or intelligent agents, represent a set of AI-powered systems that can understand human behavior and make decisions on our behalf. Current technologies in this field include virtual assistants like Alexa, Cortana, Siri and Google

10 Now as well as chatbots and automated robotic systems. For now, they are quite simple, but over the next five years they will become much better at making decisions on our behalf in more complex scenarios, which will enable mass adoption of breakthroughs like self-driving cars.

15   These robots can be helpful for companies looking to cut costs, but not so good if you're an employee working in a simple-to-automate field.

"By 2021 a disruptive tidal wave will begin. Solutions powered by AI/cognitive technology will displace jobs, with the biggest impact felt in transportation, logistics, customer service and consumer services," said Forrester's Brian Hopkins in the report.

The Inevitable Robot Uprising has already started, with at least 45% of US online adults saying they use at least one of the aforementioned digital concierges. Intelligent agents can access calendars, email accounts, browsing history, playlists, purchases and media viewing history to create a detailed view of any given individual. With this knowledge, virtual agents can provide highly customized assistance, which is valuable to shops or banks trying to deliver better customer service.

Forrester paints a picture of the not-too-distant future.

"The doorbell rings, and it's the delivery of a new pair of running shoes, in the right style, color and size, just as you needed to replace your old ones. And here's the kicker: you didn't order them. Your intelligent agent did."

In the transportation industry, Uber, Google and Tesla are working on driverless cars, while similar technology is creeping its way into trucking to replace expensive human drivers.

It's easy to get dazzled by such innovations, but what happens to the 6%? The call center staff, the taxi drivers and the truckers. There may be new jobs created to oversee and maintain these automated systems, but they will require an entirely different skillset.

"Six percent is huge. In an economy that's really not creating regular full-time jobs, the ability of people to easily find new employment is going to diminish. So we will have people wanting to work and struggling to find jobs because

My Thoughts

_____
_____
_____
_____
_____
_____
_____
_____
_____
_____
_____
_____
_____
_____
_____
_____
_____
_____
_____
_____
_____
_____
_____
_____

the same trends are beginning to occur in other historically richer job creation areas like banking, retail and healthcare,"

50   said Andy Stern, the former president of the Service Employees International Union.

"It's an early warning sign and I think it just portends a massive wind of change in the future."

Studies have shown that higher rates of unemployment

55   are linked to less volunteerism and higher crime. Taxi drivers around the world have already reacted with violent protest to the arrival of ride-hailing app Uber. Imagine how people react when Uber eliminates drivers from its fleet.

"There is a lot of correlation between unemployment and

60   drug use," said Stern. "Clearly over time, particularly in urban settings, the lack of employment is tinder for lighting a fire of social unrest."

The challenge posed by automation is not being taken seriously enough at a policy level, Stern added. "Politicians

65   would rather talk about getting a college degree and technical skill training, things that are probably five to 10 years too late. We don't really have a plan and we don't appreciate how quickly the future is arriving."

FIRST RESPONSE: KEY IDEAS AND DETAILS

According to the passage, how could widespread unemployment affect society? Record your answer in your response journal.

TECH-CONNECT

As directed by your teacher, send a question you had about the article to Poll Everywhere or post it on your class website.

Focus on Analyzing the Development of Central Ideas

In nonfiction, a central idea is an idea that an author wants readers to understand fully. Some nonfiction texts, like the article you just read, have two or more central ideas.

The central idea in the first half of the article is this: by 2021, robots will eliminate 6% of jobs.

What do you think is the central idea in the second half of the passage?

CONNECT TO ESSENTIAL QUESTION

The article focuses on the negative effects of automation. Are there positive effects to society that the article does not describe?

Authors develop, or say more about, a central idea with information such as details, examples, quotations, and so on. By developing a central idea, the author gives readers a fuller understanding of the idea and its importance.

The diagram below restates the first central idea of the passage and one of its supporting details. Complete the diagram with two other supporting details.

REFLECT

You might have heard the expressions "the bare bones of an idea" and "fleshing out an idea." How are those expressions related to the development of a central idea?

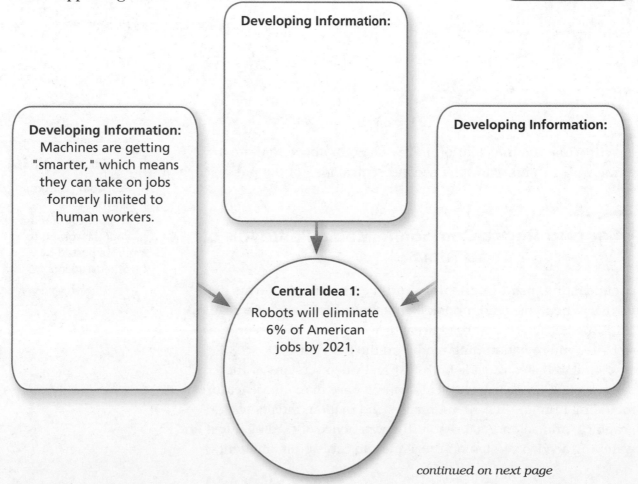

Developing Information:

Developing Information:
Machines are getting "smarter," which means they can take on jobs formerly limited to human workers.

Developing Information:

Central Idea 1:
Robots will eliminate 6% of American jobs by 2021.

continued on next page

Work with a partner to fill out the following diagram. When you're finished, the diagram should identify the second central idea of the passage and three pieces of information that help develop that central idea.

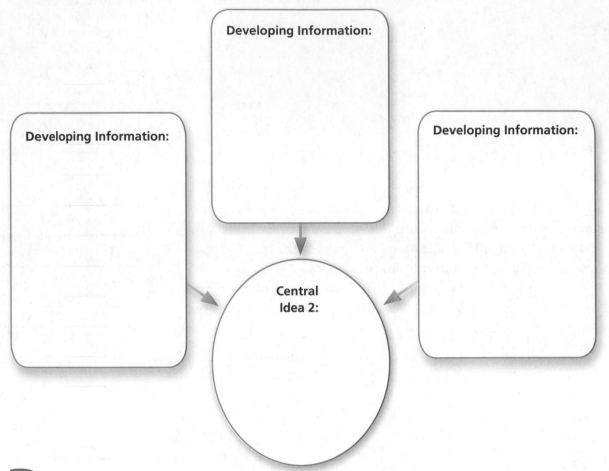

Developing Information:

Developing Information:

Developing Information:

Central Idea 2:

▼**Write** Use the information in the diagram above to write a paragraph summarizing the second central idea of the passage.

TECH-CONNECT

Post your paragraph on your class webpage. Compare your paragraph to those posted by other students.

Second Read: Comparing Media Portrayals of a Topic

Broadcasting, print publishing, and the Internet are forms of media. When you read a book or magazine article, you're reading print media. When you read an article or watch a video on a website, you're consuming media on the Internet.

Some websites provide both text and video versions of the same topic. Compared with texts, videos have many more features, including human presenters, images and motion, music, text graphics, and so on. As a result, the experience of reading a text and watching a video version on the same subject is quite different.

Objective: First, read the article that follows. As you read, circle any words or phrases that show the author's personality or express a mood. After you read the text, you will watch a video version of this article.

Robots Are Slowly Taking Over the Job Market
by Lindsey Pulse, Newsy.com

	My Thoughts

1   Robots are taking over the work world, but that doesn't mean machines will take everyone's jobs—for now.

    A study by Forrester Research found 6 percent of all U.S. jobs will be replaced by robots by 2021—starting with those in
5 customer service.

    Forrester found that eventually, robots will take over most craftsmen and factory jobs. They'll also come for taxi and truck drivers. Uber is already at the forefront of that innovation.

    And while these robots can be good for companies looking
10 to cut costs and increase efficiency, where does that leave employees who get the boot?

    The argument for a more automated workforce is that it will create new jobs in robot creation and robot management. But that argument can really only apply to those capable
15 of becoming engineers. Not everyone can create artificial intelligence software.

    And there's not a lot anyone can do to stop artificial intelligence from seeping into the work world.

    McDonald's has been using self-service ordering kiosks in
20 various locations since last year. Other food chains followed suit.

    And right now, most robots are pretty basic. They can take commands, like Amazon's Alexa or Apple's Siri. But over the next several years, those robots will learn how to do even more.

    That includes the ability to predict human behavior and
25 figure out complex scenarios.

For now, it appears jobs that require physical interaction, like management, are in the clear, along with jobs that can be unpredictable, like construction work—but for how long, we can't really say.

_____

_____

Before you watch the video version of the article, make a prediction: What mood will the video have? Will it portray the topic in a way that alarms, amuses, reassures, or excites? Or will there be no apparent mood at all? Explain your prediction.

Review the questions in the chart. As you watch the video, record notes in the chart on how the video presents information. **Note:** Search using the title of the article. The video is found on the Newsy.com site. The video is less than two minutes long. Watch it at least three times to gather enough information to complete the chart.

Video Version of "Robots Are Slowly Taking Over the Job Market"
During Viewing
Presenter: What is the presenter's tone? How does she want to make you feel?
Music: Is there music? Describe what it sounds like. Is it intended to affect your reception of the information? If so, how?

Video Version of "Robots Are Slowly Taking Over the Job Market"
Text Graphics: Are there text graphics? What do they say? What purposes do they seem to have? Are they helpful?
Other Images: What people or things does the video show? What do they add to the presentation of the information?
After Viewing
Overall Impressions: What did you think of the video clip? What emotions did you experience? Was the tone of the video a good match for the information presented? Why or why not?

Focus on Comparing Media Portrayals of a Topic

When watching the video at Newsy.com, you probably noticed that the text of the article is found under the video. This digital text has different features from the print version found in this book. It includes links to the Forrester Research study cited in the article. It also provides links to other articles on the same topic. You can click on the buttons under SHARE to share the article's URL on social media or send it to yourself via email. How could you use these features if you were conducting a research report on this topic?

Use this chart on the following page to gather information to help you compare and contrast the article and the video. The first row has been completed for you.

continued on next page

Question	Article	Video
What is the central idea of each version?	Robots are taking over more and different types of jobs.	Robots are taking over more and different types of jobs.
Do you get a sense for the personality of the author (article) or the speaker (video)? If so, describe that personality.		
Describe the tone with which the subject matter is portrayed.		

Speak and Listen Although the article and the video present the same information, their portrayals of the subject matter are clearly quite different. With a group of three or four classmates, share your charts and discuss how the article and the video differ.

Write Based on your discussion with your classmates, write a paragraph that describes what you think is the most important difference between the article and the video's portrayal of the subject. Refer specifically to the video's use of music, text graphics, and imagery in your answer. Complete your paragraph by explaining one likely reason the producers made the video so different from the article.

> **REFLECT**
>
> Which portrayal was more informative? Which portrayal was more entertaining? If you were doing research for an essay about robots and society, which would you find more useful?

Third Read: Analyzing Presentations of the Same Topic

The two articles you read present much of the same information, but they differ in their presentation of that information. But in what ways do they differ?

Objective: Read the two articles again. (You do not need to watch the video again.) As you read, circle any supporting details that are similar. In the "My Thoughts" column, jot down your observations about how the conclusions of each article are different.

> **TECH-CONNECT**
>
> Post your paragraph on your class website. Read other students' responses and comment positively on two or more of them.

Focus on Analyzing Presentations of the Same Topic

The two articles in this chapter are similar, but there are some important differences in the conclusions they reach about robots and the job market. Complete the chart below to compare and contrast the articles.

Question	"Robots Will Eliminate 6% of All U.S. Jobs"	"Robots Are Slowly Taking Over the Job Market"
On what report are both articles based?		
Identify statistics (numbers) that appear in both articles.		
Identify the kinds of jobs the articles say will disappear.		
What examples of artificial intelligence does each article give?		
Who does each article quote? What are their names and jobs?		

continued on next page

Question	"Robots Will Eliminate 6% of All U.S. Jobs"	"Robots Are Slowly Taking Over the Job Market"
What does each article claim about whether society is ready for the change?		
What idea does each article want the reader to take from it?		

(Speak and Listen Form a small group and discuss the important differences between the two articles. Consider these questions:

- Are the articles similar or different in how they interpret the facts?

- Does one article go further in its interpretation of the facts than the other?

REFLECT

Which article made you ponder your own future more? Why?

Language: Subject and Verb Agreement

In the present tense, subjects and verbs must agree with each other in number. Plural subjects take plural verbs, and singular subjects require singular verbs. Following this rule becomes more difficult when the subject and verb are separated or when the sentence has multiple subjects.

Two or more subjects in a clause form a compound subject. Depending on how the subjects are related, a compound subject may take a singular or a plural verb. Consider the following sentences with compound subjects.

- Alexa, Cortana, Siri, and Google Now are virtual assistants.

- If Alexa or Siri hears its name, it listens for a command.

In the first sentence, the subjects are joined by the word *and*, making the compound subject plural. In the second sentence, the subjects are joined by *or*, showing a choice between the subjects. They are not acting together, so the compound subject is singular. Remember, in a complex sentence like this one, the subject and verb in the dependent clause must agree and the subject and verb in the independent clause must agree. Study the following sentence.

- Virtual assistants like Alexa, Cortana, Siri, or Google Now are quite simple, but over the next five years they will become much better.

In this sentence, the subject is *virtual assistants*, which is plural. The names may appear to be a compound subject, but the names are the objects in the prepositional phrase. The word *like* is used as a preposition.

In the following sentences, underline the subject and circle the correct verb.

1. The car full of teenagers (pulse / pulses) with loud music even though two police cars (follow, follows) behind.

2. Jeremy, the oldest of six kids, (love / loves) to babysit.

3. Shelly, Mika, and I (wants / want) to see the school play.

4. Jobs that require physical interaction, like management, (is / are) in the clear.

5. A robot or a computer program like a self-service ordering kiosk (replaces / replace) several human workers.

Project-Based Assessments

Op-Ed

An op-ed is a written opinion published by a newspaper or magazine that typically appears opposite the editorial page. It has a named author and focuses on an issue of importance.

Research the following question. Then write an op-ed for your local newspaper.

- What is the proper role of government, if any, in helping large groups of workers replaced by robots?

Follow these steps to help you.

1. Read two op-eds from a local newspaper. Study how an op-ed is written. How does it start? How does the opinion develop? What reasons and information does it give?
2. Research. Find three reliable sources on how governments have assisted workers who lost their jobs to robots.
3. Take careful notes and put the ideas into your own words.
4. Once you've done research, state your opinion on the question above.
5. Write your op-ed. It should be between 200 and 300 words.

> **CONNECT TO ESSENTIAL QUESTION**
>
> On balance, is the human world improved or hurt by the spread of robots?

continued on next page

6. Ask two people to read your op-ed and give you feedback. Revise your op-ed based on their suggestions.

7. Check your writing for mistakes in grammar usage, punctuation, transitions, and spelling.

Use the following guidelines for your op-ed.	
To receive the highest score (4.0), the op-ed must meet all of these criteria.	Your op-ed • includes a clearly stated opinion. • acknowledges an opposing opinion/counterargument. • demonstrates the appropriate structure and length of an op-ed. • uses evidence to support your opinion. • uses correct grammar, punctuation, and spelling.

Job Fair Pamphlet

The second article states, "Not everyone can create artificial intelligence software." That's probably true. But not everyone *wants* that job. What is your dream job? What education or training would you need in order to get it?

Research a job you are interested in. Then use a word processing program to create a trifold, double-sided pamphlet to present information about the job. Imagine you are making the pamphlet for a job fair, which is an event where people come to learn about jobs.

Research the Job

1. Brainstorm jobs. Investigate what really interests you. Would you like to be an astronaut, a politician, a movie star, or a professional athlete? For this activity, the sky is the limit.

2. Visit the U.S. Bureau of Labor Statistics' online Occupational Outlook Handbook (OOH) at bls.gov/ooh/.

3. Spend time exploring the OOH Page. You can search for jobs by data such as pay, education level, and growth rate. You can also browse through "Occupation Groups" such as "Arts and Design" or "Entertainment and Sports." Use the features of these digital texts including links and pop-up explanations to enhance your understanding of what you are reading.

4. Once you've settled on an interesting job, record as much information as you can gather about it from the OOH website.

Make the Pamphlet

1. Find the trifold template in your word processing program and choose a style.

2. Your brochure will open in a new file. Save and name the

file. Locate the front page of the brochure and add a title and a picture. (Pictures can be downloaded from the Internet.)

3. Design the inside and back of the brochure and include the following information:

- the name of the job

- a brief description of what people in the job typically do

- the minimum amount of training or education required to get started in the job, e.g., high-school diploma, two-year degree, apprenticeship, four-year degree, graduate degree, or more

- the average starting salary

- the future prospects for the job, e.g., whether robots will likely displace human workers

- at least two visual aids to support your text, such as photos of people performing the job or graphs showing trends over time

Use the following guidelines for your job fair pamphlet.	
To receive the highest score (4.0), the pamphlet must meet all of these criteria.	Your pamphlet • contains the name and description of the job. • includes the minimum education required to get started. • displays the average beginning salary. • discusses the future prospects for the job. • includes at least two visuals that support an understanding of the job. • is well organized, neat, and professional. • uses correct grammar, punctuation, and spelling.

On Your Own: Integrating Ideas

1. As mentioned at the beginning of this chapter, the word *robot* was first used in the 1920 play *R.U.R.* (*Rossum's Universal Robots*) by Karel Čapek. You can find a public domain recording of the play at Archive.org.

2. Robots are the subject of many famous science-fiction stories, but the writer Isaac Asimov wrote many of the most celebrated, beginning with his short story collection *I, Robot* (1950), which is still in print and can probably be found in your school library. Asimov imagined that advanced robots would be programmed to obey three laws that would protect people from harm. Select and read some of Asimov's stories or read another text about intelligent robots.

> **REFLECT**
>
> As you get older, how can you respond to the problem of automation in the workplace? Are there things you can do to make sure you have a good chance of keeping a job?

Connect to Testing

In this chapter, you analyzed the development of central ideas, compared media portrayals of a topic, and analyzed presentations of the same topic. When you take assessments, you will be tested over these skills.

1. **Part A:** Which sentence from "Robots will eliminate 6% of all US jobs by 2021" best summarizes one of that article's two central ideas?

   A. *These robots, or intelligent agents, represent a set of AI-powered systems that can understand human behavior and make decisions on our behalf.*

   B. *Intelligent agents can access calendars, email accounts, browsing history, playlists, purchases and media viewing history to create a detailed view of any given individual.*

   C. *"It's an early warning sign and I think it just portends a massive wind of change in the future."*

   D. *Imagine how people react when Uber eliminates drivers from its fleet.*

   Part B: Which sentence offers details that develop the central idea in Part A?

   A. *These robots can be helpful for companies looking to cut costs, but not so good if you're an employee working in a simple-to-automate field.*

   B. *Current technologies in this field include virtual assistants like Alexa, Cortana, Siri and Google Now as well as chatbots and automated robotic systems.*

   C. *In the transportation industry, Uber, Google and Tesla are working on driverless cars, while similar technology is creeping its way into trucking to replace expensive human drivers.*

   D. *We don't really have a plan and we don't appreciate how quickly the future is arriving.*

2. How is the experience of watching the video of "Robots Are Slowly Taking Over the Job Market" different from reading the article? Refer to specific ways the video helps you understand the concepts in the article.

3. Read the sentences below. Choose the sentence where the subject and verb do **not** agree.

    A. Artificial intelligence, or AI, is an area of computer science.

    B. Two of the activities computers with artificial intelligence is designed for include speech recognition and problem solving.

    C. Robotics, or the design and operation of robots, is also a field related to artificial intelligence.

    D. Industrial robots used in manufacturing are just one type of robot.

4. **Part A:** What central idea can be found in **both** articles about robots?

    A. Robots will replace a significant number of workers at their jobs.

    B. Widespread unemployment will lead to crime and social unrest.

    C. Forrester Research released a report with disturbing findings.

    D. Robots will become able to do more sophisticated jobs over time.

    Part B: Select one sentence from each article to support the answer to Part A.

    A. *By 2021, robots will have eliminated 6% of all jobs in the US, starting with customer service representatives and eventually truck and taxi drivers.* (article 1)

    B. *For now, they are quite simple, but over the next five years they will become much better at making decisions on our behalf in more complex scenarios, which will enable mass adoption of breakthroughs like self-driving cars.* (article 1)

    C. *Studies have shown that higher rates of unemployment are linked to less volunteerism and higher crime.* (article 1)

    D. *A study by Forrester Research found 6 percent of all U.S. jobs will be replaced by robots by 2021—starting with those in customer service.* (article 2)

    E. *But over the next several years, those robots will learn how to do even more.* (article 2)

    F. *For now, it appears jobs that require physical interaction, like management, are in the clear, along with jobs that can be unpredictable, like construction work—but for how long, we can't really say.* (article 2)

5. Which of these describes an important difference between the two articles about robots?

    A. *The Guardian* article explains how society should respond to automation.

    B. *The Guardian* article draws a connection between unemployment and crime.

    C. The Newsy article discusses how robots are changing customer service jobs.

    D. The Newsy article describes how robots are growing more sophisticated with time.

Chapter 14

Determining Theme

Preview Concepts

It is hard for young people to remember a time without the Internet, websites, and social media such as Facebook or Instagram. You have probably never known life without such technology. And like all technologies, it can be good or bad for individuals and society.

1. Describe one way in which the technology of the Internet has led to a more interesting world.

2. Now describe one way in which the Internet might actually be harmful to people who use it a lot.

Making Connections

Read the following sentences.

> Extreme boredom provides its own antidote.
>
> —François de La Rochefoucauld, a 17th-century
> French author

> If life . . . were possessed of any positive intrinsic value, there would be no such thing as boredom at all: mere existence would satisfy us in itself, and we should want for nothing.
>
> —Arthur Schopenhauer, a 19th-century German philosopher

> Isn't "not to be bored" one of the principal goals of life?
>
> —Gustave Flaubert, a 19th-century French author

> A well-stocked mind is safe from boredom.
>
> —from *Childhood's End* by Arthur C. Clarke

The quotations above show that some great minds have thought about boredom's importance, meaning, and solutions. Choose one of the sentences above. Restate in your own words what the sentence means. Then state whether you agree with the author's point of view, and explain why.

> **MAKING CONNECTIONS**
>
> As you read the excerpt from the novel in this chapter, think about how the narrator's struggles with boredom help to develop the theme.

First Read: Comparing Points of View

Before reading a text, you should preview the headers and the genre and make predictions about the text. This excerpt is from the science-fiction novel *Feed*. A teenager named Titus lives in a future world where everyone has the Internet connected wirelessly into their brains. As the story begins, Titus and his friends take a trip to the Moon, where Titus meets a girl named Violet. A strange event at a dance club knocks the friends out, and when they wake up, they find themselves disconnected from the feed.

Objective: Preview the section headers and make predictions about the main character's point of view. As you read, identify characters who feel differently than Titus does about feednet and write "might feel differently" in the margin. As you read, make predictions about what will happen next based on other science-fiction novels you have read.

from
Feed

by M. T. Anderson

	My Thoughts

1 **Awake**

The first thing I felt was no credit.

I tried to touch my credit, but there was nothing there.

It felt like I was in a little room.

5   My body—I was in a bed, on top of my arm, which was asleep, but I didn't know where. I couldn't find the Lunar GPS to tell me.

Someone had left a message in my head, which I found, and then kept finding everywhere I went, which said that

10   there was no transmission signal, that I was currently disconnected from feednet. I tried to chat Link and then Marty, but nothing, there was no transmission signal, I was currently disconnected from feednet, of course, and I was starting to get scared, so I tried to chat my parents, I tried to chat them on

15   Earth, but there was no transmission etc., I was currently etc.

So I opened my eyes.

College Try

"Nothing," she said.

I had gotten up and was sitting on a chair beside her. We

20 were in a hospital. We took up a ward.

Link was still asleep. Nurses went by.

I said, "I can't see anything. Through the feed."

. . . .

We'd been up for fifteen or twenty minutes. Everything in

25 my head was quiet. . . .

"What do we do?" she asked.

I didn't know.

Boring

There was nothing there but the walls. We looked at them,

30 and at each other. We looked really squelch. Our hair and

stuff. We had remote relays attached to us to watch our blood

and our brains.

There were five walls, because the room was irregular. One

of them had a picture of a boat on it. The boat was on a pond

35 or maybe lake. I couldn't find anything interesting about that

picture at all. There was nothing that was about to happen or

had just happened.

I couldn't figure out even the littlest reason to paint a

picture like that.

40 ## Still Boring

Our parents had been notified while we were asleep. Only

Loga hadn't been touched by the hacker. She hadn't let him

touch her, because he looked really creepy to her, so she stood

way far away. There were also others, people we'd never met,

45 who had been touched, and they were in the wards, too. He

had touched thirteen people in all.

My Thoughts

There was a police officer there, waiting in a chair. He told us that we would be off-line for a while, until they could see what had been done and check for viruses, and decrypt the

50 feed history to get information to use against the guy in court. They said that they had identified him, and that he was a hacker and a naysayer of the worst kind.

We were frightened, and kept touching our heads. Suddenly, our heads felt real empty. At least in the hospital

55 they had better gravity than the hotel.

Missing the Feed

I missed the feed.

I don't know when they first had feeds. Like maybe, fifty or a hundred years ago. Before that, they had to use their hands

60 and their eyes. Computers were all outside the body. They carried them around outside of them, in their hands, like if you carried your lungs in a briefcase and opened it to breathe.

People were really excited when they first came out with feeds. It was all *da da da, this big educational thing, da da*

65 *da, your child will have the advantage, encyclopedias at their fingertips, closer than their fingertips, etc.* That's one of the great things about the feed—that you can be supersmart without ever working. Everyone is supersmart now. You can look things up automatic, like science and history, like

70 if you want to know which battles of the Civil War George Washington fought in and [stuff].

It's more now, it's not so much about the educational stuff but more regarding the fact that everything that goes on, goes on on the feed. All of the feedcasts and the instant news,

75 that's on there, so there's all the entertainment I was missing without a feed, like the girls were all missing their favorite

feedcast, this show called *Oh? Wow! Thing!*, which has all these kids like us who do stuff but get all pouty, which is what the girls go crazy for, the poutiness.

80   But the braggest thing about the feed, the thing that made it really big, is that it knows everything you want and hope for, sometimes before you even know what those things are. It can tell you how to get them, and help you make buying decisions that are hard. Everything we think and feel is taken

85   in by the corporations, mainly by data ones like Feedlink and OnFeed and American Feedware, and they make a special profile, one that's keyed just to you, and then they give it to their branch companies, or other companies buy them, and they can get to know what it is we need, so all you have to do

90   is want something and there's a chance it will be yours.

      Of course, everyone is like, *da da da, evil corporations, oh they're so bad*, we all say that, and we all know they control everything. I mean, it's not great, because who knows what evil [things] they're up to. Everyone feels bad about that.

95   But they're the only way to get all this stuff, and it's no good getting [mad] about it, because they're still going to control everything whether you like it or not. Plus, they keep like everyone in the world employed, so it's not like we could do without them. And it's really great to know everything about

100   everything whenever we want, to have it just like, in our brain, just sitting there.

      In fact, the thing that made me [mad] was when they couldn't help me at all, so I was just lying there, and couldn't play any of the games on the feed, and couldn't chat anyone,

105   and I couldn't do a . . . thing except look at that stupid boat painting, which was even worse, because now I saw that there

My Thoughts

_____
_____
_____
_____
_____
_____
_____
_____
_____
_____
_____
_____
_____
_____
_____
_____
_____
_____
_____
_____
_____
_____
_____
_____
_____
_____

was no one on the boat, which was even more stupid, and was kind of how I felt, that the sails were up, and the rudder was, well, whatever rudders are, but there was no one on board to
110 look at the horizon.

<u>**FIRST RESPONSE: KEY IDEAS AND DETAILS**</u>

Based on your first reading, how does Titus feel about feednet? Correct or confirm the predictions you made before reading the text. Record your first response in your journal.

CONNECT TO ESSENTIAL QUESTION

Does *Feed* depict a society in which technology has brought wonderful things? Or has technology brought about something terrible? Could it be both?

Focus on Comparing Points of View

A character's *point of view* is the set of thoughts and feelings he or she has about something. The text offers ample evidence about how Titus feels about feednet because he is the narrator and spends most of his time talking about himself and how he feels.

How does Titus feel about feednet?

How do you know Titus feels this way? What are some words, phrases, or sentences in the text that support your claim about his point of view?

REFLECT

Would you want to live in a society in which you were constantly connected to a feed of information and products? Do you already?

☾**Speak and Listen** The hacker might have a different point of view about feednet. The excerpt isn't clear on the hacker's motivations, but there is one possible clue. In line 52, Titus says the police called him "a hacker and a naysayer of the worst kind." A naysayer is someone who says "no." But what could the hacker be saying "no" to?

With a partner, talk about the possible motivations of the

hacker, that "naysayer of the worst sort." What could he be saying "no" to? How might it be related to feednet?

▼**Write** Based on your discussion, write a prediction in your response journal. If you were to continue reading *Feed*, what do you think the hacker's point of view about the feed would be? How would it differ from Titus's opinion? Use what you know about science-fiction dystopian novels to inform your predictions.

Second Read: Analyzing the Effects of Setting

Feed is set roughly 100 years in the future. As with most science-fiction stories, the setting strongly shapes the behaviors of the characters and the plot events.

Objective: Read the text a second time. Write the abbreviation "FS" for "Future Setting" next to any character behavior or plot event that is possible only because of the future setting.

Focus on Analyzing the Effects of Setting

You can describe two settings in *Feed*: The larger setting (the type of reality the characters live in) and the local setting (where the character Titus is currently narrating events from).

1. What is the larger setting of *Feed*?

2. What major event in the story makes sense only because of the larger setting of *Feed*?

3. How does living in the larger setting seem to have shaped Titus's personality?

continued on next page

©Perfection Learning® • No Reproduction Permitted

TECH-CONNECT

Conduct an Internet search to find a quote about corporations and consumerism. Choose a favorite and tweet it to your teacher or classmates as per your teacher's instructions, or post it to a pin board or class website.

4. The larger setting of *Feed* sets the stage for what happens in the local setting. What is the local setting of the excerpt from *Feed*?

5. Why is Titus in the local setting? What does he do and think while there?

6. Does being in the local setting without contact with feednet have an effect of Titus? If so, what?

☾**Speak and Listen** With a partner, read aloud the two times that Titus describes the picture of the boat. Then discuss this question:

- Has Titus changed between his first and second descriptions of the picture? If so, how?

▼**Write** Based on your discussion, write a paragraph describing how Titus either did or did not change during the excerpt. Support your response with details from the text.

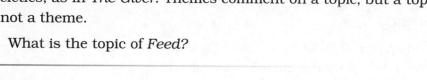

Third Read: Determining Theme

Titus, the main character in this excerpt from *Feed*, has a fairly clear point of view about feednet. But does everyone feel as Titus does about feednet?

Objective: As you read the text a third time, think about what message the author might be trying to express. Underline any sentences that seem to suggest such a message.

Focus on Determining Theme

Before identifying the theme of a story, you need to be clear on what a theme *is* and what it *isn't*. First, let's define some concepts people commonly mistake for theme.

A topic is not a theme. Topics are ideas such as liars and their lies, as in *Catch Me If You Can*, and individualism within societies, as in *The Giver*. Themes comment on a topic, but a topic is not a theme.

What is the topic of *Feed*?

A summary is not a theme. Summaries tell readers the main characters and events in a story. Understanding what happens in a story is only one step in determining the theme.

The author's purpose is not a theme. Authors may write to entertain, inform, or teach, but theme is separate from purpose.

Identify the author's main purpose in writing *Feed*.

A moral is not a theme. Morals appear in fables and folktales. They are obvious and often stated at the very end of the story. Themes, in contrast, are not stated. You need to analyze the elements of the story to determine the theme.

continued on next page

You probably know the fable "The Tortoise and the Hare" or the folktale "The Boy Who Cried Wolf." Identify the moral of *one* of these stories.

CONNECT TO ESSENTIAL QUESTION

Although *Feed* is set in the future, do its ideas about technology and society seem relevant today?

A conflict or problem is not a theme. The central conflict or problem that the main character tries to overcome is extremely important to the theme, but it is not the same as the theme.

At this point, you're asking yourself: "Well, what is theme, anyway? How can I figure it out?"

Theme is the author's message. It is a truth or insight about life that the author wants to convey. A story's theme is not as obvious as a moral, because you have to analyze the story to figure it out. So how can you determine a story's theme?

- **First, decide what the central conflict is.** What central problem or obstacle is the main character trying to overcome? How does the conflict resolve? In success or failure?

- **Second, summarize the plot.** Write a short description of the beginning events, the characters, conflict, and how the conflict resolves.

- **Third, think about how the main character grows or changes throughout the story.** The theme is often revealed through changes in the main character over the course of the story. Consider what lessons the character learned or how his or her thinking about life changed. In some stories, theme arises based on a lesson the character failed to learn.

- **Fourth, look for repeated ideas or images throughout the work.** Ideas are usually statements a character or narrator explicitly states. Images are often objects or events that happen to a character.

After you follow these steps, you'll likely have gathered enough information to figure out the theme. Remember, all of the above must be supported by evidence from the text.

TECH-CONNECT

Post your sentence describing the theme of *Feed* on your class website. It will form the basis of an all-class discussion.

Fill in the chart to help you determine the theme of the excerpt from *Feed*. Some sentence starters are included for you.

Steps to Finding Theme	Your Response
Describe the central conflict. What main problem or obstacle is the character trying to overcome?	Titus wants Titus's main problem is Titus feels
Summarize the plot. Write a short description of the beginning and what happens before the resolution.	*Feed* is the story of
What repeated ideas or images are there?	
Does the main character, Titus, change or grow during the story? If so, how? If not, why not? [Hint: Think about the image you identified above.]	
Review your responses above. Then finish the following sentence. The theme of this excerpt from *Feed* is. . . .	

Speak and Listen Share your answers from the chart in a class discussion.

Discuss this question:

- What is the theme of this excerpt from *Feed*?

Refer to words, phrases, and sentences from the text in your class discussion. Use hand signals to indicate when you want to talk. Thumbs up means you want to share something new.

Language: Using Context Clues

Roughly 100 years ago, if you were walking down the street of a city, you might hear people saying things such as:

- "He's the bee's knees." (He's an extraordinary person.)

- "That's the cat's meow." (That's really great.)

- "Don't take any wooden nickels." (Don't do anything stupid.)

These days, the only place you might hear these phrases are in movies, television shows, or plays set in the 1920s. Such slang, or informal speech, is no longer part of everyday life.

So, if the past has its own slang, what about the future? M. T. Anderson, the author of *Feed*, came up with slang terms that, while unfamiliar, a reader can use context clues to figure out.

In the table below, use the context clues to write a definition of the underlined slang term.

Sentences	Definition of Slang Term
There was nothing there but the walls. We looked at them, and at each other. We looked really <u>squelch</u>. *Our hair and stuff. We had remote relays attached to us to watch our blood and our brains.*	squelch:
But the <u>braggest</u> *thing about the feed, the thing that made it really big, is that it knows everything you want and hope for, sometimes before you even know what those things are.*	braggest:

TECH-CONNECT

Send a private email to your teacher telling him or her how the class discussion went. Be polite and specific. Describe one thing that went well. Give one recommendation for how to make the next all-class discussion better.

Project-Based Assessments

Response Essay

Although Feed is set in the future, much of what Titus talks about easily applies to the present day. Read the excerpt below from *Feed*.

> Everything we think and feel is taken in by the corporations. . . . Of course, everyone is like, *da da da, evil corporations, oh they're so bad*, we all say that, and we all know they control everything. I mean, it's not great, because who knows what evil [things] they're up to. Everyone feels bad about that. But they're the only way to get all this stuff, and it's no good getting [mad] about it, because they're still going to control everything whether you like it or not. Plus, they keep like everyone in the world employed, so it's not like we could do without them. And it's really great to know everything about everything whenever we want, to have it just like, in our brain, just sitting there.

Write a one-page response to Titus's ideas about the role of corporations in our lives. First, accurately summarize Titus's ideas. Then explain whether you agree or disagree with his ideas. Support your ideas with examples from your life and the lives of your friends and family. Organize your essay clearly, using a good introduction, body, and conclusion.

Use the following guidelines for your response essay.	
To receive the highest score (4.0), the essay must meet all of these criteria.	**Your essay should** • accurately summarize Titus's ideas about the role of corporations in our lives. • explain your own position on Titus's ideas. • be supported with examples from your life and the lives of your friends and family. • end with a satisfying conclusion. • maintain a formal style. • contain correct grammar, spelling, and punctuation.

continued on next page

Write a Book Chapter

The motivations of the hacker in *Feed* remain mysterious. All we know about him is from the following excerpt.

> Our parents had been notified while we were asleep. Only Loga hadn't been touched by the hacker. She hadn't let him touch her, because he looked really creepy to her, so she stood way far away. There were also others, people we'd never met, who had been touched, and they were in the wards, too. He had touched thirteen people in all.
>
> There was a police officer there, waiting in a chair. He told us that we would be off-line for a while, until they could see what had been done and check for viruses, and decrypt the feed history to get information to use against the guy in court. They said that they had identified him, and that he was a hacker and a naysayer of the worst kind.

Write a chapter for *Feed* written from the point of view of the hacker. Your chapter must

- be based on the events described in the excerpt above.
- describe the dance club setting where the events take place.
- make clear the hacker's motivations for separating Titus and others from the feed.
- have a clear ending.

Use the rubric below to guide your writing.

Use the following guidelines for your book chapter.	
To receive the highest score (4.0), the book chapter must meet all of these criteria.	Your chapter • is based on the events of the excerpt from *Feed*. • is written from the hacker's point of view. • clearly shows the hacker's motivations. • uses narrative techniques, such as dialogue and description, to develop experiences, events, and characters. • uses descriptive details and sensory language to convey experiences and events. • provides a conclusion that follows from the events narrated. • contains correct grammar, spelling, and punctuation.

On Your Own: Integrating Ideas

1. Sherry Turkle, a professor at the Massachusetts Institute of Technology (MIT), has spent most of her career considering how modern communications technologies affect our personal relationships. Her presentation "Connected, but alone?" discusses how modern communication technologies can actually isolate us from each other: https://www.ted.com/talks/sherry_turkle_alone_together.

2. In *Feed*, people are controlled not through being deprived of goods and services but by having all their needs and pleasures met. The book *Brave New World* by Aldous Huxley, published in 1932, explores similar themes, and it is a classic of dystopian literature. Search for it in your school or public library.

3. What do doctors mean when they talk about "Internet addiction disorder"? Is it a true addiction, as some people are addicted to drugs and alcohol? Or should it be called something else? Do some research on the Internet to answer these questions.

REFLECT

Have you ever been bored while on the web or the Internet? If so, how was that possible, given everything that's available on it?

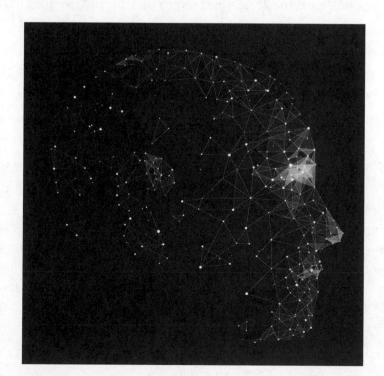

Connect to Testing

In this chapter, you determined the theme of a story, examined the interaction of the setting on characters and events, and analyzed point of view. When you take assessments, you will be tested over your ability to analyze texts in these ways and support your analysis with textual evidence.

1. **Part A:** Which of the following is the main theme statement represented by this excerpt of *Feed*?

    A. Only through struggle can young people grow into adults.

    B. Making art is a way to strengthen the mind and improve the heart.

    C. Constant technological stimulation can dull our ability to amuse ourselves.

    D. The history of human society is one of progress, but some people will always resist it.

    Part B: Which sentences from *Feed* best support the answer to Part A? Select **two** choices.

    A. *I couldn't figure out even the littlest reason to paint a picture like that.*

    B. *They said that they had identified him, and that he was a hacker and a naysayer of the worst kind.*

    C. *They carried them around outside of them, in their hands, like if you carried your lungs in a briefcase and opened it to breathe.*

    D. *That's one of the great things about the feed—that you can be supersmart without ever working.*

    E. *But the braggest thing about the feed, the thing that made it really big, is that it knows everything you want and hope for, sometimes before you even know what those things are.*

    F. *In fact, the thing that made me [mad] was when they couldn't help me at all, so I was just lying there, and couldn't play any of the games on the feed, and couldn't chat anyone, and I couldn't do a . . . thing. . . .*

2. According to the excerpt from *Feed*, how has the invention of feednet most affected human society in the future?

    A. It has improved medical treatments.

    B. It has made a few people amazingly wealthy.

    C. It has caused people to resist new technologies.

    D. It has bound people and technology more closely.

3. **Part A:** Read these sentences from the beginning of the excerpt from *Feed*.

   The first thing I felt was no credit.

   I tried to touch my credit, but there was nothing there.

   Which word has the closest meaning to the word *credit* as it is used in these sentences?

   A. belief

   B. contact

   C. mind

   D. debt

   Part B: Which detail from *Feed* best supports the answer to Part A?

   A. *My body—I was in a bed, on top of my arm, which was asleep, ...*

   B. *Someone had left a message in my head, which I found, ...*

   C. *I tried to chat Link and then Marty, but nothing, there was no transmission signal, ...*

   D. *So I opened my eyes.*

4. **Part A:** Which of the following best describes Titus's point of view regarding the corporations that make profiles for feednet?

   A. He finds it frightening that he has no choice in whether to use their technology.

   B. He believes that corporations do more good than harm in his world.

   C. He assumes corporations do bad things, but believes no alternatives exist.

   D. He welcomes the idea that corporations help people learn more about their own wants.

   Part B: Which of the sentences from *Feed* best supports the answer to Part A?

   A. *We were frightened, and kept touching our heads.*

   B. *But the braggest thing about the feed, the thing that made it really big, is that it knows everything you want and hope for, sometimes before you even know what those things are.*

   C. *Of course, everyone is like, da da da, evil corporations, oh they're so bad, we all say that, and we all know they control everything.*

   D. *But they're the only way to get all this stuff, and it's no good getting [mad] about it, because they're still going to control everything whether you like it or not.*

5. How does Titus mostly respond to being disconnected from feednet over time?

   A. He is mostly bored.

   B. He is mostly angry.

   C. He is mostly frightened.

   D. He is mostly lonely.

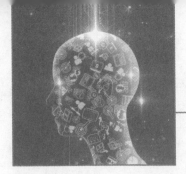

Chapter 15

Analyzing Different Interpretations of Evidence

Preview Concepts

This unit is about how technology affects society. Here is a question adults ask all the time about you and your classmates:

- How are new communication technologies affecting our kids?

1. Think of a time when an adult was worried about your watching a video, visiting a website, or playing a video game. Why did the adult have that point of view about the video, site, or game? Did he or she give any reasons or evidence to support that point of view?

2. Did you agree with that adult's point of view? Did you agree with the reasons or evidence offered?

Making Connections

When trying to convince a reader, writers sometimes make logical fallacies. A logical fallacy is committed when a writer relies on emotion and incorrect thinking to convince the audience that his or her point of view is correct. Two examples of logical fallacies are loaded language and sweeping generalizations.

CHAPTER GOALS

In this chapter you will

- cite textual evidence to support an analysis of a text.
- determine an author's point of view and purpose.
- examine how authors writing on the same topic can interpret the same evidence differently.
- correct misplaced modifiers.

PREVIEW ACADEMIC VOCABULARY

point of view

purpose

Loaded Language: Words that have strong positive or negative connotations: *dangerous influence, innocent children*

Overgeneralization: Concluding that what is true in one case (or for one person) is true for all other situations (or people): *My mom is a really bad driver. All women are worse drivers than men.*

Below are excerpts from two letters from the 1950s that citizens wrote to their senators about the dangers of comic books. Read them and then answer the questions that follow.

My dear Senator Hendrickson,

I believe that the [Parent–Teacher Associations] all over the country could unite to have these comics banned, many cities have done this and as Dr. [Wertham] says, we have laws that prohibit selling poison, why can't we prohibit these people from selling poison to our children's minds?

—Eugenia Y. Genovar, November 24, 1953

Dear Sir.

I have been reading comic books for seven to nine years. Every kind of book that was written. I have never robbed a bank or things like that. My personal opinion is I think reading crime books makes a young or old person not want to commit a crime, because in every story the old saying "Crime don't pay" is carried out. The person or persons committing the crime are always caught. The fear of this stops crime and stops juvenile delinquency. . . .

—Robert Merdian, June 22, 1954

What is each writer's point of view about whether comic books cause young people to commit crimes? Identify any loaded language or overgeneralizations in the letters.

> **MAKING CONNECTIONS**
>
> In this chapter, you'll explore how authors on different sides of an issue shape their arguments.

First Read: Finding Supporting Evidence

Dr. Nicholas Kardaras is an expert on addiction, a condition in which a person becomes dependent on a chemical such as a drug. Addiction can drive people's behavior and cause them to suffer without the chemical. In the following editorial, Kardaras argues that screen technologies are as addictive as cocaine or heroin, two dangerous illegal drugs. It is a controversial claim, as you will see later in the chapter.

Objective: As you read, underline two sentences with evidence based on personal experiences—either the author's or those of other people. Write PE (for "personal experience") next to each sentence. Then, draw a box around two sentences with evidence based on scientific research. Write SR (for "scientific research") next to those sentences. Record any questions you have in the My Thoughts column.

excerpt
It's 'digital heroin': How screens turn kids into psychotic junkies
by Dr. Nicholas Kardaras, in the *New York Post*,
August 27, 2016

My Thoughts

1   Many parents intuitively understand that **ubiquitous** glowing screens are having a negative effect on kids. We see the aggressive temper tantrums when the devices are taken away and the wandering attention spans when children are

5   not perpetually stimulated by their hyper-arousing devices. Worse, we see children who become bored, apathetic, uninteresting and uninterested when not plugged in.

But it's even worse than we think.

We now know that those iPads, smartphones and Xboxes

10   are a form of digital drug. Recent brain imaging research is showing that they affect the brain's frontal cortex—which controls **executive functioning**, including impulse control—in exactly the same way that cocaine does. . . .

---
ubiquitous: found everywhere
executive functioning: decision-making

This addictive effect is why Dr. Peter Whybrow, director

15 of neuroscience at UCLA, calls screens "electronic cocaine" and Chinese researchers call them "digital heroin." In fact, Dr. Andrew Doan, the head of addiction research for the Pentagon and the US Navy—who has been researching video game addiction—calls video games and screen technologies

20 "digital pharmakeia" (Greek for drug).

That's right—your kid's brain on *Minecraft* looks like a brain on drugs. No wonder we have a hard time peeling kids from their screens and find our little ones agitated when their screen time is interrupted. In addition, hundreds of clinical

25 studies show that screens increase depression, anxiety and aggression and can even lead to psychotic-like features where the video gamer loses touch with reality.

In my clinical work with over 1,000 teens over the past 15 years, I have found the old axiom of "An ounce of prevention

30 is worth a pound of cure" to be especially true when it comes to tech addiction. Once a kid has crossed the line into true tech addiction, treatment can be very difficult. Indeed, I have found it easier to treat heroin and crystal meth addicts than lost-in-the-matrix video gamers or Facebook-dependent

35 social media addicts.

According to a 2013 Policy Statement by the American Academy of Pediatrics, 8- to 10-year-olds spend 8 hours a day with various digital media while teenagers spend 11 hours in front of screens. One in three kids are using tablets or

40 smartphones before they can talk. Meanwhile, the handbook of "Internet Addiction" by Dr. Kimberly Young states that 18 percent of college-age internet users in the US suffer from tech addiction.

My Thoughts

Once a person crosses over the line into full-blown

45 addiction—drug, digital or otherwise—they need to **detox**

before any other kind of therapy can have any chance of

being effective. With tech, that means a full digital detox—no

computers, no smartphones, no tablets. The extreme digital

detox even eliminates television. The prescribed amount of

50 time is four to six weeks; that's the amount of time that is

usually required for a hyper-aroused nervous system to reset

itself. But that's no easy task in our current tech-filled society

where screens are ubiquitous. A person can live without

drugs or alcohol; with tech addiction, digital temptations

55 are everywhere.

_____

detox: let the body rid itself of a harmful substance

My Thoughts

FIRST RESPONSE: KEY IDEAS AND DETAILS

Based on your first reading of this text, what do you think of Kardaras's argument? How well does it match with your personal experience? Record your first response in your journal.

TECH-CONNECT

Post your First Response answers on your class webpage. Compare your answers to those posted by other students.

Focus on Finding Supporting Evidence

Kardaras's claim is explicit: video screen addiction is a real problem among young people, and it can be as difficult to treat as heroin addiction. He supports this claim with evidence of two kinds: evidence based on personal experience and evidence based on scientific research.

The chart on the next page divides the evidence into personal experience and scientific research. The shaded cells are completed for you and list the researchers and those who had the personal experience. Complete the unshaded cells to explain what the research said and describe the experiences.

Claim: Video screen addiction is a real problem among young people, and it can be as difficult to treat as heroin addiction.			
Personal Experience		Scientific Research	
Who had the experience?	What was the experience?	Who did the research?	What did that research say?
parents		Dr. Kimberly Young	
Dr. Nicholas Kardaras		Brain-imaging researchers	

Speak and Listen With a partner, discuss the evidence that Kardaras presents to support his claim that video game addiction is a serious problem. What evidence is most convincing? What is least convincing?

Write Based on the results of your conversation, write a paragraph in which you explain which piece of evidence you found least convincing. Give one reason you found the evidence unconvincing. If necessary, use these sentence frames to get started.

- The evidence I found least convincing is . . .

- I believe this evidence is least convincing because . . .

Second Read: Determining Point of View and Purpose

When reading any text, it's important to distinguish between an author's point of view and his or her purpose for writing.

- An author's point of view is the attitude (opinions and feelings) the author has toward the topic he or she is writing about.

CONNECT TO ESSENTIAL QUESTION

About 200 years ago, some thinkers actually made the same claims about reading stories and novels that Kardaras is making about digital screens. What does this tell you about how people sometimes receive new technologies?

continued on next page

- An author's purpose is why the author is writing the text—what the author hopes the text will accomplish. Part of determining an author's purpose is looking at both what the author says and the language the author uses to say it.

Objective: Read the text a second time.

- Underline one sentence that provides evidence of the author's point of view. Write the abbreviation POV by that sentence.

- Circle two phrases that seem intended to have a powerful emotional effect on the audience.

REFLECT

Do you think anyone might disagree with Kardaras's argument? Why might someone disagree with it?

Focus on Determining Point of View and Purpose

Kardaras's point of view about the topic is not subtle. It might be one you have encountered from adults or even your peers.

1. In the space below, state both the topic and Kardaras's point of view about it. As evidence of his point of view, quote the sentence you underlined.

Kardaras's purpose in writing this editorial is only slightly less obvious than his point of view. When determining an author's purpose, focus on not just what the text says but how it says it. And Kardaras has a pretty powerful way with words. Just look at some of what he says:

- *But it's even worse than we think.*

- *a form of digital drug*

- *"electronic cocaine"*

- *"digital heroin"*

- *psychotic-like features*

- *your kid's brain on* Minecraft *looks like a brain on drugs*

Kardaras uses loaded language to stir up a strong response in the reader. These emotional words are meant to persuade the audience to agree with the author. However, sometimes loaded words can be manipulative and indicate bias on the part of the author.

2. In the space below, answer these questions:

- Who is Kardaras's primary audience?

- Based on his word choice, what effect do you think Kardaras intended this editorial to have on his audience?

(Speak and Listen With a partner, discuss how Kardaras's word choice could affect what his audience thinks of him, not of the topic. Give reasons to support your ideas.

Write Write a paragraph in which you explain both Kardaras's point of view and his purpose in writing the editorial. Focus on how he uses emotionally powerful words and phrases to try to achieve that purpose.

Third Read: Analyzing Interpretations of Evidence

Kardaras made a powerful claim, and powerful claims tend to earn strong responses. Three days after his editorial appeared in the *New York Post*, the following response was published on *The Verge*, a website devoted to news about technology, science, art, and culture. The writer, Rachel Becker, is a trained scientist who has reported for several reputable science magazines and websites.

Objective: Read the excerpt that begins on the next page from Becker's editorial. Then go back to Kardaras's editorial and read it a third time. This time, look for any evidence that both Kardaras and Becker both cite in their editorials and write "BE" (for "Both Editorials") next to the evidence in both excerpts.

excerpt
Why calling screen time 'digital heroin' is digital garbage

by Rachel Becker, *The Verge*, August 30, 2016

1   The supposed danger of digital media made headlines over the weekend when psychotherapist Nicholas Kardaras published a story in the *New York Post* called "It's 'digital heroin': How screens turn kids into psychotic junkies." In

5   the op-ed, Kardaras claims that "iPads, smartphones and Xboxes are a form of digital drug." He stokes fears about the potential for addiction and the ubiquity of technology by referencing "hundreds of clinical studies" that show "screens increase depression, anxiety and aggression." We've seen

10   this form of scaremongering before. People are frequently uneasy with new technology, after all. The problem is, screens and computers aren't actually all that new. There's already a whole generation—millennials—who grew up with computers. They appear, mostly, to be fine . . . If computers

15   were "digital drugs," wouldn't we have already seen warning signs? . . .

This style of manipulation is most obvious in Kardaras' use of statistics: "According to a 2013 Policy Statement by the American Academy of Pediatrics, 8- to 10-year-olds spend

20   8 hours a day with various digital media while teenagers spend 11 hours in front of screens," he writes. His article takes general aim at screens, but specifically stokes fears about video games and the internet. . . . He makes no mention of television, which remains the predominant form of media for

25   children and teens, according to a 2013 policy statement from the American Academy of Pediatrics. . . .

Kardaras' op-ed goes on to warn that exposure to screens can cause "addiction," and he quotes researchers analogizing screen time to heroin and cocaine. "That's right—your kid's

30　brain on *Minecraft* looks like a brain on drugs," he writes. This is, strictly speaking, true—at least, from a neuroimaging standpoint. This is a **hoary old trope** in science writing, and it's apparently loosely based on **fMRI**, which is hardly the most accurate discipline. The brain's reward center, the ventral

35　striatum, is what makes you feel good when you eat, . . . take cocaine, or play video games.

Yale psychiatrists Robert Leeman and Marc Potenza write in a 2013 review paper that there are neurobiological and genetic parallels between substance abuse and problematic

40　behaviors, like excessive . . . internet use. But because these are things pretty much everyone engages in, it's hard to draw a line between one person's activity and another person's addiction.

Kardaras' loose talk on addiction is what makes his

45　argument so tough to believe. About 1.6 percent of Americans use heroin, but a quarter of them wind up addicted, according to an estimate from the National Institutes of Drug Addiction. Something like 16 percent of cocaine users become dependent on the drug within 10 years of trying it for the first time, say

50　scientists in the journal *Neuropsychopharmacology*. Digital devices, as well as video games, are far more widespread than either of these drugs. If they were, in fact, comparable, we should be seeing a lot more people displaying "catatonia," with their iPads dropped dramatically beside them.

My Thoughts

_____

---

hoary old trope: frequently used idea
fMRI: functional magnetic resonance imaging, a way of scanning the brain and measuring its activity

55   The tech-as-addiction metaphor is sloppy, though it might not be wrong. The problem is we don't have a good handle on what qualifies as tech addiction—if it exists at all, how common it is, and what kind of environmental and **physiological** conditions predispose someone to it.

---

physiological: relating to the way in which a living organism functions

Focus on Analyzing Interpretations of Evidence

Becker's editorial is a rebuttal to Kardaras's editorial. *Rebut* means "to contradict." One way Becker rebuts Kardaras's claim is to suggest that the evidence might be flawed and that his interpretation of it may be misleading.

1. Remember that Kardaras provides two kinds of evidence: personal experience and research. Whose personal experience does Kardaras cite as evidence?

Both Kardaras and Becker use the readers' personal experience as evidence. Did you notice how often each uses the word *we*?

- Kardaras: "We see the aggressive temper tantrums when the devices are taken away . . ."

- Kardaras: "No wonder we have a hard time peeling kids from their screens . . ."

- Becker: "We've seen this form of scaremongering before."

- Becker: "If computers were 'digital drugs,' wouldn't we have already seen warning signs?"

Using *we* suggests that the readers share the same experience and already know (and agree with) what the author is saying. Kardaras is saying that his fellow parents have observed these troubling behaviors. Becker, on the other hand, says that readers have evidence that disproves Kardaras's claim.

> **REFLECT**
>
> The editorials discuss screen use among children and teenagers. But what about adults and their screen use? Should we be concerned about them, as well?

2. How do you feel about the authors calling on your personal experience as evidence? Do you agree that what they have seen is the same as what you have seen?

3. Becker does not mention the other type of personal experience that Kardaras uses in his editorial. Speculate: Why do you think she didn't mention that evidence?

4. In your opinion, whose use of personal experience as evidence is more convincing for their claim: Kardaras's or Becker's? Why do you think so?

Becker also analyzes Kardaras's evidence—specifically, whether the evidence means what he says its means. Different authors can look at the same evidence and reach different conclusions. Authors always say what *they* believe the evidence means.

Consider Kardaras's use of brain imaging research. Kardaras says that iPads, smartphones, and Xboxes affect the brain's frontal cortex in exactly the same way that cocaine does. That sounds scary, right? But look at what Becker says about Kardaras's use of that research:

> This is, strictly speaking, true—at least from a neuroimaging standpoint. This is a hoary old trope in science writing, and it's apparently loosely based on fMRI, which is hardly the most accurate discipline. The brain's reward center . . . is what makes you feel good when you eat, . . . take cocaine, or play video games.

continued on next page

If you read it closely, Becker says Kardaras's use of evidence is weak in two ways:

- The research isn't "the most accurate." This means that evidence comparing cocaine use and screen use might not be trustworthy or true.

- And, even if the evidence is accurate, it doesn't necessarily mean using screens is as harmful as using cocaine. According to Becker, eating food also affects the brain's "reward center." So, maybe playing video games is more like eating food than it is like doing drugs.

TECH-CONNECT

Use an online polling site to compare which editorial your classmates agree with more: Kardaras's or Becker's. Post your results on your class website.

In other words, Becker suggests the brain imaging research is flawed and that Kardaras is choosing the scariest evidence to make his case.

The last two rows of the chart below will help you continue to examine Becker's interpretation. The blue-shaded cells have been completed for you. Complete the sentence starters in the other cells.

Source and Evidence	What Kardaras says the evidence means	What Becker says about the evidence
Source: Brain imaging research **Evidence:** iPads, smartphones, and Xboxes affect the frontal cortex the same way cocaine does	Digital screens are as harmful and addictive as cocaine.	• The research method might be flawed, leading to bad evidence. • He ignores the fact that safer pleasures, like eating, also affect the brain's reward center. Video games might be more like food than drugs.
Source: Hundreds of clinical studies **Evidence:** Screens increase	That screens	• She calls it "scaremongering." • She says that Kardaras and others are just uneasy with new technology. • She says that a generation of computer users "appear, mostly, to be fine."
Source: 2013 Policy Statement by the American Academy of Pediatrics **Evidence:**	That excessive screen use	The same 2013 Policy Statement

Speak and Listen At the end of her editorial, Becker writes, "The tech-as-addiction metaphor is sloppy, though it might not be wrong."

- Why do you think she says this?

- Why admit that Kardaras might be right?

Discuss these questions with a partner.

Language: Comma Usage

Commas are used to create a break between elements in a sentence. They set off introductory words and transitions from the main clause and separate clauses in a sentence.

Commas After Introductory Words and Phrases

Study the sentence below from "It's 'digital heroin.'"

> In fact, Dr. Andrew Doan, the head of addiction research for the Pentagon and the US Navy, calls video games and screen technologies "digital pharmakeia."

In this sentence, the phrase *in fact* is used as an introduction to the clause that follows. (Remember, a clause is a complete thought with a subject and verb.) Introductory words and phrases require a comma to set them off from the rest of the sentence.

How do you know when a word or phrase is introductory? An introductory element is not necessary to understand the rest of the sentence. If the phrase *in fact* were removed from the example, the sentence would still function and make sense.

Introductory phrases often double as transitions—words that show a connection between a sentence and the one before it. Phrases like *in fact*, *for example*, and *in addition* connect ideas, but they are not strictly necessary for understanding the sentence. Take a look at another example:

> In addition, hundreds of clinical studies show that screens increase depression, anxiety and aggression . . .

Again, the phrase *in addition* could be removed from the sentence without disrupting its meaning. It shows the relationship between this sentence and the previous sentence and introduces the main clause.

Commas That Separate Clauses in a Sentence

A compound sentence consists of two independent clauses connected with a conjunction (such as *and, but,* and *or*). A comma is placed after the first clause and before the conjunction.

continued on next page

CONNECT TO ESSENTIAL QUESTION

What do you think is the most important *positive* effect of all these screens in our lives? What about the most important *negative* effect?

Study the example sentence below. Each independent clause is underlined.

About 1.6 percent of Americans use heroin, but a quarter of them wind up addicted . . .

The following sentences contain comma errors. Rewrite each one, and place the comma correctly.

1. On the other hand video gaming has its benefits.

2. I enjoy using my smartphone but, I try not to overuse it.

3. Although, there are drawbacks to screen use people are unlikely to unplug altogether.

4. You can try to set limits for yourself or you can use apps that monitor your use.

5. Of course people lived full lives for thousands of years, before digital devices existed.

6. As Rachel Becker says the majority of digital users, are not showing the troubling signs of addiction.

Project-Based Assessments

Develop a Public Service Announcement

A public service announcement (PSA) is a short audio or video advertisement intended to alert the public about a social problem and to suggest a solution. Kardaras's editorial about "digital heroin" is not a PSA, but he clearly wants to alert the public to a problem. (In the full article, he suggests steps parents should take, but that section does not appear in the excerpt.) Imagine that Kardaras's message were turned into an audio PSA, one that describes the problem and recommends a solution. What would it sound like?

For this project, you will create a 30-second audio PSA to raise awareness of "digital heroin" and what you can do to fight the problem.

Follow these steps to create your own audio PSA:

1. Visit the website psacentral.org/campaigns to find PSAs from the past and present. Find topics that interest you and watch the PSAs about them. This will help you think about how to develop your PSA and how your voice should sound.

continued on next page

2. Write a 30-second announcement that is 85 to 100 words in length. Practice reading your announcement until it sounds professional and is within the time limit. Read clearly and with the appropriate feeling. Should you sound serious, sad, anxious, or friendly? The tone of your voice needs to match the tone of your words.

3. Record the announcement on a smartphone voice memo app or on a computer using recording software. Your announcement must be between 28 and 32 seconds in length.

4. If you have access to audio editing software, you could add music or sound effects to increase the effectiveness of your PSA.

5. Before submitting your PSA as your teacher directs, play it for another student or an adult. Ask for feedback using the rubric below as a guide. Change your PSA based on this feedback.

6. Submit your digital recording and text electronically to your teacher or present it to the class as instructed.

Use the following guidelines for your public service announcement.	
To receive the highest score (4.0), the public service announcement must meet all of these criteria.	Your announcement • clearly and creatively explains the problem using facts and/or personal examples. • offers a reasonable solution to the problem that people can follow easily. • is digitally recorded and is 30 seconds in length. • sounds professional, with clear speech and good vocal variety to communicate ideas.

Roundtable Discussion

Participate in a roundtable discussion on the following questions:

> What do you think about the central claim that Kardaras and Becker's editorials debate—that screens are "digital heroin"?
>
> What experiences or observations about screens make you think this way?

In a roundtable discussion, all students are equal and everyone participates. Arrange your seats in a circle. Your teacher or a discussion leader may sit in the middle. Come to the discussion with an open mind. You will be evaluated on the following:

Expectations for Discussion	
Listening	**Speaking**
Listen respectfully	Speak at least once
Look at the speaker	Give reasons or examples
Take notes on what the speaker is saying	Ask questions
Write down follow-up questions	Explain and justify (offer reasons to support your idea)
	Invite comment

Instructions for a Roundtable Discussion

1. The discussion leader (teacher or student) begins by asking the following questions:

> What do you think about the central claim that Kardaras and Becker's editorials debate—that screens are "digital heroin"?
>
> What experiences or observations about screens make you think this way?

2. Allow each member the chance to reply to the questions.
3. Take notes on comments you disagree with or you have questions about. Record what was said and who said it.
4. Go around the circle again and allow everyone to ask a follow-up question. Questions should be directed to the person who made the original comment. Try phrasing your questions in this way:
   - Explain what you mean by . . .
   - Who agrees/disagrees with (name of participant)? Why?
5. Close the discussion by having everyone respond to the following questions:

> Did your opinion change during the roundtable discussion? Why or why not?

Use the following guidelines for the roundtable discussion.	
To receive the highest score (4.0), the discussion must meet all of these criteria.	During the discussion, you should • listen carefully when others speak; make notes about what they said. • offer thoughtful feedback and encourage everyone to participate. • share reasonable opinions and support your opinion with examples. • speak to the question or point at hand in a clear, concise manner.

On Your Own: Integrating Ideas

1. Kardaras's main concern about screens is that they are addictive. But perhaps a more common concern is whether playing violent video games can encourage violent behavior. The website ProCon.org is one place to start looking into this topic. Visit videogames.procon.org and see what the evidence is.
2. To learn more about the history and impact of video games, check out this site from the Public Broadcasting System: www.pbs.org/kcts/videogamerevolution. A companion program, *The Video Game Revolution*, might be available in your school media center or at your public library.
3. Read the Slate.com article "The Caped Crusader: Fredric Wertham and the Campaign Against Comic Books" by Jeet Heer. Consider how concerns about video games are similar to and different from the "great comic-book scare."

Connect to Testing

In this chapter, you cited evidence to support an analysis, determined an author's point of view and purpose, and examined how authors on different sides of an issue interpret the same evidence. When you take assessments, you will be tested over your ability to use these skills.

1. One central idea from Kardaras's editorial is that excessive screen time harms the mental health of children. Which sentence from the editorial provides the strongest evidence to support this claim?

    A. *Many parents intuitively understand that ubiquitous glowing screens are having a negative effect on kids.*

    B. *We now know that those iPads, smartphones and Xboxes are a form of digital drug.*

    C. *This addictive effect is why Dr. Peter Whybrow, director of neuroscience at UCLA, calls screens "electronic cocaine" and Chinese researchers call them "digital heroin."*

    D. *In addition, hundreds of clinical studies show that screens increase depression, anxiety and aggression and can even lead to psychotic-like features where the video gamer loses touch with reality.*

2. Rewrite the following sentence correcting comma errors.

    Even though, Mrs. Rodriquez wanted to limit her son's screen time she knew he needed his phone in case of an emergency and he couldn't do his homework without his laptop.

3. What two sources of evidence does Nicholas Kardaras mention in his editorial "Digital Heroin" that Rachel Becker in "Digital Garbage" does not?

    A. the personal experience of parents

    B. brain imaging research

    C. a 2013 Policy Statement by the American Academy of Pediatrics

    D. hundreds of clinical studies

    E. his clinical work with more than 1,000 teenagers

    F. research by the National Institutes of Drug Addiction

4. **Part A:** Which sentence from "Digital Heroin" most clearly states Nicholas Kardaras's point of view about digital screens?

   A. *But it's even worse than we think.*

   B. *We now know that those iPads, smartphones and Xboxes are a form of digital drug.*

   C. *Once a kid has crossed the line into true tech addiction, treatment can be very difficult.*

   D. *A person can live without drugs or alcohol; with tech addiction, digital temptations are everywhere.*

   Part B: Which sentence from "Digital Garbage" most clearly shows Rachel Becker distinguishing her position from Kardaras's position?

   A. *In the op-ed, Kardaras claims that "iPads, smartphones and Xboxes are a form of digital drug."*

   B. *People are frequently uneasy with new technology, after all.*

   C. *Kardaras' op-ed goes on to warn that exposure to screens can cause "addiction," and he quotes researchers analogizing screen time to heroin and cocaine.*

   D. *Kardaras' loose talk on addiction is what makes his argument so tough to believe.*

5. **Part A:** Which source do Kardaras and Becker both cite?

   A. Dr. Peter Whybrow

   B. Chinese researchers

   C. American Academy of Pediatrics

   D. Dr. Kimberly Young

   Part B: How does Becker criticize Kardaras's use of evidence from the source cited in Part A?

   A. She claims that Kardaras is not considering all the facts from that source.

   B. She claims the source that produced the evidence is biased.

   C. She claims that the research producing that evidence is flawed.

   D. She claims the evidence actually proves the opposite of what Kardaras claims.

Writing a Fictional Narrative

Technology can be our best friend, and technology can also be the biggest party pooper of our lives.
—**Steven Spielberg**

The real danger is not that computers will begin to think like men, but that men will begin to think like computers.
—**Sydney Harris**

The nonfiction selections in this chapter dealt with problems and solutions—specifically, how technologies can solve problems while at the same time creating others. And in *Feed*, the fiction selection in the chapter, Titus struggles with fear, loneliness, and boredom after being disconnected from feednet.

A variety of fiction stories feature technology. Some involve characters who face more dramatic problems—artificial intelligence taking over society, for example, or scientists rushing to cure a plague or blow up an asteroid. In still other stories, the problem with technology may be less serious. Maybe the main character bickers with a lazy robot that doesn't want to do its job. Or perhaps the story is about the robot itself, putting up with human foolishness. And some stories about technology root themselves in the real world, exploring what happens when robots put people out of work or when teenagers post something regrettable to social media.

In this chapter, you will write a fictional narrative in which a character confronts some problem related to technology.

WRITING PROMPT

Write a story in which the main character confronts a problem related to a technology. Your narrative:

- must have a vivid setting, a main character, and a clearly depicted problem.

- should show the character confronting and trying to solve the problem.

- must depict how the problem is resolved (with or without success) and the logical outcomes from that resolution.

Your narrative should also make use of thoughtful description, realistic dialogue, and careful pacing. The final product will be two to three typed pages, double-spaced, using a standard-sized font.

Prepare to Write

Read the prompt closely. Underline key words that explain what you must do. Break it down based on purpose, audience, content, and additional requirements by filling in the chart below.

Purpose	to write a fictional story about a character confronting a problem relating to technology
Audience	classmates, teacher
Content Requirements	
Additional Requirements	

▼ The Writing Process

Brainstorm

To get started with your story, read through the chart below. It lists possible problems, settings, technologies, main characters, and people or things that might oppose the main character. Circle options that look interesting.

Note: You are not limited to the ideas in this chart. If you are interested in ideas that do not appear here, write those ideas in the margins.

> **CONNECT TO ESSENTIAL QUESTION**
>
> What is more interesting to you: exploring how a technology affects an entire society, or exploring the relationship between an individual and a technology?

Common Problems
• A character has a technology that can change society and must decide how to use it.
• A character has a technology that can change society and is hunted by others who want it for their own purposes.
• A character encounters a technology (possibly but not necessarily intelligent) that threatens society.
• A character who fears the effect of a new technology and fights to stop its spread.
• A society dependent on a technology approaches disaster when the device breaks or gets stolen.
• A society adopts a technology that seems wonderful at first but hides a terrible secret.

Settings	
• the past, present, or future	• a large, real-world city
• a planet, space station, or spaceship	• an undiscovered civilization
• another dimension	• a local, real-world place: your home, school, mall, library, hospital, etc.
• your hometown or city	

continued on next page

Technologies	
• **Technology of the mind:** reading, controlling, or manipulating other minds	
• **Technology of transportation:** time travel, space travel, teleportation (instantly moving from one place to another)	
• **Technology of the body:** mental connection to the Internet, devices that enhance physical abilities (strength, intelligence) or any of the five senses, invisibility	
• **Technology of transformation:** nanites (microscopic machines that can destroy or build any type of matter), artificial viruses, weapons of all sorts	
• **Technology that comes to life:** anything from toasters to elevators to artificial satellites	

Main Characters	People or Things Opposing the Main Character
• you, a friend, or a relative	• the technology itself
• someone modeled after a famous person you admire	• a large corporation
• a mysterious outsider	• a powerful government or agency
• an intelligent machine	• individuals seeking profit
• a scientist who has lost control of the technology	• a person or group against the technology
• a person nobody would expect	• a person or group seeking to ruin the world
	• a person or group seeking to change the world in ways that benefit only themselves

Generate Ideas

To help you generate ideas, try the following creative prewriting activities. **Note:** As you write your story, you might find your ideas changing. This is fine; go where the story takes you.

The Problem

Which problem in the chart on pages 325–326 appeals to you most? (If none appeal, write your own.)

Why does the problem appeal to you? What about it is interesting? Be specific.

The Setting

What setting in the chart appeals to you most? Why? (If none appeal, explain one of your own.)

In the space below, brainstorm the setting. What kind of world produces the problem you wrote about above? What sorts of things would your main character see, hear, and feel?

The Technology

Which technology in the chart appeals to you most? (If none appeal, develop and explain your own.)

What does the technology look like? Write notes about its size, weight, shape, color, and any other features worth description. Be as specific as you can: Instead of saying "large," say "the size of a minivan." Instead of saying "red and shiny," say "gleaming like polished copper." You can also draw a picture of the technology.

The Main Character

Who in the chart on pages 325–326 will be the main character? (If none appeal, come up with your own.)

From what point of view will you write: first or third person?

Describe your character. Young or old? Male or female? Is the character joking and confident, quiet and thoughtful, or angry and brave? Be specific.

People or Things Against the Main Character

Who or what in the chart on pages 325–326 will oppose the main character? (If none appeal, come up with your own.)

Describe the person, group, or thing opposing the main character. What does this person, group, or thing want, and why?

Organize Ideas

Fiction writers often use story maps to plan their details. A story map helps them ensure that the story elements work together well.

Your Story Map	
Setting:	Main Character:
Problem:	
Beginning (introduces the main character, the setting, and the problem): **Middle** (builds the story as the character tries to deal with the problem): **End** (wraps up the story and tells how the problem is resolved):	

First Draft

Use your story map to write a draft of your fictional narrative.
Here are some hints:

- Refer to your notes while drafting.

- Write quickly. You will revise and proofread later.

continued on next page

- Write on every other line, or double-space if working on a computer. This will make it easier to make revisions.

- If you take a break and then return to drafting, reread what you have written before continuing. This will help you resume the flow of thought.

- Mark this version of your narrative Draft 1.

Revision

Have others (other students, your teacher, or your relatives) read your narrative. Listen carefully to their questions and comments. Applying their advice can help refine your writing. You can put your narrative through the three types of review that follow.

Draft 1: Group Peer Review

This review will evaluate whether your story is engaging and its sequence of events is logical. In a group of two to three people, complete the following steps:

Steps for Peer Review

1. Select a timekeeper. Each writer gets 15 minutes. Respect the time limit.

2. One writer begins by reading aloud the first two sentences of the story while other people listen.

3. Pause. The same writer reads the first two sentences aloud a second time.

4. The writer asks, "Does the beginning of my narrative make you want to know more?" As each member responds, the writer takes notes on the draft.

5. The writer reads aloud the entire story once. As the writer reads, members take notes.

6. The writer asks, "What questions do you have about the events of the story? Is there anything you'd like to see better developed or described?" The writer jots down replies.

7. The members hand over their notes to the writer.

8. Repeat Steps 1–7 with the next member, who becomes the writer.

As soon as possible after the group peer review, revise your draft based on your peers' questions and comments. Mark this paper Draft 2.

Draft 2: Markup Review

For Draft 2, you will conduct a markup review to improve your word choice and sentence variety.

Tools needed: colored pencils

Step 1: With a green colored pencil, bracket [ ] the first word of each sentence. Make a list of these words on a separate sheet of paper. Identify their parts of speech.
Evaluate: Are a variety of words used? Which word(s) appear most?
Action: Reduce the number of identical first words by half. Try starting sentences with descriptive phrases or clauses.

Step 2: Underline each sentence in the paper with alternating blue and orange colored pencils. Sentence 1—orange, sentence 2—blue, sentence 3—orange, and so on.
Evaluate: Do the sentence lengths vary? Are most sentences the same length? Are any too long and wordy?
Action: Add variety by combining short sentences or breaking up long ones. Strive for a balance of long and short sentences.

Step 3: Circle all the *being* verbs with red pencil. Use this list to help you.

> **am, is, was, were, be, being, been**

Evaluate: Are *being* verbs overused? Can they be replaced with any action verbs?
Action: Reduce the number of *being* verbs by half.

Step 4: Choose a black pencil and draw a box around "dead" words. Refer to the following list of overused words below.

> **a lot, also, awesome, awful, cool, fun, funny, get, good, got, great, have to, like, really, very**

Evaluate: Can dead words be replaced with more specific ones? Use a thesaurus to find more interesting substitutes.
Action: Reduce the number of dead words by half.

When you finish the steps above, mark the version Draft 3.

REFLECT

A good narrative opens by pulling the reader into the action. Try the following:

- Begin with dialogue. Example: "I always knew this mind-reading technology would embarrass me!" said Xorn, furious.

- Begin at the most suspenseful part, then describe events leading up to the crisis. Example: As the nanites melted her shoes, Rania's mind flashed back to her mom's warning.

- Begin in the middle of the action. Example: After five minutes of matching wits with the elevator, I began to realize how outclassed I was.

Draft 3: Individual Peer Review

Ask one student to read Draft 3 and rate it using the rubric below.

Use the following guidelines for your fictional narrative.	
To receive the highest score (4.0), the narrative must meet all of these criteria.	The narrative should • introduce a narrator and one or more characters. • establish a setting and context for the story. • organize an event sequence that unfolds logically. • use techniques such as dialogue, pacing, and description. • use precise words and phrases, details, and sensory language to capture action and convey events. • provide a conclusion that follows from the events. • use correct grammar, usage, punctuation, and spelling.

REFLECT

Good pacing means the story flows at the right rate. It doesn't drag or move too quickly. Use description to slow down the pace. Use dialogue or describe action to pick up the pace. Try reading your narrative aloud to judge whether the action is happening too quickly or too slowly.

Proofread

As you prepare a final draft, make sure you have used standard grammar and punctuation. Proofread carefully for omitted words and punctuation marks. If you used a word processing program, run spell check, but be aware of its limitations. Proofread again to detect the kinds of errors the computer can't catch.

Final Narrative

Share your completed narrative with audiences beyond your classroom. Read it to your family and friends. Upload your finished digital copy to your class website. If you have a school or personal blog, share it with your readers.

Practice Performance Task

A performance task evaluates your ability to comprehend selections of literature or informational text and then demonstrate your knowledge in writing. The task may begin with several multiple-choice or short-answer questions on key vocabulary and the central ideas of the passage(s). The task culminates with a writing assignment.

Complete the following performance task based on selections from Unit 3. You will read three sources and answer questions. Finally, you will complete a longer writing task.

Source #1

Read the following excerpt from *Smarter Thank You Think by* Clive Thompson from Chapter 11 of this unit.

One way [teachers can get more one-on-one time with students] is by using new-media tools to invert the logic of instruction. Instead of delivering all her math lessons to the entire class, Thordarson has them watch Khan videos and work on the online problems. This way, the students who quickly "get it" can blast ahead—and Thordarson can focus more of her class time on helping the students who need coaching. Other teachers are even more aggressive about inverting their classes: They assign videos to be watched at home, then have the students do the homework in class, flipping their instruction inside out.

This makes curious psychological sense. A video can often be a better way to deliver a lecture-style lesson, because students can pause and rewind when they get confused—impossible with a live classroom lesson. In contrast, homework is better done in a classroom, because that's when you're likely to need to ask the teacher for extra help. (Or to ask another student: Thordarson and her colleagues noticed students helping one another, sharing what they'd learned, and tutoring each other.)

"Kids get to work in their place where they're most comfortable," says Thordarson as we wander around her class. "They're allowed to jump ahead. It gives kids who are above grade level a chance to just soar! And for kids who struggle, it gives them a chance to work through some of those issues without everybody watching."

1. Read the sentence below.

> One way [teachers can get more one-on-one time with students] is by using new-media tools to invert the logic of instruction.

What is the meaning of the phrase <u>invert the logic of instruction?</u>

   A. help students enjoy class more than they normally would

   B. make the teacher work harder outside class than during class

   C. let the struggling students do what they want during class

   D. change which tasks are done during and outside class

2. **Part A:** How has technology changed how Tami Thordarson runs her classroom?

   A. She shows videos during her lectures.

   B. She tutors more during class time.

   C. She works directly with advanced students.

   D. She assigns more homework.

   Part B: Which of the following **best** supports the answer to Part A?

   A. *Instead of delivering all her math lessons to the entire class, Thordarson has them watch Khan videos and work on the online problems.*

   B. *This way, the students who quickly "get it" can blast ahead—and Thordarson can focus more of her class time on helping the students who need coaching.*

   C. *(Or to ask another student: Thordarson and her colleagues noticed students helping one another, sharing what they'd learned, and tutoring each other.)*

   D. *"Kids get to work in their place where they're most comfortable," says Thordarson as we wander around her class.*

3. **Part A:** What is the author's point of view regarding the use of videos in the classroom?

   A. Few students benefit from their use.

   B. Most students benefit from their use.

   C. Struggling students benefit from their use.

   D. High-performing students benefit from their use.

Part B: Which of the following best supports the answer to Part A? Select two choices.

A. *One way [teachers can get more one-on-one time with students] is by using new-media tools to invert the logic of instruction.*

B. *Instead of delivering all her math lessons to the entire class, Thordarson has them watch Khan videos and work on the online problems.*

C. *Other teachers are even more aggressive about inverting their classes: They assign videos to be watched at home, then have the students do the homework in class, flipping their instruction inside out.*

D. *A video can often be a better way to deliver a lecture-style lesson, because students can pause and rewind when they get confused—impossible with a live classroom lesson.*

E. *"It gives kids who are above grade level a chance to just soar!"*

F. *"And for kids who struggle, it gives them a chance to work through some of those issues without everybody watching."*

Continue the performance task by reading a second source and answering questions.

Source #2

Read the following excerpt from "Robots will eliminate 6% of all US jobs by 2021, report says," by Olivia Solon from Chapter 13.

By 2021, robots will have eliminated 6% of all jobs in the US, starting with customer service representatives and eventually truck and taxi drivers. That's just one cheery takeaway from a report released by market research company Forrester this week. . . .

"Six percent is huge. In an economy that's really not creating regular full-time jobs, the ability of people to easily find new employment is going to diminish. So we will have people wanting to work and struggling to find jobs because the same trends are beginning to occur in other historically richer job creation areas like banking, retail and healthcare," said Andy Stern, the former president of the Service Employees International Union. "It's an early warning sign and I think it just portends a massive wind of change in the future."

Studies have shown that higher rates of unemployment are linked to less volunteerism and higher crime. Taxi drivers around the world have already

continued on next page

reacted with violent protest to the arrival of ride-hailing app Uber. Imagine how people react when Uber eliminates drivers from its fleet.

"There is a lot of correlation between unemployment and drug use," said Stern. "Clearly over time, particularly in urban settings, the lack of employment is tinder for lighting a fire of social unrest."

4. Which sentence uses a word that means the same as *relationship*?

    A. *That's just one cheery takeaway from a report released by market research company Forrester this week. . . .*

    B. *In an economy that's really not creating regular full-time jobs, the ability of people to easily find new employment is going to diminish.*

    C. *Imagine how people react when Uber eliminates drivers from its fleet.*

    D. *"There is a lot of correlation between unemployment and drug use," said Stern.*

5. What are two central ideas of the article? Select two choices.

    A. Society will create more full-time jobs.

    B. Protests can have dangerous outcomes.

    C. Unemployment and crime are connected.

    D. Automation will lead to more leisure time.

    E. The jobs of truck and taxi drivers are at risk.

    F. Automation will cause more unemployment.

Continue the performance task by reading a third source and answering questions.

Source #3

Read the following excerpt from *Feed* by M. T. Anderson from Chapter 14.

But the braggest thing about the feed, the thing that made it really big, is that it knows everything you want and hope for, sometimes before you even know what those things are. It can tell you how to get them, and help you make buying decisions that are hard. Everything we think and feel is taken in by the corporations, mainly by data ones like Feedlink and OnFeed and American Feedware, and they make a special profile, one that's keyed just to you, and then they give it to their branch companies, or other companies buy them, and they can get to know what it is we need, so all you have to do is want something and there's a chance it will be yours.

Of course, everyone is like, *da da da, evil corporations, oh they're so bad*, we all say that, and we all know they control everything. I mean, it's not great, because who knows what evil [things] they're up to. Everyone feels bad about that. But they're the only way to get all this stuff, and it's no good getting [mad] about it, because they're still going to control everything whether you like it or not. Plus, they keep like everyone in the world employed, so it's not like we could do without them. And it's really great to know everything about everything whenever we want, to have it just like, in our brain, just sitting there.

6. What is the central idea of this excerpt from *Feed*?
   A. The feed corporations don't care about society.
   B. Corporations have both positive and negative effects on society.
   C. People should be making the decisions that are now being made by corporations.
   D. Most people don't fully understand how corporations affect society.

7. Read the following sentence from *Feed*.

   Of course, everyone is like, *da da da, evil corporations, oh they're so bad*, we all say that, and we all know they control everything.

What impact does this sentence have on the paragraph in which it appears?
   A. It shows Titus totally agrees with the arguments against corporations.
   B. It shows Titus wants corporations to play less of a role in society.
   C. It shows Titus thinks corporations are making human beings less free.
   D. It shows Titus doesn't take the arguments against corporations too seriously.

8. How does the author develop Titus's mixed point of view about the feed? Choose two answers.
   A. Titus briefly admits problems with corporations.
   B. Titus totally agrees with the claims that corporations are mostly bad.
   C. Titus argues that corporations are essential to his life.
   D. Titus openly mocks the idea that corporations are evil.

Your Assignment

WRITING PROMPT

Technology has both positive and negative effects on society. Your assignment is to write an essay in which you argue whether technology is shaping modern society in ways that are *mostly* positive or *mostly* negative. Use textual evidence from three sources within the chapters in the unit to support your claim. (You can use sources other than those provided in this Performance Task.)

Before you begin writing, revisit all the works you studied in Unit 3, keeping the purpose of this writing task in mind. Decide which three selections best lend themselves to your argumentative essay.

Read the prompt carefully. Underline words that indicate ideas that should be included in your essay. Before you begin writing, create a list of sources and the evidence they provide supporting your claim to help you organize your ideas. Be sure to identify the source of each idea.

Your writing will be evaluated on the following qualifications. Read these before you begin writing. Then use them to evaluate your finished essay.

Reading Comprehension:
- How well did you understand the texts?
- Does your writing reflect your understanding of the sources?

Writing Expression:
- Does your argumentative essay address the requirements of the prompt?
- Does your essay make a claim based upon an opinion?
- Is your claim supported with reasons and evidence?
- Is your essay clearly organized with ideas that fit together to create a well-constructed argument?
- Does the writing style contain precise, accurate language and content appropriate to the purpose, task, and audience?

Writing Conventions:
- Does your writing follow the rules of standard English for grammar, usage, and spelling?

Unit 4

Essential Question
What does history tell us about ourselves?

When you study history or read and learn about decisions that were made by those who came before you, what does it mean to you? Is history just a set of facts and figures to be memorized? Is history just a series of events that took place a long time ago? How is history relevant to you and your life?

When our country was no more than thirteen colonies and facing the decision of whether to remain under Great Britain's rule or gather troops to fight for independence, the patriot Patrick Henry pointed to England's history with the colonies. Over and over, King George had abused the rights of the colonists. In a passionate speech, Henry stated: "I have but one lamp by which my feet are guided; and that is the lamp of experience. I know of no way of judging of the future but by the past." In this same way, you base decisions in your own life on the lessons of the past.

History can also teach you how to stand up for what you believe in. The Revolutionary War, for instance, would not have taken place if a group of colonists hadn't decided to rebel against unfair treatment by Great Britain. Similarly, the Civil Rights Movement would never have taken place in the United States if citizens hadn't stood up for equal rights.

In this unit you will consider the question: What does history teach us about ourselves? You will explore several works of historical fiction and compare nonfiction texts on similar topics. You will read about real and imagined historical figures who endured injustice and war and how these events affected them and their families. You will also research and write about a person from history and identify elements in his or her story that inspires you.

GOALS

- To understand how the setting shapes conflict and characters in literature.
- To compare a fictional account of historical events with a nonfiction account.
- To determine the theme of a passage and analyze how it is developed through setting and conflict.
- To compare how an author develops characters' points of view.
- To analyze how authors use figurative language, sensory language, dramatic irony, and dramatic techniques to create meaning.
- To analyze how the format and structure of a play communicate theme.
- To write a research paper on the impact of a historical figure.

Chapter 16

Discovering How Story Elements Shape Literature

Preview Concepts

How does the setting of a story affect the characters and the plot?

Think about the following popular books. How does the setting of the story—the time and place where the action takes place—affect the characters and the conflict? Could the plot have occurred anywhere or does the setting directly shape the events and the conflict?

Work with a partner to complete the chart below and analyze how setting affects other story elements. The first row has been completed for you. Fill in the rest of the chart. In the final two rows, add stories or books you have read recently.

Book/Story	Setting	How does the setting affect the characters and the conflict?
Little Women	A family living in a small town in New England in the years before and after the Civil War, approximately 1861–1876	Because of the Civil War, the girls' father is away. As a result, they struggle to earn a living without him and they worry about his safety. Their lives are influenced by the uncertainty of war.
Harry Potter books		
The Hunger Games books		

©Perfection Learning® • No Reproduction Permitted

Making Connections

The following is from the short story by Edgar Allan Poe. This excerpt shares details of the torture chamber in which the narrator finds himself. As you read, underline words and phrases that describe characteristics of the setting.

PREVIEW ACADEMIC VOCABULARY

conflict

historical fiction

nonfiction

point of view

setting

All this I saw indistinctly and by much effort: for my personal condition had been greatly changed during slumber. I now lay upon my back, and at full length, on a species of low framework of wood. To this I was securely bound by a long strap . . . . It passed in many convolutions about my limbs and body, leaving at liberty only my head, and my left arm to such extent that I could, by dint of much exertion, supply myself with food from an earthen dish which lay by my side on the floor. . . .

A slight noise attracted my notice, and, looking to the floor, I saw several enormous rats traversing it. They had issued from the well, which lay just within view to my right. Even then, while I gazed, they came up in troops, hurriedly, with ravenous eyes, allured by the scent of the meat. From this it required much effort and attention to scare them away.

—"The Pit and the Pendulum" by Edgar Allan Poe

What is the effect of the setting on the conflict the narrator faces? Will this setting be to his advantage or disadvantage? Explain.

MAKING CONNECTIONS

In this chapter you will analyze how the setting of a story impacts the characters and conflict.

First Read: Analyzing How Setting Affects Conflict

This passage is from *The Lions of Little Rock*, a novel about Marlee and Liz who live in segregated Little Rock, Arkansas, in the late 1950s. The girls' friendship is tested when it is revealed that Liz has been passing for, or pretending to be, white.

Objective: As you read the first passage, underline words and phrases that explain the setting of the story.

from
The Lions of Little Rock
by Kristin Levine
Chapter 15: "Talking to Daddy"

My Thoughts

1   I woke up the next morning in a good mood. The presentation was over, and I'd done my part. Everything was as it should be. Except my teeth felt fuzzy, like I hadn't brushed them before bed. But I *always* brushed them before bed, even

5   when . . . then I remembered.

I went into the kitchen and made myself a bowl of oatmeal. Daddy was reading the paper. There was an article about the election the weekend before on the front page:

Little Rock votes against integration 19,470 to 7,561.

10   *Schools to be closed indefinitely.*

Daddy slammed down the paper, making me jump. "Sorry," he said. But he scowled as he said it, and I realized then, certain as could be, that when asked if Negroes and whites should go to school together, he had voted yes. "Are

15   you ready to go, Marlee?"

I nodded, even though I'd only had two spoonfuls of my oatmeal.

It was quiet in the car. Daddy gripped the steering wheel like he was driving in a snowstorm. Not that it snowed much

20   in Little Rock, but I'd seen a movie where there was one once,

and the actor clutched the steering wheel so tight, his knuckles turned white.

"Daddy?" I asked.

"What?"

25 "Can you find her for me? Maybe get her phone number?"

Daddy shook his head. "Marlee, you need to leave that girl alone."

"But she's my best friend."

30 "She *was* your friend. Now she's someone else."

No, she wasn't. Liz was funny and outspoken and clever, and I didn't see how all that had changed, just because people were now calling her colored. But Daddy and I usually got along so well. I trusted him. "I don't know," I said finally.

35 "I want to hear her side of the story first."

"Marlee, you can't still be friends with Liz."

"Why not?"

"**Segregationists** don't take kindly to Negroes who try to pass as white. Liz and her family are in real danger. The farther

40 away you stay from them, the better."

"You're worried about me?" I asked.

"Yes, I am," said Daddy. "Why do you think I drive you to school every day?"

I shrugged.

45 Daddy ran a hand through his hair. "Do you remember when I invited that colored minister, Pastor George, to come speak at our church?"

I nodded.

---

segregationists: people who believed that white people and black people should be kept separate, in schools, restaurants, buses and other public locations

My Thoughts

"The next day there was a note tucked in with our paper.

50 It said, *You let your youngest walk to school tomorrow, she won't make it*. And it was signed, *KKK*."

"The Ku Klux Klan is in Little Rock?"

Daddy nodded.

"Who's in it?"

55 "Hard to tell, since it's a secret organization. However, the Capital Citizens' Council, or CCC, is not a secret club. Their avowed purpose is to support segregation in Little Rock. It seems reasonable to assume that some of their members are Klan **sympathizers**, at the very least."

60 "Do we know any CCC members?" I asked.

"Mr. Haroldson, from next door."

He was a nice old man who sometimes gave me penny candy. At least, I'd always thought he was nice.

"And Mrs. McDaniels, Sally's mother, is a member of the

65 Mothers' League."

"What's that?" I asked.

"A women's group, associated with the CCC, that formed last year to oppose integration at Central."

This was a lot to take in. "Isn't everyone allowed to have

70 their own opinion?"

"Of course," said Daddy. "But the reason there were police all over David's graduation last May was not because people have different opinions. The FBI was there to protect Ernest Green because they were worried that someone was going to

75 try to kill him."

I had never really thought about why we'd gotten so few tickets to David's graduation that Granny hadn't even

---

sympathizers: people who agree with and uphold the views of a particular group or individual

been able to go. Apparently, there was a lot I hadn't thought about.

80 "But you still support integration, right?"

"I do," said Daddy. "And I still talk to Pastor George. He's Betty Jean's husband, you know."

I hadn't known. How could I? "Why haven't you ever told me any of this?"

85 "These are issues for grown-ups to deal with, not children."

"The Little Rock Nine weren't much older than me."

Daddy sighed, but he didn't answer.

"I thought things settled down at Central once they called the soldiers in."

90 "Somewhat," said Daddy. "At least that was the official story. But things were not ever pleasant for them there. Minnijean Brown got expelled."

She was the colored girl who'd dumped a bowl of soup on the boys who were picking on her. That was something Liz

95 would do.

"If they were still being harassed, why didn't they complain?"

Daddy shrugged. "Maybe they did and nothing was done. Maybe they thought if they showed any weakness, it would only get worse. In any case, last year the pictures from Central told the

100 whole world Little Rock is filled with hate. And now the town's gone and voted against opening the schools. We are not *just* a town of racists, but those of us who believe in integration . . ." He shook his head. "We can't seem to find our voice."

Daddy was so upset, for a minute I thought he was going

105 to cry. That scared me as bad as anything he'd said. I knew what it was like to have trouble finding your voice, so I reached over and patted his arm. He didn't look at me.

"I mean it, Marlee. I don't want to scare you too much—I'll keep you safe—but I do want you to be careful. Which means

110 you stay away from Liz."

I nodded to show him I understood what he was saying.

But I didn't promise that I would.

My Thoughts

_____
_____
_____
_____

FIRST RESPONSE: KEY IDEAS AND DETAILS

Based on your first read of the passage, describe the relationship between Marlee and her father in your response journal. Support your description using evidence from the text.

TECH-CONNECT

Post your description to your class website. View two of your classmates' descriptions and comment positively on them.

Focus On Analyzing How Setting Affects Conflict

The setting of a story includes the time and place where events take place. The story's setting often influences the conflicts in the story. Then the conflicts influence the choices the characters make. As you know, there are many different types of conflict. Here are just a few:

- person vs. person—a character struggles against another character.

- person vs. nature—a character struggles against forces in nature, often fighting for his or her life

- person vs. self—a character struggles with a quality within his or her own personality. Examples include fear, anger, hatred, worry, or insecurity.

- person vs. society—a character struggles against the rules of society or the laws of the government.

In the graphic organizer on the next page, describe the setting by filling in the top three boxes. Then think about how the setting reveals conflict between groups in the city of Little Rock and also the personal conflicts that Marlee faces.

Time	Place	Situation

↓

Conflicts/Type of conflict

⟨Speak and Listen Discuss your answers to the chart above with a partner. Consider the following question:

- How are the time and place responsible for the conflict in the story?

▼**Write** Write two or three paragraphs explaining how the setting of the story affects the conflicts in the story. Use evidence from the story to support your response, including paraphrasing the text and directly quoting it.

▌Second Read: Analyzing How Point of View Affects a Story

This passage is written from first person point of view, meaning that one of the characters is telling the story. The narrator is Marlee. Marlee's version of events is influenced by who she is—a young white girl. The reader is seeing the events and interactions from Marlee's perspective—which is different from other characters' perspectives.

Objective: Read the passage again or listen as your teacher reads the passage aloud. Think about Marlee's reactions to what her father tells her, and write R next to Marlee's responses.

Focus on Analyzing How Point of View Affects a Story

Consider this example.

> A car and a truck enter a busy intersection. The person driving the red car makes a left turn and is hit by the blue pickup. The person driving the red car says he was in the middle of the intersection waiting to make a left turn, which he did when the light turned yellow. The person driving the pickup says she entered the intersection with the sun in her eyes, and the red car turned right in front of her.

The story changes, then, depending on who tells it. The two versions of the events are told from different points of view.

In the same way, your opinion as a reader is shaped by Marlee's opinions about the events going on around her. If Marlee's dad were telling the story, you as a reader would get an entirely different perspective.

In the graphic organizer below, several sentences from the passage are provided in the left column. In the right column, explain what they reveal about Marlee's point of view of the conflicts taking place in Little Rock. In the third column, explain what the lines indicate about Daddy's point of view.

Lines from Passage	Marlee's Point of View	Daddy's Point of View
"She was your friend. Now she's someone else." *No, she wasn't. Liz was funny and outspoken and clever, and I didn't see how all that had changed, just because people were now calling her colored. But Daddy and I usually got along so well. I trusted him. "I don't know," I said finally. "I want to hear her side of the story first."*		

Lines from Passage	Marlee's Point of View	Daddy's Point of View
This was a lot to take in. "Isn't everyone allowed to have their own opinion?" "Of course," said Daddy. "But the reason there were police all over David's graduation last May was not because people have different opinions. The FBI was there to protect Ernest Green because they were worried that someone was going to try to kill him." I had never really thought about why we'd gotten so few tickets to David's graduation that Granny hadn't even been able to go. Apparently, there was a lot I hadn't thought about.		
Daddy was so upset, for a minute I thought he was going to cry. That scared me as bad as anything he'd said. I knew what it was like to have trouble finding your voice, so I reached over and patted his arm. He didn't look at me. "I mean it, Marlee. I don't want to scare you too much—I'll keep you safe—but I do want you to be careful. Which means you stay away from Liz." I nodded to show him I understood what he was saying. But I didn't promise that I would.		

Write Use the chart to help you analyze how the author develops the points of view of Marlee and Daddy in the story. Focus on how they each view Liz and the events going on in Little Rock. Use your notes from the chart you completed to write a few paragraphs. On the next page are some sentence starters to help you get started.

continued on next page

- Marlee's and Daddy's points of view are . . . .

- Marlee sees Liz as . . . . For instance, ...

- From Daddy's point of view, Liz is . . . .

- Marlee wants . . . . because she says . . . .

- Daddy is worried about . . . . He says . . . .

Speak and Listen With a small group of students, take turns reading your paragraphs aloud. Each group member should offer a compliment and a suggestion for improvement. Listen and record these comments. Edit your paragraphs based on your classmates' suggestions.

Third Read: Comparing and Contrasting Historical Fiction and Nonfiction

Reread the passage from the novel a third time. Then read the following historical timeline of the Little Rock Nine.

Objective: As you read, underline historical details that refer to people and events discussed by the characters in the *The Lions of Little Rock*.

Little Rock Central High School
National Historic Site
Crisis Timeline
from www.nps.gov

1 **May 17, 1954**

The United States Supreme Court rules racial segregation in public schools is unconstitutional in *Brown v. Board of Education of Topeka*. Five days later, the Little Rock School

5 Board issues a policy statement saying it will comply with the Supreme Court's decision. In May 1955, The Supreme Court further defines the standard of implementation for **integration** as being "with all **deliberate** speed," in *Brown II* and charges the federal courts with establishing guidelines for compliance.

My Thoughts

_____

_____

_____

_____

_____

_____

_____

_____

_____

---

integration: combining of black and white citizens, in this case, in schools
deliberate: carefully and considerate of the consequences

August 23, 1954

10   Under the direction of Pine Bluff attorney Wiley Branton, chairman of the state's **NAACP** Legal Redress Committee, the NAACP **petitions** the Little Rock School Board for immediate integration.

May 24, 1955

15   The Little Rock School Board adopts the Blossom Plan of gradual integration beginning with the high school level (starting in September 1957) and the lower grades during the next six years.

February 8, 1956

20   Federal Judge John E. Miller dismisses the NAACP suit (*Aaron v. Cooper*), declaring that the Little Rock School Board has acted in "utmost good faith" in setting up its plan of gradual integration. In April, the Eighth Circuit Court of Appeals upholds Judge Miller's dismissal.

August 27, 1957

25   The segregationist Mother's League of Central High School holds its first public meeting. They seek a temporary court order to stop school integration. Two days later, the courts approve the order on the grounds that integration could

30 lead to violence. Federal Judge Ronald Davies reverses the court order and tells the School Board to proceed with its desegregation plan.

September 2, 1957 – (Labor Day)

    Governor Orval Faubus orders the Arkansas National

35 Guard to prohibit African American students from entering Central High School and announces his plans in a televised speech.

My Thoughts

NAACP: National Association for the Advancement of Colored People, a group that works for the human rights of African Americans

September 3, 1957

The Mother's League holds a "sunrise service" at Central

40 High attended by members of the Citizen's Council, parents

and students. On September 20, Federal Judge Ronald

Davies rules that Governor Faubus has not used the troops

to preserve law and order and orders them removed.

Faubus removes the Guardsmen and the Little Rock Police

45 Department moves in.

September 23, 1957

An angry mob of over 1,000 whites gathers in front of

Central High School, while nine African American students

are escorted inside. The Little Rock police remove the nine

50 children for their safety. President Eisenhower calls the rioting

"disgraceful" and orders federal troops into Little Rock.

September 24, 1957

One thousand, two hundred members of the

101st Airborne Division, the "Screaming Eagles" of Fort

55 Campbell, Kentucky, roll into Little Rock. These federal troops

take over and the Arkansas National Guard must follow their

lead.

September 25, 1957

Under troop escort, the "Little Rock Nine" are escorted

60 back into Central High School for their first full day of classes.

May 25, 1958

Senior Ernest Green becomes the first African American

student to graduate from Central High School.

June 3, 1958

65 Highlighting numerous discipline problems during the

school year, the school board asks the court for permission to

delay the desegregation plan in *Cooper v. Aaron*.

My Thoughts

June 21, 1958

70 Judge Harry Lemley grants the delay of integration until January 1961. The judge states that while the African American students have a constitutional right to attend white schools, the "time has not come for them to enjoy [that right.]"

September 12, 1958

75 The United States Supreme Court rules that Little Rock must continue with its desegregation plan. The School Board orders the high schools to open on September 15. Governor Faubus orders four Little Rock high schools closed as of 8:00 a.m., September 15, 1958, until the public could vote on integration.

80 **September 16, 1958**

The Women's Emergency Committee to Open Our Schools (WEC) forms and begins to solicit support for reopening the schools.

September 27, 1958

85 Citizens vote 19,470 to 7,561 against integration and the schools remain closed.

May 5, 1959

Segregationist members of the school board vote not to rehire 44 teachers and administrators they say supported 90 integration.

May 8, 1959

The WEC and local businessmen form Stop This Outrageous Purge (STOP) and work to get voter signatures to remove the three segregationist board members. Segregationists form the 95 Committee to Retain Our Segregated Schools (CROSS).

May 25, 1959

Through the efforts of STOP, three segregationists are voted off the school board and three moderate members are retained.

August 12, 1959

Little Rock public high schools reopen, nearly a month

100 early. Segregationists rally at the State Capitol where Faubus

advises them that it is a "dark" day, but they should not give

up the struggle. They then march to Central High School where

the police and fire departments break up the mob. Twenty-one

people are arrested.

My Thoughts

_____

_____

_____

_____

_____

Focus on Comparing and Contrasting Historical Fiction and Nonfiction

Study the chart below. The first column lists a fact from the nonfiction timeline and the second column explains how that fact is treated in the historical fiction novel excerpt. Complete the chart with facts from the timeline and corresponding textual evidence from the novel excerpt. For the second column, paraphrase or quote directly from the novel excerpt.

Little Rock Central High School National Historic Site Crisis Timeline	The Lions of Little Rock (historical fiction)
1. September 25 - Under troop escort, the "Little Rock Nine" are escorted back into Central High School for their first full day of classes.	Marlee states, "I thought things settled down at Central once they called the soldiers in."
2.	
3.	
4.	

Fiction and nonfiction texts approach their subjects differently. Nonfiction texts:

- are primarily intended to supply information, so writers focus on accurately explaining facts.

- capture the big picture of a historical event by explaining actions taken by leaders and how their actions cause other events.

- often rely on print features, such as headers, graphics, and charts to communicate key ideas.

Historical fiction texts:

- take a narrower focus.

- usually describes events, both real and imaginary, by focusing on the lives of characters.

- feature interactions between characters to provide a glimpse into the motivations and emotions experienced by people involved in history.

- engage the imagination and entertains the reader, while often providing historically accurate information.

Speak and Listen Work with a partner to fill in the following Venn diagram, comparing the two texts. Consider the purpose, focus, format, writing style, and the point of view contained in each text.

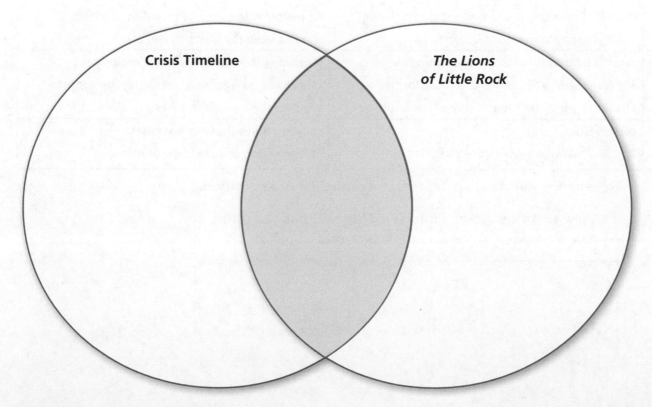

Crisis Timeline

The Lions of Little Rock

Write Work with your partner to write a summary of your comparison of the two texts. Present your summary to the class.

Language: Capitalization

The excerpt from *The Lions of Little Rock* shows off a variety of uses for capital letters—in personal titles such as Pastor George, names such as the Mothers' League, and place names such as Little Rock. Capital letters begin a sentence, a proper noun, and each major word in a title. These rules are simple enough to remember. The tricky rules often concern when not to capitalize words. Common nouns and seasons are generally lowercase, but what about job titles or directional words?

The chart below contains some tips about when—and when not—to capitalize.

Capitalize . . .	Do not capitalize . . .
the first word in a quotation of a complete sentence. He asked, "When will we get there?"	**the first word in a quotation of an incomplete sentence.** She explained they would "get there when we get there."
nouns that form part of a name. We visited the Gateway Arch last summer. I rode with Aunt Ana and Uncle Miguel. We also saw Badlands National Park.	**nouns that are not part of a name.** We walked under the arch, staring up in awe. I enjoy spending time with my aunt and uncle. There are 59 national parks in this country.
titles for specific individuals. In 1797, President Washington stepped down. I had an appointment with Doctor Li.	**titles that do not name individuals.** At the time, the president had no term limit. She has been my doctor for years.
directions that refer to specific regions. My father got a job in Northern California. Elizabeth rarely sees her family in the South.	**directions that do not refer to regions.** The window faced east, revealing the sunrise. We bike the trail on the western edge of town.
course titles. Are you taking Algebra I this year?	**subject names that are not titles.** I like algebra, but I prefer geometry.

Rewrite the following sentences, correcting the capitalization.

1. A few years ago, after winning a Writing Contest, I got to visit the State Capitol and meet Governor Tanaka.

2. To find the Public Library, head northwest on baker street until you reach the Town Square and then look for the Statue of Ben Franklin.

3. Janelle always had trouble with Geography, but when she took professor Martinez's class, global studies, she found Geography easier to understand.

4. Despite the terrible review he read in the Newspaper, Ahmed called the movie "One heck of a ride!"

Project-Based Assessments

Historical Background

Write an explanation of the process of integration in the schools in Little Rock, Arkansas. Your report should provide background information that would help readers of the novel *The Lions of Little Rock* to understand the events, leaders, and community groups involved in the excerpt you read in this chapter.

continued on next page

Here are some steps to help you.

1. Begin by rereading the excerpt from the novel. Take notes about the people, places, and events mentioned. Write questions you have that aren't answered by the excerpts.

2. Conduct research to find answers to your questions. As much as possible, use primary sources for your research.

   - A *primary source* is an eyewitness account of historical events. Examples include journals, biographies, government documents, and newspaper articles from the time period.

   - Primary sources tend to be more accurate because they were written by people who witnessed the events. For example, a good primary source is *The New York Times* from September 25, 1957, which can be found online at nytimes.com.

   - Government websites, academic websites, and established periodicals are also good sources for historical research.

   - Keep records of all of your sources.

3. Use notes from your research to write a one to two page historical companion to the book *The Lions of Little Rock*. Present your information in a way that is appealing to your audience—seventh-graders reading the book. Include text features such as headers, bullet points, quotations, and photos to support your written text. Use a word processing or design program to make your project visually appealing.

4. Include a list of sources used in your research. Follow your teacher's instructions for formatting these sources.

Use the following guidelines for your historical background report.	
To receive the highest score, the report must meet all of these criteria.	Your report • presents accurate background information related to the events, groups, and people mentioned in *The Lions of Little Rock*. • includes two or more primary sources as well as other reliable sources. • includes text features (photos, headers, bullet points) that support the writing. • is appropriate for a seventh-grade audience. • is visually appealing. • uses correct grammar, word usage, spelling, and punctuation.

Historical Fiction

Write an imaginary conversation between two people involved in the events surrounding the integration of Central High in Little Rock. Your characters might be real people, such as one of the Little Rock Nine. Or they might be imaginary characters based on real people, such as students or teachers at Central High School. Use the dialogue from *The Lions of Little Rock* as a model for your writing.

Here are some suggestions to help you:

1. Conduct research on the Little Rock Nine and the events that took place in September 1957. Use reliable sources, including primary sources when possible, and keep a record of your source information. (See an explanation of primary sources under the Historical Background project.)

2. Think about possible conversations you might write about. Suggestions include, but aren't limited to
   - one of the Little Rock Nine and his or her parent the night before the first day of school
   - two of the Little Rock Nine as they approach the school or at school during the first day
   - two students attending Central High on September 25

3. In your dialogue, communicate how the characters feel about the events and how they respond to the conflict. Are they brave, worried, anxious, or angry? Your writing should be entertaining as well as historically accurate.

4. Include a list of works used in your research. Follow your teacher's instructions for the formatting of sources.

Use the following guidelines for your historical fiction conversation.	
To receive the highest score, the historical ficiton must meet all of these criteria.	Your historical fiction conversation • presents an imaginary conversation related to the events, groups, and people mentioned in *The Lions of Little Rock*. • accurately represents historical events mentioned. • includes dialogue between two characters involved in the events. • communicates the feelings and motivations of the characters. • uses correct grammar, word usage, and punctuation.

On Your Own: Integrating Ideas

1. Read the entire book *The Lions of Little Rock* by Kristin Levine. Visit the author's website to learn more about the book.

2. Read *Warriors Don't Cry* by Melba Pattillo Beals, one of the Little Rock Nine who became a journalist. The book explains her first year at the school and her determination in the face of abuse.

3. Research oral histories about the Civil Rights movement in Little Rock during the 1960s. Visit the Library of Congress website to watch videos of those involved in Civil Rights and the integration of schools.

Connect to Testing

Tests may require you to answer questions about setting, point of view, or the differences and similarities between a historical fiction excerpt and a nonfiction text on the same subject. Here are some examples of these types of questions.

1. **Part A:** How does the setting of *The Lions of Little Rock* affect Marlee's father's state of mind?

   A. It makes him want to protect his family.

   B. It makes him want to get involved in the Civil Right movement.

   C. It makes him less trusting of other people.

   D. It makes him curious about what will happen next locally.

   Part B: Which of the following provides the strongest evidence for the answer to Part A?

   A. *"She was your friend. Now she's someone else."*

   B. *A women's group, associated with the CCC, that formed last year to oppose integration at Central.*

   C. *This was a lot to take in. "Isn't everyone allowed to have their own opinion?"*

   D. *"I mean it, Marlee. I don't want to scare you too much—I'll keep you safe—but I do want you to be careful."*

2. How would *The Lions of Little Rock* most likely be different if it were told from Marlee's father's point of view?

   A. It would involve a more biased opinion.

   B. It would include more historical analysis.

   C. It would be more informative about civil rights.

   D. It would be boring.

3. **Part A:** According to the timeline, Marlee's conversation with her dad takes place in

   A. September 1957.

   B. September 1958.

   C. May 1959.

   D. August 1959.

Part B: Which of the following provides the strongest evidence for the answer to Part A?

A. *There was an article about the election the weekend before on the front page: Little Rock votes against integration 19,470 to 7,561. Schools to be closed indefinitely.*

B. *"But the reason there were police all over David's graduation last May was not because people have different opinions. The FBI was there to protect Ernest Green because they were worried that someone was going to try to kill him."*

C. *"I thought things settled down at Central once they called the soldiers in."*

D. *In any case, last year the pictures from Central told the whole world Little Rock is filled with hate.*

4. Read the following entry from the timeline.

> May 25, 1958
>
> Senior Ernest Green becomes the first African American student to graduate from Central High School.

How does the conversation between Marlee and her father further develop the facts in this entry of the timeline? In your answer refer to specific details from the excerpt.

continued on next page

5. How does the setting influence the conflict between Marlee and society and Marlee and her father? In your answer, explain the conflicts and how specific elements of the setting cause the conflicts. Support your conclusions with evidence from the text.

Chapter 17

Learning About History Through Fiction

Preview Concepts

We make inferences every day in all kinds of situations. Read the following situation and make inferences based on what you read in the text and your own experience.

> Crack! Thunder struck and rain poured. Max stared blankly out the window, trying to contain his emotions that raged like the weather. He was beginning to lose it. Dropping the kite from his hand, Max broke out into sobs. His mother comforted him, "It's okay. We'll just find something else to do." She began to unpack the food from a basket on the counter and offered him a sandwich. Max snapped, "I don't wanna sand-mich!" Boom! A flash lit up the living room. Max screamed and covered his ears.

Inferences about Max:

Evidence from text:

Inferences about the situation:

Evidence from text:

Making Connections

Read the following excerpt.

This was a lofty chamber, lined and littered with countless bottles. Broad, low tables were scattered about, which bristled with retorts, test-tubes, and little Bunsen lamps, with their blue flickering flames. There was only one student in the room, who was bending over a distant table absorbed in his work. At the sound of our steps he glanced round and sprang to his feet with a cry of pleasure.

"I've found it! I've found it," he shouted to my companion, running towards us with a test-tube in his hand. "I have found a re-agent which is precipitated by hemoglobin, and by nothing else." Had he discovered a gold mine, greater delight could not have shone upon his features.

"Dr. Watson, Mr. Sherlock Holmes," said Stamford, introducing us.

"How are you?" he said cordially, gripping my hand with a strength for which I should hardly have given him credit. "You have been in Afghanistan, I perceive."

"How on earth did you know that?" I asked in astonishment.

"Never mind," said he, chuckling to himself.

—*A Study in Scarlet*, by Arthur Conan Doyle

What did you already know about the character of Sherlock Holmes before reading this excerpt?

What inference might you make about Sherlock Holmes, based on the way he acts in this excerpt? Underline details in the text that support your response.

MAKING CONNECTIONS

In this chapter you will make inferences based on evidence from a text.

First Read: Making Inferences

This story was written by Ray Bradbury, an author best known for writing science fiction. What inferences can you make about the characters, setting, and situation based on the text?

Objective: As you read, make inferences about the setting and the boys' feelings. Write two inferences in the My Thoughts column. Underline lines in the text that support your inferences.

excerpt
The Drummer Boy of Shiloh
by Ray Bradbury

My Thoughts

1   In the April night, more than once, blossoms fell from the orchard trees and lit with rustling taps on the drumskin. At midnight a peach stone left miraculously on a branch through winter flicked by a bird fell swift and unseen struck once like

5   panic, which jerked the boy upright. In silence he listened to his own heart ruffle away away—at last gone from his ears and back in his chest again.

After that he turned the drum on its side, where its great lunar face peered at him whenever he opened his eyes.

10   His face, alert or at rest, was solemn. It was a solemn time and a solemn night for a boy just turned fourteen in the peach orchard near Owl Creek not far from the church at **Shiloh**. . . .

The boy turned on his side. A moth brushed his face, but it was a peach blossom. A peach blossom flicked him, but it was

15   a moth. Nothing stayed put. Nothing had a name. Nothing was as it once was.

If he stayed very still, when the dawn came up and the soldiers put on their bravery with their caps, perhaps they ★ might go away, the war with them, and not notice him living

20   small here, no more than a toy himself.

Shiloh: a small town in southwest Tennessee

"Well, by thunder now," said a voice. The boy shut his eyes to hide inside himself, but it was too late. Someone, walking by in the night, stood over him. "Well," said the voice quietly, "here's a soldier crying *before* the fight. Good. Get it over.

25 Won't be time once it all starts."

And the voice was about to move on when the boy, startled, touched the drum at his elbow. The man above, hearing this, stopped. The boy could feel his eyes, sense him slowly bending near. A hand must have come down out of the

30 night, for there was a little *rat-tat* as the fingernails brushed and the man's breath fanned the boy's face.

"Why, it's the drummer boy, isn't it?"

The boy nodded, not knowing if his nod was seen. "Sir, is that you?" he said.

35 "I assume it is." The man's knees cracked as he bent still closer. He smelled as all fathers should smell, of salt-sweat, tobacco, horse and boot leather, and the earth he walked upon. He had many eyes. No, not eyes, brass buttons that watched the boy.

He could only be, and was, the general. "What's your

40 name, boy?" he asked.

"Joby, sir," whispered the boy, starting to sit up.

"All right, Joby, don't stir." A hand pressed his chest gently, and the boy relaxed. "How long you been with us, Joby?"

"Three weeks, sir."

45 "Run off from home or join legitimate, boy?"

Silence.

"Fool question," said the general. "Do you shave yet, boy? Even more of a fool. There's your cheek, fell right off the tree overhead. And the others here, not much older. Raw, raw, the

50 lot of you. You ready for tomorrow or the next day, Joby?"

My Thoughts

"I think so, sir."

"You want to cry some more, go on ahead. I did the same last night."

"You, sir?"

55 "It's the truth. Thinking of everything ahead. Both sides figuring the other side will just give up, and soon, and the war done in weeks and us all home. Well, that's not how it's going to be. And maybe that's why I cried."

"Yes, sir," said Joby.

60 The general must have taken out a cigar now, for the dark was suddenly filled with the Indian smell of tobacco unlighted yet, but chewed as the man thought what next to say.

"It's going to be a crazy time," said the general. "Counting both sides, there's a hundred thousand men—give or take

65 a few thousand—out there tonight, not one as can spit a sparrow off a tree, or knows a horse clod from a **Minie ball**. Stand up, bare the breast, ask to be a target, thank them and sit down, that's us, that's them. We should turn tail and train four months, they should do the same. But here we are,

70 taken with spring fever and thinking it **bloodlust,** taking our **sulphur** with cannons instead of with molasses, as it should be—going to be a hero, going to live forever. And I can see all them over there nodding agreement, save the other way around. It's wrong, boy, it's wrong as a head put on

75 **hindside** front and a man marching backward through life. Sometime this week more innocents will get shot out of pure **Cherokee** enthusiasm than ever got shot before. Owl Creek

---

Minie ball: a kind of bullet used during the Civil War
bloodlust: desire for bloodshed
sulphur: a chemical given as a medicine
hindside: the backside or backwards
Cherokee: a Native American tribe

was full of boys splashing around in the noonday sun just a few hours ago. I fear it will be full of boys again, just floating,

80 at sundown tomorrow, not caring where the current takes them."

The reconstructed Shiloh Church, Shiloh, Tennessee

FIRST RESPONSE: KEY IDEAS AND DETAILS

How does the author portray the battle that will soon take place? What lines foreshadow the coming battle? Write your answer in your response journal. Be ready to defend your analysis using evidence from the passage and also be ready to explain the evidence if needed.

Focus on Making Inferences

Consider what you can infer about the characters and the setting in the excerpt from "The Drummer Boy of Shiloh." Use the graphic organizer on the next page to identify inferences and specific sentences and details that support your inferences. The first row has been completed for you.

TECH-CONNECT

Tweet a detail that most clearly communicates the author's portrayal of the coming battle or post it to your class website. Include an explanation of why you chose it.

Inferences about the boy	Evidence
1. The boy is scared about the battle that will take place the next day.	*His face, alert or at rest, was solemn. (line 10)* *perhaps they might go away, the war with them, and not notice him living small here (lines 18–19)*
2.	

Inference about the general	Evidence
1.	
2.	

Inferences about the battle	Evidence
1.	
2.	

Write The Battle of Shiloh was fought on April 6–7 in 1862. Based on the passage, make inferences about the situation and actual outcome of the battle based on the excerpt from "The Drummer Boy of Shiloh." Explain which words or details led you to make your inferences.

TECH-CONNECT

Conduct online research to check your inferences about the Battle of Shiloh.

Second Read: Analyzing an Author's Use of Language

As you read the text again, pay attention to how the use of language reveals the author's voice and style.

Objective: Underline examples of language that create a picture in your mind. Place a star by examples of figurative language that compare objects in the story to other objects.

REFLECT

What is your favorite line from the excerpt? Why?

Focus on Analyzing an Author's Use of Language

Bradbury chooses his words carefully. He wants the reader to experience what it's like to be a fourteen-year-old waiting to fight in his first battle. Here are some of the literary devices Bradbury uses.

sensory language: language that appeals to the senses, helps the reader see, feel, and smell the scene being described

metaphor: comparison of two unalike things

repetition: repeating a word or phrase for emphasis

foreshadowing: when a writer gives an advance hint of what is to come later in the story

Complete the chart below with examples from the excerpt.

Literary Device	Word or Phrase	Effect on Reader
sensory language	1. 2.	
metaphor	1. 2.	
repetition	1. 2.	
foreshadowing	1. 2.	

Speak and Listen Share your answers to the chart with a partner. Then discuss the following questions:

- What emotions do you feel as you read the passage?

- Is his language effective at communicating these emotions? Why or why not?

Third Read: Analyzing a Fictional Account of a Historical Event

Reread the excerpt from "The Drummer Boy of Shiloh" a third time. Then read the excerpt below. It is a nonfiction article about drummer boys during times of war.

Objective: Underline ideas that provide information that helps you better understand details from the short story.

excerpt
Drummer Boys
by Stephen Currie

My Thoughts

1   Throughout much of American history, drummer boys made a small but important contribution to American military units. These children, some as young as nine years old, courageously faced the enemy with little more than a drum and a pair of
5   sticks. A few became the first to fall in the line of duty.

Early American armies were largely volunteer affairs. Few formal age restrictions existed, and youngsters who lied about their age were often enlisted with little scrutiny. Those who were clearly underage sometimes became drummers. A typical
10   drummer boy was between twelve and sixteen years old, although a few even younger boys managed to enlist.

Drummers served in all our early conflicts—the Revolutionary War, frontier battles, the War of 1812, the Mexican War, and the Civil War. These young soldiers
15   played a vital role, as they served as the primary means of communication between officers and men. The drum and **fife** called troops to arms, signaled changes in strategy, and provided the **cadence** for marching. . . .

By the Civil War, drumbeats had become more
20   sophisticated. Drummer boys sounded the daily calls and

---

fife: small flute-like instrument

cadence: a beat or rhythm used to keep soldiers in step when marching

provided beats for marching drills. A well-trained **regiment** could maneuver expertly without spoken commands, with only the drumbeats transmitting the orders.

The boys also performed a number of less colorful duties.
25 Most helped with camp chores such as carrying water, and one even served as a barber, while another peddled sweets to the soldiers. After a battle, the youngsters faced more serious tasks. They helped remove and care for the wounded, sharpen the surgeon's instruments, and bury the dead.

30 Several heroic or tragic tales involving drummer boys emerged from the Civil War. Most of these were romantic works of fiction. One famous ballad, for example, claimed to tell the mournful end of "The Drummer Boy of Shiloh." Historic research indicates that no such individual existed. . . .

35 The new weapons of the Civil War helped end the days of children soldiers. War had become a more professional and deadly business. An act of Congress passed in March 1864 prohibited the enlistment of anyone under age sixteen. The echo of young drumbeats faded as **bugles**, telegraphs, and,
40 later, radios guided the infantry into battle.

The drummer boys played a crucial role in our early American armies. They joined up for the excitement of soldiering and aged quickly in the harsh realities of war. They risked, and sometimes lost, their lives for the cause of freedom
45 at an age when most children now think only of school or play. Today we can look with pride on the drummer boys' bravery when the United States, like the boys themselves, was a youngster filled with dreams of glory.

_____

regiment: a military unit

bugles: a valveless brass instrument similar to a trumpet

My Thoughts

Focus on Analyzing a Fictional Account of a Historical Event

Writers of historical fiction who base their stories on actual events usually alter or adapt them to fit their purposes. The goal of historical fiction is to entertain. So the author often takes liberty with characters and events to make the story more engaging.

Fill in the following graphic organizer, contrasting the way details are represented in the first and the second passages. Use direct quotations from the texts or paraphrase the information. Include line numbers for reference.

Idea	The Drummer Boy of Shiloh by Ray Bradbury	Drummer Boys by Stephen Currie
Age of drummers		
Duties in and after battle		
The person known as "The Drummer Boy of Shiloh"		
Drummer boys' responses to fighting in a war		

Speak and Listen Review your answers to the chart with a partner. Then discuss the following question:

- Should the fact that children were allowed to serve as drummer boys in wars be celebrated or condemned?

Support your opinion with evidence from the texts.

Write Write several paragraphs analyzing how the short story represents, or does not represent, the facts presented in "Drummer Boys" by Stephen Currie.

Language: Spelling

It is important to use correct spelling when writing assignments for school or when writing emails and other communication with community leaders and business people. Informal spelling and abbreviations are fine to use when texting with family and friends. However, in most other situations, including correspondence about job opportunities, you should use correct spelling and complete words and phrases.

Basic Spelling Rules

1. Most of the time, you should place *i* before *e* in words, except after *c*.
   Examples: *re<u>cei</u>pt, de<u>cei</u>ve, fri<u>e</u>nd, bel<u>ie</u>ve*

2. When forming the plural of a word, most of the time you simply add *s*.
   Examples: *dogs, tractors, pears, rocks*

3. If a word ends in *-s, -x, -z, -ch*, or *-sh*, add *-es* to make it plural.
   Examples: *coa<u>ches</u>, wi<u>shes</u>, gra<u>sses</u>, bo<u>xes</u>*

4. If a noun ends in *y*, change the *y* to an *i* and add *-es* to make the plural.
   Examples: *fly/flies, factory/factories, story/stories, baby/babies*

Also remember that spell-check is a helpful tool, but it is not a substitute for carefully proofing your writing. Spell-check doesn't catch mistakes in words that are often confused such as *their*, *there*, and *they're* or *your* and *you're*. Read the following commonly confused words.

Commonly Confused Words

whose—possessive for "of who"	*who's*—contraction for "who is"
Whose book is this?	Who's going to the game?

your—possessive for "of you" Your bike is in the yard.	*you're*—contraction for "you are" You're going to be late for school.
their—possessive form of "they" Their shoes were by the front door.	*there*—in that place The baseball is over there.
they're—contraction for "they are" They're going to be home soon.	
passed—past tense of "to pass" I passed the vegetables to my mom.	*past*—at a previous time The past month has been very rainy.
its—possessive form of "it" The dog buried its bone by the tree.	*it's*—contraction for "it is" It's never too late to try.

Read the sentences below. Circle any misspelled or incorrect
words, and rewrite the sentence correctly in the space provided.

1. I can't beleive that they're team won the game.

REFLECT

What words do
you often confuse?
Add them to the
list of Commonly
Confused Words.

2. The two deputys had not seen are stolen cars.

3. I saw so many churchs that day and recieved so many
complements on my camera that I was exhausted.

continued on next page

4. When I red you're writing, it was easy to see why you one first place in the essay contest.

5. The advise of the coachs was to weight and continue the meat after the rain stoped.

Project-Based Assessments

Response Essay

The writer of "Drummer Boys" claims "Most of the tales involving drummer boys were romantic works of fiction." Is Bradbury's account an example of one of these "romantic works of fiction" or is it a realistic portrayal of the people and battles involved? Provide evidence from the text to support your point of view.

Write a thesis statement that makes a claim about whether Bradbury's story portrays war as a romantic adventure. Then use direct quotations from the text as evidence to support your claim.

Use the following guidelines for your response essay.	
To receive the highest score, the essay must meet all of these criteria.	Your response essay • makes a claim about whether Bradbury's portrayal of war is romantic or realistic. • provides strong evidence from the text, including direct quotations. • demonstrates an understanding of the ideas found in both texts in the chapter. • uses correct grammar, word usage, punctuation, and spelling.

Argumentative Essay

The writer of "Drummer Boys" claims "One famous ballad, for example, claimed to tell the mournful end of "The Drummer Boy of Shiloh." Historic research indicates that no such individual existed. . . ." Research to find facts that support or disprove the idea that the drummer boy of Shiloh was a fictional character.

As much as possible, use primary sources such as journals, letters, and newspaper articles from the time period or from eyewitnesses. Also use secondary sources about the Civil War from reliable Internet sources. Keep a thorough record of all sources you consult during your research.

Based on your research, make a claim about whether the drummer boy of Shiloh was a real person. Support your answer with evidence. Follow your teacher's instructions for citing your sources and creating a Works Cited page.

	Use the following guidelines for your argumentative essay.
To receive the highest score, the essay must meet all of these criteria.	Your argumentative essay • makes a claim about the reality of the drummer boy of Shiloh. • supports the claim with evidence from primary and secondary sources. • is based on relevant and sufficient evidence. • is clearly organized and easy to follow. • uses correct grammar, word usage, punctuation, and spelling.

On Your Own: Integrating Ideas

1. Read the rest of *The Drummer Boy of Shiloh*. How does this excerpt affect your understanding of the entire short story?
2. Watch a documentary about either the Revolutionary War or the Civil War. Ken Burns' *The Civil War* is an award-winning account of the conflict. Episode Two: A Very Bloody Affair (1862) covers the Battle of Shiloh.
3. Find online recordings of Revolutionary War or Civil War marches. As you listen, try to hear the cadence of the drums.

Connect to Testing

In this chapter you practiced making inferences, analyzing literary devices, and comparing and contrasting historical fiction and historical nonfiction. You will be tested on these skills on reading tests. Answer these questions to help you practice these skills.

1. **Part A:** Which of the following is the best inference about Joby based on the information in the excerpt from "The Drummer Boy of Shiloh"?

   A. He is highly confident and ready for the task ahead of him.

   B. He is somewhat nervous and afraid.

   C. He does not like the idea of heading into battle.

   D. He has fought in several other battles before the current one.

   Part B: Which of the following provides the best evidence for the answer to Part A?

   A. *After that he turned the drum on its side, where its great lunar face peered at him whenever he opened his eyes.*

   B. *"Well," said the voice quietly, "here's a soldier crying before the fight. Good. Get it over. Won't be time once it all starts."*

   C. *"All right, Joby, don't stir." A hand pressed his chest gently, and the boy relaxed. "How long you been with us, Joby?"*
   "Three weeks, sir."

   D. *"Raw, raw, the lot of you. You ready for tomorrow or the next day, Joby?"*
   "I think so, sir."

2. **Part A:** What can you infer about the general's experience, based on the evidence in the excerpt from "The Drummer Boy of Shiloh"?

   A. He is relatively new in the armed forces.

   B. He has been through many battles.

   C. He loves being in the midst of battle.

   D. He would like to lead more soldiers than he does.

Part B: Provide two examples of evidence from the text that supports the answer to Part A.

3. What is one piece of information included in both *The Drummer Boy of Shiloh* and *Drummer Boys*?

    A. Drummer boys could be quite young.

    B. Drummer boys transmitted messages.

    C. Drummer boys sometimes did chores in camps.

    D. Drummer boys often helped wounded soldiers.

4. Which of the following could you infer about drummer boys, based on the information in *Drummer Boys*?

    A. They were generally ambitious but were not always able to survive war.

    B. They were clever and resourceful.

    C. They were brave, sometimes surprisingly so.

    D. They were able to walk long distances without feeling tired.

Read the following excerpt then answer the question that follows:

> The man's knees cracked as he bent still closer. He smelled as all fathers should smell, of salt-sweat, tobacco, horse and boot leather, and the earth he walked upon. He had many eyes. No, not eyes, brass buttons that watched the boy.

5. **Part A:** The author's description of the general indicates that he is a(n)

    A. ruthless fighter who loves violence.

    B. godlike figure who is worshiped by his men.

    C. nurturing person who understands his soldiers.

    D. old man who is tired of war.

Part B: Provide evidence from the excerpt above to support the answer to Part A.

Chapter 18

Analyzing the Structure of a Story

Preview Concepts

With a partner, share what you know about World War I from classes, books, and other sources.

This picture is a reenactment of a World War I battle. What can you infer about the conditions of the war based on this photo?

CHAPTER GOALS

In this chapter, you will

- analyze a story within a story.
- determine the theme of a passage and analyze how it is developed.
- determine the meaning of figurative language in a text.

PREVIEW ACADEMIC VOCABULARY

connotation

figurative language

mood

theme

Making Connections

Read the following excerpt from the poem "Dulce et Decorum Est" by Wilfred Owen, a British soldier who fought in World War I. The title refers to a Latin phrase "It is sweet and fitting to die for one's country."

> Bent double, like old beggars under sacks,
>
> Knock-kneed, coughing like hags, we cursed through sludge,
>
> Till on the haunting flares we turned our backs,
>
> And towards our distant rest began to trudge.
>
> Men marched asleep. Many had lost their boots,
>
> But limped on, blood-shod. All went lame; all blind;
>
> Drunk with fatigue; deaf even to the hoots
>
> Of gas-shells dropping softly behind.
>
> Gas! GAS! Quick, boys!—An ecstasy of fumbling
>
> Fitting the clumsy helmets just in time,
>
> But someone still was yelling out and stumbling
>
> And flound'ring like a man in fire or lime.—
>
> Dim through the misty panes and thick green light,
>
> As under a green sea, I saw him drowning.

Which words and phrases best describe what it is like to be a soldier in World War I? Which words best communicate the author's unique voice?

> ### MAKING CONNECTIONS
>
> In this chapter you will read a story about a soldier who fought in World War I.

The second stanza of the poem describes a gas attack. How does the picture on page 380 help you understand what is happening in this stanza?

First Read: Analyzing Parallel Stories

This story is about an artifact from World War I and the importance that artifact has for a family.

Objective: Think about how the author tells the story of Jacko from World War I at the same time as he describes the story of Jacko's family and the journal.

excerpt
Our Jacko
by Michael Morpurgo

My Thoughts

1   Hidden away under more Christmas decorations, my mother had found a large brown envelope. She gave it to my father. He opened it and took something out.

"It's here," he said. "The notebook." He turned to the first

5   page and read out loud: *"This book belongs to Lt. Jack Morris, actor, Shakespeare Memorial Theatre, Stratford-upon-Avon.* That's Our Jacko! It's got a title: *In my mind's eye. Thoughts of home, some poems I know and love."* He turned the notebook over and looked at the back." It says, *To whoever may find*

10   *this, please return it to the theater in Stratford, where I work; or to Ellie, my dear wife, and to Tom, our little son, at Mead Cottage, Charlecote Road, Hampton Lucy. I should be forever grateful. Lt. Jack. Morris, Sherwood Foresters. Ypres, Belgium.* It's his writing, Our Jacko's handwriting, from a hundred years

15   ago," my father said, in a whisper almost.

At that moment, something fell out of the notebook and onto the table. I picked it up. It was a photograph. A young man in uniform stood there, hand resting on a table beside him, stiff and stern, looking at me out of his black-and-white

20   world. Looking me straight in the eye, knowing—I could see it—that he was going to die, that he was telling me so, too. He looked more like a boy dressing up than a soldier.

"Here," my father went on, handing the notebook to Otto, "you read it. It's in pencil. I can't read it too well."

25 Otto began to read in a hushed voice. We all listened.

"June 18, 1915

Dearest Ellie,

I hope one day, when all this is over, to come home and bring this little notebook with me. Should it come home

30 *without me, then you will know forever how much you and little Tom are in my thoughts; you, and the walks we went on down the river, and the poems we loved to read together. I will write nothing of this place or of the war. It is a nightmare that one day I shall wake from and then forget. And if I don't*

35 *wake, then you shall never know. I don't want you ever to know.*

I want only to write of the good times, to see them and you again in my mind's eye; to read them again and again, to remind me that there is goodness and beauty and love in this

40 *world, to remind me of you and of our Tom."*

Otto paused for a moment, and then read on:

"Our first walk together:

In my mind's eye . . . I am walking down through the meadows along the river beyond Half Moon Spinney, where

45 *I walked when I was a boy, where I walked with you, Ellie, where one day you and Tom and I will walk together, and I will pick a buttercup and hold it under his chin to see if he likes butter or pick a dandelion clock and puff on it to tell the time.*

It is best as it is now in the early morning, the cows

50 *wandering legless through the mist. I am alone with them and with birdsong. I am walking where Will Shakespeare walked, where he fished, where he dreamed the dreams of*

his plays and his poems, along the bank where he sat and
wrote, maybe. A kingfisher flew for him, too, and it flew for
55 *us once—do you remember, Ellie? As it flies for me now, in my*
mind's eye. Straight like an arrow on fire out of the mist. And
a heron lifts off, unhurried. Heron, kingfisher, they were both
taught to fish as I was, by their fathers—and mothers—and I
shall teach Tom, when I come home. The river flows slow now,
60 *in gentle eddies, unhurried. She's taking her time. The aspen*
trees are quivering in the breeze. The whole world along the
river trembles with life."

No one spoke, not for a long time. Otto was turning the
pages of the notebook. . . .

65 I had been looking at the photo of Our Jacko all the time
Otto was reading. It was as if I could hear his voice in every
word. I turned the photo over. On the back was written: *Jack*
Morris, my husband, father of Tom, son, actor, soldier. Our
Jacko. Born: September 23, 1892, Stratford. Killed: October 20,
70 *1915, Ypres. He may have no known grave, but he rests in our*
hearts forever.

We then had the most intense family discussion I can ever
remember, about whether I should or should not take it to
school for the exhibit. My father said I could take in the tin
75 hat and the shell case, but that the rest was private and too
precious. I argued that no one had thought the notebook
precious when it had been stuffed away in an old envelope for
years.

It surprised me how adamant my father was about it—but I
80 was even more surprised when Otto piped up in my defense.

"The photo and the notebook may be precious and unique
and irreplaceable," he said, "but they tell Our Jacko's story.
Everyone should know his story."

My Thoughts

World War I helmet

FIRST RESPONSE: KEY IDEAS AND DETAILS

Why does the author tell this story? Write an answer in your response journal. Be sure to use details to support your response, and be ready to defend or explain your answer with the help of those details.

TECH-CONNECT

Post your ideas about the author's purpose to the class website. Include some details that helped you to infer the author's purpose.

Focus on Analyzing Parallel Stories

The excerpt from "Our Jacko" begins with a story about Jacko's ancestors. Then it flashes back to Jacko's experiences during World War I. The author structures the narrative so two parallel stories are being told at the same time. This technique is sometimes called a story-within-a-story. Use the following graphic organizer to analyze the two stories.

Story Element	Jacko	Jacko's Ancestors
Setting		
Characters		
Conflict		

☾Speak and Listen With a partner, discuss the following question:

- How are the two conflicts in the story related?

Summarize your discussion in the space below.

▼**Write** Write a paragraph in which you explain the relationship between the two stories in the excerpt from "Our Jacko."

⌐Second Read: Exploring Theme

Read the story again or listen as your teacher or your classmates read it.

Objective: Underline details and sentences that reveal the theme of the story.

Focus on Exploring Theme

Review the concept of theme by studying the following chart.

What is theme?
Theme
• is the central idea of a story, poem, or other piece of writing.
• can be stated as a sentence that expresses a general, universal truth explored by the author.
• is usually inferred rather than directly stated.
• is supported by the characters, conflict, and resolution.
Theme is NOT
• the topic. Examples: love, friendship, war.
• a summary of what happens.
• the purpose.
• the moral.
• the conflict or problem.

Use the graphic organizer on the following page to help you analyze the theme of this story. Identify details about the characters and the conflict in the text. Then record the theme of the story.

Characters:
Conflict:
Theme:

▼**Write** Write a short paragraph in which you explain and defend your decision about the theme of the passage. Refer to details from the passage that you used to determine the theme.

CONNECT TO ESSENTIAL QUESTION

Why would someone want to prevent historical facts and personal experiences from being shared?

Third Read: Analyzing Figurative Language

In this story, the writer creates the voice (or perspective) of the narrator Jacko by using figurative language. This in turn contributes to the mood of the story.

Objective: As you read the passage a third time, focus on the section that begins "Our first walk together: . . ." in which Jack describes walking by the river with his wife. Think about the author's use of language in this section of the passage.

Focus on Analyzing Figurative Language

Writers use many kinds of figurative language to make their writing come alive.

- **Simile:** Compares two seemingly different things using *like* or *as*: *as fast as the speed of light, bursting on the scene like a tsunami.*

- **Metaphor:** Says that one thing *is* another: *my love for this city is a firmly rooted tree; the general was a cheetah on the prowl.*

- **Personification:** Gives human qualities to nonhuman things: *The leaves danced in the fall breeze. The trees spread their arms and waved away the birds.*

REFLECT

How do you think Jacko would feel about his journal being put on display?

continued on next page

Authors generally use figurative language to create the emotional mood of their writing. Mood is the feeling that a work of literature creates in the reader. Some words create strong emotional impressions. The emotional impression of a word or phrase is also called *connotation*.

Fill in the following graphic organizer, identifying three examples of figurative language from "Our Jacko," what they mean, and what effect they achieve through their connotation.

Figurative Language	Meaning	Emotional Effect

(**Speak and Listen** With a partner, review your answers to the graphic organizer. Based on your answers, what is the mood of the story?

▼**Write** Write a paragraph describing how the figurative language in the passage creates an overall mood. Use your examples from the organizer above as support for your conclusions.

REFLECT

If the emotional effect of the writing in the journal had been different, would the family have been more likely to share the journal?

Language: Word Meanings

Writers have one main tool to help them communicate their ideas to readers—words. Words may be used in a number of ways, some more subtle or imaginative than others. The chart below contains some tips about word relationships and nuances of meaning. Understanding the uses of language will make you a better reader and writer.

Word Relationships	
Two words that mean the same thing are called *synonyms*.	*wild* and *feral* *tired* and *weary*
Two words that have opposite meanings are called *antonyms*.	*dim* and *bright* *polite* and *rude*
An analogy uses a comparison to communicate a relationship or to explain complex ideas.	*I am to this town what Hadrian was to his wall: a builder.*
Nuanced Meanings	

Words have a *denotation* (dictionary definition) and a *connotation* (positive or negative association). Writers choose words with connotations that fit their point of view and influence the reader. Consider the difference between a *cheap trinket* and an *inexpensive figurine*. Which phrase paints the object in a more positive light?

Which of the following words communicates a greater degree of anger?

His racist comments <u>bothered</u> me.

His racist comments <u>infuriated</u> me.

Choose words that fit the nuanced meaning you want to communicate.

Read the sentences below, all of which contain examples of figurative language. Answer the questions after each sentence.

1. After wandering around for several hours, we came to the movie theater, only to find that it was completely empty. Rewrite the sentence with an antonym for *empty?*

What different impression does the sentence give?

2. The <u>disobedient</u> child was <u>disciplined</u> by the teacher.
   What are the connotations or nuanced meanings of the
   underlined words in the sentence?

Rewrite the sentence, replacing the underlined words to give
the sentence a different connotation.

3. Explain the following analogy from J. K. Rowling:
   "Longbottom, if brains were gold, you'd be poorer than
   Weasley, and that's saying something."

Project-Based Assessments

Letter

Write a letter from the narrator of the story to Jacko. The letter
should describe the narrator's feelings about Jacko's bravery, as
well as his happiness to have Jacko's notebook. Include questions
that the narrator might want to ask Jacko. The letter could tell
something about life in the present day, as well.

Begin by conducting research on WWI so that you can
ask appropriate questions in your letter. When searching for
information to add to your letter, use search terms such as *World
War I* and *Ypres*. You can also search for other details from Jacko's
story, such as *Stratford-upon-Avon*.

Next, write a letter that has at least three paragraphs, each
exploring a different topic or question.

As you edit your letter, review the rubric on the next page so
that you will know what is expected of you.

Use the following guidelines for your letter.	
To receive the highest score, the letter must meet all of these criteria.	Your letter • contains examples and details that show that you understand the characters in the original story. • includes questions to Jacko about the war and his experiences. • is logically organized and formatted as a letter. • uses correct grammar, word usage, punctuation, and spelling.

Oral Presentation

Imagine you are the narrator of the story and must give a presentation about Jacko and World War I in class. Write a presentation that explains who the notebook belonged to, why the notebook was returned to the narrator's family, and what the notebook means to the narrator. Base your presentation on the story and fill in missing details as needed.

When developing the presentation, stay focused on the subject. Your goal is to teach fellow students about World War I as well as describing the notebook and the life events associated with it.

Include visual aids, such as pictures of soldiers and artillery. Make sure your pictures are appropriate and not overly graphic.

Practice your presentation so that you can speak confidently. Use note cards as needed, but make eye contact with your audience.

Use the following guidelines for your presentation.	
To receive the highest score, the letter must meet all of these criteria.	Your presentation • contains examples and details that show that you understand the original story and where the narrator fits in it. • includes visual aids that help your audience understand your subject. • is presented in a professional manner that demonstrates adequate preparation. • uses correct grammar, word usage, punctuation, and spelling.

On Your Own: Integrating Ideas

1. Read a first person account by a soldier who served in World War I, preferably at Ypres. What do you learn from this account that the story doesn't necessarily tell you?
2. Find other letters written by World War I soldiers to their families. What do these letters tell you about the war?
3. Read poetry written by soldiers who fought in WWI. A good resource is warpoetry.co.uk. Share your favorite with your classmates.

Connect to Testing

Questions on reading tests may ask you to analyze the structure of a story, identify theme, and analyze the effects of figurative language. Often a second part of the question will test your ability to find textual evidence that supports the correct inference. Answer the following questions.

1. **Part A:** Based on the passage, what would you most likely infer about the narrator's father?

    A. He is possessive of his personal items.

    B. He respects and honors Jacko.

    C. He prefers to get his own way in family conflicts.

    D. He doesn't like the narrator's school assignment.

    Part B: Which of the following lines from the excerpt best supports the answer to Part A? Choose two.

    A. *It's his writing, Our Jacko's handwriting, from a hundred years ago," my father said, in a whisper almost.*

    B. *I will write nothing of this place or of the war. It is a nightmare that one day I shall wake from and then forget.*

    C. *It was as if I could hear his voice in every word. I turned the photo over. On the back was written:* Jack Morris, my husband, father of Tom, son, actor, soldier.

    D. *We then had the most intense family discussion I can ever remember, about what I should or should not take it to school for the exhibit.*

    E. *My father said I could take in the tin hat and the shell case, but that the rest was private and too precious.*

2. Which of the following best describes the theme of the story?

    A. Stories from the past should be shared with future generations.

    B. Love rises above all earthly conflicts.

    C. Loyalty to one's country is the greatest virtue.

    D. At times one must have courage when courage seems impossible.

3. **Part A:** Jacko's journal is used as a

    A. record of wartime events.

    B. notebook to keep his poems and writings in.

    C. list of things he wanted to do when he got home.

    D. way to focus on the people he loved.

Part B: Which of the following lines from the excerpt best support the answer to Part A? Choose two.

A. *I hope one day, when all this is over, to come home and bring this little notebook with me.*

B. *you will know forever how much you and little Tom are in my thoughts; you, and the walks we went on down the river, and the poems we loved to read together.*

C. *I want only to write of the good times, to see them and you again in my mind's eye . . .*

D. *It is best as it is now in the early morning, the cows wandering legless through the mist . . .*

E. *The aspen trees are quivering in the breeze. The whole world along the river trembles with life.*

4. Describe the relationship between the two stories in the excerpt. How does one story affect the other? Refer to details from the text to support your answer.

Chapter 19

Analyzing an Author's Portrayal of War

Preview Concepts

Irony is a literary term that has to do with a difference between expectations and reality. One type of irony is dramatic irony. Dramatic irony is a difference between what the reader or audience knows and what one or more of the characters know. Dramatic irony can add suspense or humor to a story.

Suppose you are watching a sit-com in which Jack and Maggie are sitting in Maggie's apartment. They kiss. Suddenly there is a knock on the door. It's Emma, Jack's girlfriend! Jack hides in the bathroom. Emma comes in. Upset, she tells Maggie that she thinks Jack is cheating on her. Maggie reassures Emma that Jack is faithful. Emma then goes into detail about what a great friend Maggie is as Maggie tries to come up with supportive answers.

With a partner, discuss how this is an example of dramatic irony. What does the audience know that Emma doesn't know?

What emotions does this create in the viewer?

Can you think of any other examples of dramatic irony from books, memes, or movies?

CHAPTER GOALS

In this chapter, you will

- make inferences about characters.
- analyze how setting affects characters and conflicts.
- compare characters' points of view.
- understand the impact of humor and dramatic irony.

PREVIEW ACADEMIC VOCABULARY

appositive phrase

dramatic irony

point of view

prepositional phrase

verbal phrases

Making Connections

Read the following excerpt from Lyndon Baines Johnson's speech about the Vietnam War from April 7, 1965.

Why are we in South Vietnam?

We are there because we have a promise to keep. Since 1954 every American president has offered support to the people of South Vietnam. We have helped to build, and we have helped to defend. Thus, over many years, we have made a national pledge to help South Vietnam defend its independence.

And I intend to keep that promise.

To dishonor that pledge, to abandon this small and brave nation to its enemies, and to the terror that must follow, would be an unforgivable wrong.

With a partner, discuss the following questions.

1. How does Johnson answer the question about why America is fighting in Vietnam?

2. What do you know about the Vietnam War based on what you've seen and read?

> **MAKING CONNECTIONS**
>
> In this chapter you will read a story about African American soldiers in the Vietnam War and analyze their points of view of the war.

First Read: Analyzing the Impact of Setting on Conflict

The Vietnam War was a long, drawn-out conflict that started in 1954 and ended in 1975. The United States was slowly drawn into the war between communist North Vietnam and anti-Communists in South Vietnam.

This story describes fighting in 1968 Vietnam, from the point of view of Richie Perry, an African American teen. Unable to afford college, Perry enlists in the army and is sent to Vietnam where he befriends Peewee, another African American teen.

Objective: As you read, identify details about the setting. Think about how the author reveals details about what it is like to fight in Vietnam.

excerpt

Fallen Angels

by Walter Dean Myers

My Thoughts

1   Saturday. My ninth day in country. The army paper *Stars and Stripes* was full of the truce talks in Paris, but the war was still going on. In the distance F-100's streaked across the sky. I saw a lot of planes, mostly jets and helicopters, and all ours. I didn't

5   see any enemy planes. I didn't even know If they had any. . . .

I was less nervous than I was when I first got in country. We were in Nam to stop the North Vietnamese from taking over South Vietnam. I didn't feel really gung ho or anything, but I was ready to do my part.

10   One of the new guys who came in was from **Fort Dix**. He looked like one of the characters from an **Archie Andrews comic**, but he was so scared it wasn't funny. He told us his name was Jenkins.

"What's it like so far?" he asked Peewee.

15   "Ain't nothing to it," Peewee said.

"You been here long?" Jenkins asked.

Fort Dix: an Army training base in New Jersey
Archie Andrews comic: a popular comic strip during the 1950s and 1960s

"Eight months," Peewee lied. "I got to kill eight more Cong before I get my quota. Then I can go home."

20 "How many you kill so far?"

"A hundred and thirty-two," Peewee said. "I weigh a hundred and forty. Whatever you weigh, that's how many you got to kill to leave early."

"I never heard of that," Jenkins said.

25 "That ain't for regular rotation," Peewee went on. "That's just so you can leave early."

"Oh." Jenkins took it all in.

"Air force guys can get their quota in one or two days," Peewee said.

30 "What did you do, machine gun most of them?" Jenkins' eyes were wide.

"No, man," Peewee shook his head. "They issue you so many bullets per week, see? But each one you turn back in you get a quarter for. So mostly I sneak up on the suckers and cut their

35 throats. That way I save my bullets. Way I figure, by the time I get back to the World I have me enough to buy a little Chevy."

"None of that is true," Jenkins said. He was pissed at Peewee for pulling his leg.

The sergeant came in and picked three guys for guard

40 duty. The ranger volunteered again, and they got Jenkins and one other guy. Jenkins was shaking when he left the **hooch**.

"Don't forget to save your bullets!" Peewee called out to him.

That night the mosquitoes ate us up. I had bites all over my body. Back home I thought mosquitoes never bit black people.

45 Not as much as they bit white people, anyway. Maybe Vietnamese mosquitoes just bit blacks and whites and didn't bite Asians.

_____

hooch: small huts used to house soldiers

We finally got the orientation lecture. This young-looking lieutenant showed us a slide of a map of Nam. Then he showed us where we were.

50   "You are not in Disneyland," he said. "The little people you see running around over here are not **Mouseketeers**. Some of them are friendly, and some of them have a strong desire to kill you. If you remember that, and manage to kill them before they kill you, then you have a good chance of getting through

55   your year of service here.

    "Take your pills. Once a week for **malaria**, twice a week if you're too stupid to remember the day you last took them. . . .

    "Stay away from the **black market**. Anything you buy that's worth a damn will be taken away from you, or you'll

60   lose it.

    "Stay away from dope. There's only two kinds of people in Nam. People who are alert twenty-four hours a day, and people who are dead.

    "If you see anything else they got over here that we don't

65   have at home, stay away from it. What these people use on a daily basis will kill you as fast as an RPG."

    "What's an RPG?" a guy in the front asked.

    "That's a rocket-propelled grenade. Stay away from them, too. If you have any more questions, ask your unit commanders

70   when you reach them. Good luck."

    When we got outside, the mosquitoes got us. The lieutenant hadn't even mentioned them, but we had been given a supply of insect **repellent**.

Mouseketeers: actors on a television show centered around the famous cartoon character Mickey Mouse, popular in the 1950s and 1960s
malaria: a disease transmitted by the bite of a mosquito
black market: illegal trading of goods that are not allowed to be bought and sold
repellent: bug spray

My Thoughts

Orders. Me, Peewee, Jenkins, and another guy were
75   assigned to the 196th. We were going to Chu Lai. I
remembered that was where Judy Duncan was assigned.

"What's that like?" Jenkins asked the sergeant in
headquarters.

"That's First Corps," the sergeant said. "All you do up there
80   is look around for charlie, and when you see him you call the
marines. Light stuff."

"Charlie?" Jenkins looked toward me and Peewee.

"Charlie is the bad guy over here." The sergeant put his
arm around Jenkins' shoulders. He was obviously enjoying
85   himself. "Sometimes we call him charlie, sometimes we call him
Victor Charlie, sometimes we call him Vietcong. That is, unless
he sends us his business card with his full name and address
on it."

We packed our gear and lined up outside, waiting for the
90   truck to the airport. We were going to Chu Lai in a C-47. I
thought guys from other hooches were going, but there were
only the four of us.

"I bet I kill me a Cong before you get one," Peewee said.

"You can have them all," I said. . . .

95   Peewee didn't say much after that and neither did I. I was
scared. My mouth was going dry, and I could see that Peewee
was scared, too. Jenkins was crying. It made me feel a little
better to see him crying like that.

"Load 'em up!"

100   Me and Peewee got on the trucks between boxes of
peanut butter, and started to the airport and to wherever the
hell Chu Lai was.

My Thoughts

FIRST RESPONSE: KEY IDEAS AND DETAILS

Write a sentence that describes the narrator Perry's point of view of the war. Write your answer in your response journal. Include evidence from the passage that supports your inference.

TECH-CONNECT

Post your answer to the First Response question to your class website. Read two of your classmate's answers and comment positively on them.

Focus on Analyzing the Impact of Setting on Conflict

For many novels, especially historical fiction, the setting directly impacts the conflict faced by the characters. In this excerpt, the author doesn't go into great detail about the setting. The reader must infer what war-torn Vietnam is like based on what characters say and do.

1. What can you infer about the setting from the narrator's thoughts and feelings?

2. What can you infer about the setting from the orientation lecture given by the lieutenant?

3. Based on what you learn about the setting, describe the conflicts that result. Use the following types of conflict to help you.
   person vs. person—

person vs. nature—

person vs. self—

▼**Write** Summarize what it is like to fight in the Vietnam War based on the excerpt. Explain how the setting results in multiple conflicts.

Second Read: Making Inferences About Characters

With your class or a small group of students, read the text aloud assigning the parts of Perry (the narrator), Peewee, Jenkins, the lieutenant, and the sergeant.

Objective: As you read the passage, make inferences about how each character views the war and how it affects his interactions with other characters. Write your inferences in the My Thoughts sidebar. Underline evidence that supports your inferences.

Focus on Making Inferences About Characters

This excerpt reveals much about the main characters, Perry, Peewee, Jenkins, the lieutenant, and the sergeant, and their points of view of the Vietnam War.

Myers keeps his description of the characters to a minimum. Instead, he allows the readers to understand what the characters are like based on how they interact with each other. Fill in the following chart to help you analyze the characters in the story. For Perry, Peewee, and Jenkins, fill in **three** examples of what each says/does and **three** explanations of what each is like. For the lieutenant and sergeant, fill in **one** example and **one** explanation.

continued on next page

Character	What he says/does How he interacts with other characters	What is he like?	What is his point of view of the war?
Perry	1. "I was less nervous than I was when I first got in country. . . . I didn't feel really gung ho or anything, but I was ready to do my part." 2.	1. He is unsure but willing to fight.	
Peewee			
Jenkins	1. "I was less nervous than I was when I first got in country. . . .		

Character	What he says/does How he interacts with other characters	What is he like?	What is his point of view of the war?
the lieutenant			
the sergeant			

Speak and Listen Share your answers to the chart with a partner. Discuss the following questions:

- Do any of the characters change from the beginning to the end of the excerpt? Why?

- What does this change reveal about the characters?

Third Read: Analyzing Author's Use of Humor

Read the excerpt a third time.

Objective: Think about how the author uses humor in a situation that is usually not humorous. Label examples with the word **humor**.

Focus on Analyzing Author's Use of Humor

The interaction between the characters in the excerpt results in some humorous moments. Identify three humorous interactions between the characters on the next page.

continued on next page

Examples of humor:

1.

2.

3.

4. *Dramatic irony* is a literary device in which the reader
knows something that one or more of the characters don't
know. Are any of the examples of humor above examples
of dramatic irony? Explain what you know that one of the
characters doesn't know.

5. Most of the humor is at the expense of Jenkins. How do you as a reader feel about the other soldiers' treatment of Jenkins?

6. Why do you think Jenkins is the target of humor? What does it reveal about Peewee and the sergeant?

Speak and Listen With a partner discuss what effect the addition of humor has on the readers' experience of the passage. Also consider what the use of humor reveals about the personalities of the characters. Summarize your explanation in your response journal. Share your summary with the rest of the class.

Language: Using Phrases Effectively

To communicate effectively and specifically, writers use phrases and clauses. Study the following explanations and examples of commonly used phrases.

A *phrase* is a group of related words that do not contain a subject and a verb.

Here are several different types of phrases.

prepositional phrases: begin with a preposition and end with an object

Examples: in the end, up the stairs, after the storm

appositive phrases: renames or gives more information about a noun, often includes a noun and any modifiers.

Examples: Natalia, the girl standing over there, is my sister.

Somalia, a country on the coast of east Africa, is experiencing a severe famine.

verbal phrases: look like verbs but act like adjectives or nouns. Gerund and participial phrases can end in *–ing* or *–ed*; infinitive phrases begin with *to*.

Examples: KJ's goal is to become a doctor. (Infinitive phrase)

---

continued on next page

Working around the clock, the firefighters finally put out the fire. (Participial phrase)

In my free time I enjoy playing video games. (Gerund phrase)

Punctuation with phrases: Commas are often used to set off phrases.

Use a single comma with an introductory verbal phrase or with prepositional phrases of four or more words at the beginning of a sentence.

Examples: By the end of the war, he was sick of fighting.

Swimming with all her might, she finally reached the shore.

Use a pair of commas to set off phrases that fall in the middle of a sentence.

Examples: The pond, frozen over since early December, is now safe for ice-skating.

My teacher, a fine pianist, spent the summer traveling with a jazz band.

Incorrect use of commas: Do not set off phrases used as the subject of a sentence.

Incorrect: To eat dinner together, was her plan.

Incorrect: Swimming in the lake, is my favorite summer activity.

Write sentences using the following phrases correctly. Add commas as needed.

1. Use the phrase *talking on the phone* as the subject of a sentence.

2. Write a sentence with a prepositional phrase at the beginning of the sentence.

3. Use the phrase *my favorite television show* as an appositive.

4. Use the phrase *covered in mud and soaking wet* at the beginning of a sentence.

Project-Based Assessments

Diary

   Imagine what a diary by one of the soldiers depicted in the passage would be like. Would it be Perkins's diary, full of fear and concern? Or would it be the tough sergeant's diary, a record of goals achieved and milestones met? Write a diary entry as you imagine one of the soldiers writing it, using details from the passage and from your own research as needed. For example, you might read some other accounts of the Vietnam War written by young people who fought.

   When you're writing the diary entry, capture the character's style of writing based on what you infer about his personality from the excerpt. Although you want the writing to be realistic, follow your teacher's guidelines for appropriateness.

Use the following guidelines for your diary.	
To receive the highest score, the letter must meet all of these criteria.	Your diary • presents information in a way that grabs the reader's attention. • is faithful to character's voice and personality as based on the excerpt. • follows the style and format of a diary. • uses correct grammar, word usage, punctuation, and spelling.

Personal Interview

   Interview a family member or friend who fought in the Vietnam War or another war or conflict.

   Before you interview the person, prepare 7 to 10 questions to guide the conversation. As the discussion progresses, ask other questions as you think of them. Use an app and your phone to record the conversation or take good notes so you can remember the details later when you write.

continued on next page

After your interview, write a summary of the interview. Begin by introducing the interviewee. Next, include the questions you asked the interviewee and his or her responses. However, do not merely copy down the person's words. Paraphrase the responses to your questions and also use direct quotations—especially when what the interviewee said represents his or her personality or is unique. Edit out information that isn't to the point.

Use the following guidelines for your interview.	
To receive the highest score, the interview must meet all of these criteria.	Your interview • includes 7 to 10 questions. • summarizes the interviewee's answers. • includes good direct quotations and paraphrases of answers. • uses correct grammar, word usage, punctuation, and spelling.

On Your Own: Integrating Ideas

1. Read the rest of the book *Fallen Angels* by Walter Dean Myers. Check out Myers' website for information about his companion books on war, including *Invasion* (WWII) and *Sunrise Over Fallujah* (Iraq War).

2. Research the Vietnam War from a Vietnamese perspective. In the story, the sergeant says some of the locals are friendly. Is this based on fact? What were the attitudes of the local residents in Vietnamese villages toward U.S. soldiers?

3. Consider how "The Drummer Boy of Shiloh" and *Fallen Angels* deal with the effects of war on young people. Use evidence from both stories to infer similar themes. Share these themes in a online post or in a class discussion.

4. With a small group, discuss the following quotation from Walter Dean Myers:

"Memories of wars fade away, even from those who fought in them. In interviewing WWII vets for *Invasion*, I could see how often films, newspaper accounts, and documentaries influence the recollection of actual events. Heroes are created decades after the events, and stories are retold to fit the mood of the country. The human elements are often lost because they don't fit the shifting momentums of the times. Books like *Fallen Angels* help to counter this trend."

Connect to Testing

In this chapter you practiced analyzing setting and conflict, inferring characterization, and analyzing the author's use of humor. For these skills, questions on reading tests may look like the following.

1. Read the following paragraph.

> I was less nervous than I was when I first got in country. We were in Nam to stop the North Vietnamese from taking over South Vietnam. I didn't feel really gung ho or anything, but I was ready to do my part.
>
> One of the new guys who came in was from Fort Dix. He looked like one of the characters from an Archie Andrews comic, but he was so scared it wasn't funny. He told us his name was Jenkins.

Part A: How does Jenkins' point of view differ from the narrator's point of view?

A. Jenkins is shy, while the narrator wants to get to work.

B. Jenkins is very timid, while the narrator is more confident.

C. Jenkins is suspicious, while the narrator is more trusting.

D. Jenkins is concerned about combat, while the narrator is excited about it.

Part B: Which of the following provide the strongest evidence for the answer to Part A? Choose three.

A. *I was less nervous than I was when I first got in country.*

B. *We were in Nam to stop the North Vietnamese from taking over South Vietnam.*

C. *I didn't feel really gung ho or anything, but I was ready to do my part.*

D. *He looked like one of the characters from an Archie Andrews comic*

E. *but he was so scared it wasn't funny.*

F. *He told us his name was Jenkins.*

Read the following excerpt from the lieutenant's orientation speech.

> "You are not in Disneyland," he said. "The little people you see running around over here are not Mouseketeers."

2. The lieutenant says this to the new recruits in order to

A. encourage them that Vietnam is an innocent, harmless place for recreation.

B. make fun of the Vietnamese and their culture.

C. give them confidence that they are fighting an important war.

D. warn them that war is not a thrilling adventure.

continued on next page

3. **Part A:** How does the sergeant's point of view differ from the narrator's point of view?

   A. The sergeant is bored by his job, while the narrator is new to it.

   B. The sergeant is nervous about the upcoming battle, while the narrator is unconcerned.

   C. The sergeant is tough and worldly, while the narrator is more naïve.

   D. The sergeant distrusts the soldiers, while the narrator has respect for them.

Part B: Provide evidence from the text to support the answer to Part A.

4. Explain two places where Myers uses humor in his writing. Is humor expected or unexpected? Why does Myers include humor? Write a paragraph in which you answer these questions.

Chapter 20

Analyzing the Format of a Play

Preview Concepts

Read the following excerpt. Then answer the questions to help you understand the purpose of unique features of this text.

> (AT RISE: *Elizabeth stands at downstage center. If lighting is used, she stands in a spotlight. She's in her 20s and shows great determination, intelligence, and impatience. She speaks directly to the audience.*)
>
> ELIZABETH: I'm not sure exactly when I decided to become a doctor. I only know it happened. Even before I could put it into words!
>
> Maybe it was when I walked with my father around the town. I saw raggedy children with their runny noses, fever blisters, and open sores. . . .
>
> (WOMAN 1, WOMAN 2, MAN 1, *and* MAN 2 *enter stage right and left, pointing at* ELIZABETH.)
>
> WOMAN 1: Have you heard? *She* wants to be a doctor!
>
> WOMAN 2: But she's a woman!
>
> MAN 1: Women can't be doctors!
>
> ELIZABETH: (*Confronting them*) Why?
>
> WOMAN 1: (*Using a mocking tone*) Why?
>
> WOMAN 2: (*Using a mocking tone*) Why?
>
> MAN 1: (*Using a mocking tone*) Why?
>
> MAN 2: Why? Because women aren't fit to be doctors!

1. Based on the structure of the excerpt, what type of literature is this?

CHAPTER GOALS

In this chapter you will

- analyze the theme of a play.
- analyze how the format and structure of a play help to communicate theme.
- identify dramatic techniques used in a scene.
- analyze the purpose of a scene within a longer play.

PREVIEW ACADEMIC VOCABULARY

aside

chorus

conflict

dialogue

domain-specific words

monologue

multiple-meaning words

narrator

theme

2. Why are some lines in parentheses?

3. Why are the lines (*Using a mocking tone*) especially important for understanding the interaction between the characters?

4. What can you infer about the setting? Support your inference with evidence.

Discuss your answers to the questions above with a partner.

Making Connections

Read the following entry about Elizabeth Blackwell from an online biographical encyclopedia:

> Elizabeth Blackwell was born on February 3, 1821, in Bristol, England. As a girl, she moved with her family to the United States, where she first worked as a teacher. Despite widespread opposition, she later decided to attend medical college and graduated first in her class, thus also becoming the first woman to receive her M.D. in the United States. She created a medical school for women in the late 1860s, eventually returning to England and setting up a private practice. Blackwell died on May 31, 1910, in Hastings.

MAKING CONNECTIONS

In this chapter you will read and analyze the theme and format of a play about the life of Elizabeth Blackwell.

First Read: Determining Theme

This is an excerpt from a play about the life of Elizabeth Blackwell (1821–1910), who was the first woman in the United States to earn a medical degree. As you read, remember that it is meant to be experienced as a performance on stage. Pay attention to special features like stage directions. Visualize the action as if you were watching the play onstage.

Objective: As you read, underline repeated ideas that help you understand the theme of this scene.

Elizabeth Blackwell
by Cynthia Mercati

My Thoughts

1   **ELIZABETH:** Father was a very unusual man! He believed completely in the equality of people. A very strange idea for the time!

MR. BLACKWELL: (*Stepping forward and speaking to the*
5   *audience*) All human beings—black, white, men, women, rich, and poor—should have the same rights!

(*AUNT BARBARA steps forward to speak to her brother. She's a very proper and prissy lady like the other aunts.*)

AUNT BARBARA: You couldn't mean that women should
10   have the same rights as men!

THREE AUNTS: Indeed he couldn't!

MR. BLACKWELL: I certainly do! That's why I've decided to hire a **governess** for my daughters!

(*MRS. BLACKWELL steps forward. She's quieter than her*
15   *husband and daughter.*)

MRS. BLACKWELL: But, husband dear, our house is already bursting at the seams! How will we fit in one more person?!

MR. BLACKWELL: We'll just have to try! The governess will teach our girls the same subjects the boys are learning in public
20   school.

governess: a woman who takes responsibility for the care and sometimes the education of children in wealthy households

MRS. BLACKWELL: (*With mild protest*) But, husband dear. What will they do with such knowledge?

MR. BLACKWELL: They'll do all sorts of interesting things. Just like their brothers! (*He beckons to ANNA to stand next to*
25 *him.*) Anna, what do you want to be when you grow up?

ANNA: A writer!

MR. BLACKWELL: Excellent!

(*ANNA returns upstage. MR. BLACKWELL indicates for MARIAN to join him.*)

30 Marian, what do you want to be?

MARIAN: A composer of music.

MR. BLACKWELL: Wonderful!

(*MARIAN returns upstage. MR. BLACKWELL turns to ELIZABETH.*) Elizabeth?

35 (*ELIZABETH steps forward. She is a very young girl now.*)

MRS. BLACKWELL: Husband! Elizabeth is far too young to have any idea what she wants to be.

(*MRS. BLACKWELL and everyone except ELIZABETH and MR. BLACKWELL exit stage left as ELIZABETH answers.*)

40 **ELIZABETH:** I know I want to be something great, Papa!

MR. BLACKWELL: I believe you will, Elizabeth! There's a special determination about you. A special spark.

ELIZABETH: (*With a dreamy enthusiasm*) I can see myself on a big, white horse, leading a charge into battle! Or painting
45 a famous picture! Or . . . or . . . making a big, important speech while thousands of people cheer!

MAN 1: (*Entering stage left*) As if women could say anything important!

MAN 2: (*Entering stage right*) As if women could do
50 anything important!

My Thoughts

_____

(MR. BLACKWELL puts his hands on ELIZABETH's shoulders.)

MR. BLACKWELL: *(Speaking seriously)* Never forget, child. The greatest thing in life is to find a cause you believe in and fight for it!

55   **ELIZABETH:** *(To the audience)* Father works for all kinds of causes.

WOMAN 1 and WOMAN 2: *(Entering stage left and stage right)* I'll say he does!

(MR. BLACKWELL speaks to the audience as if giving a
60   *speech. The WOMEN and MEN become very angry.)*

MR. BLACKWELL: I work to end slavery!

MAN 1: Slave trade is my business. How dare you try to stop it!

MR. BLACKWELL: I work to end child labor! It's criminal
65   that children five and six years old are made to work 14 hours a day in coal mines and factories.

MAN 2: I can save all kinds of money using those children in my mine. I don't have to pay them half of what I pay adults!

MR. BLACKWELL: Everyone is entitled to earn a decent
70   living!

WOMAN 1: Stop your **jabbering** about decent wages. You'll take away some of the profits from my husband's cloth factory.

MR. BLACKWELL: Good!

WOMAN 2: Mr. Blackwell also wants to make our hospitals
75   cleaner and better run!

MAN 2: And he wants to raise our taxes to do it!

ELIZABETH: *(Proudly)* My father believes that women should be free and equal citizens. They should not be considered just the property of their husbands!

---

jabbering: to talk rapidly or unintelligibly

80   **MAN 1 and MAN 2:** Balderdash!

     MAN 1: Mr. Blackwell, you are a **crackpot**!

     ELIZABETH: How dare you say such things about my

father! He's a very great man!

     MAN 2: He's crazy as a loon!

85   *(Marching determinedly to MAN 2, ELIZABETH gives him a*

kick in the leg.)

     ELIZABETH: You take that back!

     (Quickly, MR. BLACKWELL restrains his daughter.)

     MR. BLACKWELL: It's all right, Elizabeth. When you

90   have new and different ideas, you're likely to take a lot of

punishment! *(with conviction)* But the important thing is not

to let the criticism bother you. Just keep on working for what

you believe.

     (MR. BLACKWELL exits stage right. The people on stage

95   *speak to ELIZABETH quickly and firmly. They take a step closer*

to her with every word. They soon surround her.)

     MAN 1: You better forget what he said, Elizabeth

Blackwell! The world doesn't work that way!

     MAN 2: Not for women!

100   **ELIZABETH:** *(Crossing down stage center, she folds her*

arms and looks forward.) I'm not listening to you!

     MR. BLACKWELL: *(Peeking out stage right to give this one*

line) That's the spirit, Elizabeth!

---

crackpot: an irrational and unreliable person, likely to say absurd things

FIRST RESPONSE: KEY IDEAS AND DETAILS

What is the central conflict of this scene from the play? Write
your response in your response journal.

TECH-CONNECT

Share your response
on your class website
or tweet your answer
to your teacher.

Focus on Determining Theme

Determining the theme of a play is similar to determining the theme of a story or novel. Earlier in this chapter you analyzed the theme of a short story. Use the same steps to analyze the theme of this scene from a play. Use the following graphic organizer to record important details about the characters, conflict, and repeated ideas. Finally, determine the theme of the play and write it in the final row.

Characters:
Conflict:
Repeated Ideas:
Theme:

▼ **Write** Write a paragraph that explains the theme of the excerpt. Support your conclusions with details about the characters, conflict, and repeated ideas from the text.

☾ **Speak and Listen** Read a partner's paragraph explaining the theme of the scene. Does your partner's theme meet the following characteristics? If not, offer specific suggestions for improvement.

continued on next page

A theme
- is the central idea of a story, poem, or other piece of writing.
- is stated as a sentence that expresses a general, universal truth explored by the author.
- is supported by the characters, conflict, and repeated ideas.

Second Read: Analyzing the Unique Format of a Play

This time read the play as a class. Assign the following parts to members of the class.

Elizabeth	Mr. Blackwell	Aunt Barbara	Aunt 2	Man 1	Woman 1
Aunt 3	Mrs. Blackwell	Anna	Marian	Man 2	Woman 2

Perform the play. Follow the stage directions that indicate where to move on stage and when to enter and exit. Read the parts with expression, paying attention to the directions that explain characterization. Try to match the sound of your voice to the age and personality of the character.

Objective: What is the purpose of the groups of aunts, of men, and of women? Why does the playwright include them? Write your observations in the My Thoughts Column.

Focus on Analyzing the Unique Format of a Play

Watching a play is a different experience from reading a book. Although this play is based on a real person, the author's goal is not to communicate with accuracy all of the factual details of Blackwell's life. Instead, she creatively portrays elements of Elizabeth's relationship with her father.

Drama uses a unique form and structure in which to communicate ideas. Think of a play as a relationship between the actors on stage and the audience.

Invisible Fourth Wall

Often the actors perform a story as if no one is watching. It's as if the action on stage is taking place in a room with four walls. The fourth wall that separates the actors on stage from the audience is invisible. The audience can see everything happening on stage, but the actors are unaware that the audience is there. There is no interaction between the audience and the actors on stage.

Aside

Some plays include a narrator who speaks to the audience about what is happening on stage. The narrator may just be someone who talks about the events. Or the narrator may be one of the characters who interacts with other characters and then steps out of the action to talk to the audience. Many times, no other characters hear what the character/narrator is saying. When a narrator or a character breaks out of the story to talk directly to the audience, it is called an *aside*. It is also called *breaking the fourth wall*.

Chorus

When a group of actors speaks together commenting on a character's actions or motivations, it is called a *chorus*. Use of a chorus of actors dates back to ancient Greek theater when a group of actors in masks would provide narration and explain transitions between scenes. Today, playwrights use a chorus creatively. Sometimes the chorus speaks in unison; other times individual members speak. This adds variety and interest to the scene.

Here are some common dramatic techniques used in plays.

- **narrator**—one or more actors speak directly to the audience to tell a story or give information about a scene. A character may be the narrator or a performer who is not involved in the action may be the narrator.

- **dialogue**—conversation between characters in a play

- **monologue**—a character speaks his thoughts aloud to another character or the audience

- **aside**—a short remark made by a character to the audience. No other characters hear this comment.

- **chorus**—group of actors that speak together in a play.

Think about the techniques the playwright uses to emphasize the theme of the work. Identify these techniques using the graphic organizer here and on the next page.

Element in the Play	Example from the Play (Include line numbers)	What effect does this have? Why does the playwright use this dramatic technique?
Elizabeth—narrates the play and steps into the action to play herself		

continued on next page

Element in the Play	Example from the Play (Include line numbers)	What effect does this have? Why does the playwright use this dramatic technique?
Use of a chorus—aunts, man 1 & 2, and woman 1 & 2		
Elizabeth—speaks directly to the audience		
Dialogue between characters		

1. Where does the chorus of the men and women speak together or say similar things? Cite line numbers.

2. What ideas do all of the lines of the men and women have in common?

3. What can you infer about the purpose of the chorus in this scene?

TECH-CONNECT

To help you answer the questions in the Speak and Listen activity, have each group member find a different biography of Elizabeth Blackwell from an online source. Focus on information about Blackwell's father and her early upbringing. Have each member read aloud from a different biography.

Speak and Listen With a small group, share your answers to the chart and the questions above. Then discuss the following questions:

- In what ways is reading/watching a play different from reading a biography of Elizabeth Blackwell?

- Which do you prefer? Why?

Third Read: Analyzing the Purpose of a Scene

Read the text a third time with a small group of classmates. Assign each group member parts to read.

Objective: Based on the theme of this scene, what purpose does this part play in the entire scope of Elizabeth Blackwell's life story?

Focus on Analyzing the Purpose of a Scene

This scene captures just a small part of the entire one-act play about Elizabeth Blackwell. As you know, Elizabeth Blackwell goes on to become the first woman to graduate from medical school in the United States. She was a pioneer in promoting women's advancement in the medical field in the United States and in the United Kingdom. Her entire life was spent proving that women are intelligent and capable of pursing any career opportunity they desire.

Read the flow chart on the next page. Then write a summary of the scene in the empty box in the flow chart to show how the scene fits into the story of Elizabeth Blackwell's life.

continued on next page

Life of Elizabeth Blackwell

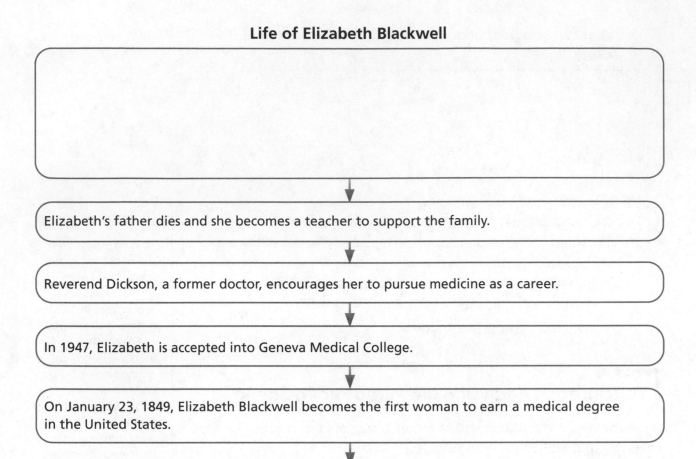

Elizabeth's father dies and she becomes a teacher to support the family.

Reverend Dickson, a former doctor, encourages her to pursue medicine as a career.

In 1947, Elizabeth is accepted into Geneva Medical College.

On January 23, 1849, Elizabeth Blackwell becomes the first woman to earn a medical degree in the United States.

Elizabeth dedicates her life to fighting prejudice against women studying and practicing medicine.

▼**Write** Write a few paragraphs in which you explain how the scene you read in this chapter is important in a play about Elizabeth's life. What is its purpose and how does it fit with the overall theme?

Language: Determining Word Meaning

In this chapter you learned words and terms that are specific to reading and performing plays. Words that have a particular meaning within an area of study or a content area are called *domain-specific*. For example, you learn vocabulary words related to science, math, or the study of literature. What terms can you name that are domain-specific for each of these subjects?

Many domain-specific words are multiple-meaning words. This means that the same word may have one meaning in one context and another meaning in another context. Sometimes these meanings are quite different. Sometimes you can determine the meaning of a domain-specific word from the context. At other times you will need to look up the word in a dictionary.

The chart beginning on the next page provides some examples of domain-specific words with their differing meanings.

Word	Means . . .	And also means . . .
strike	a labor stoppage growing out of protest of management	attack (military); hit forcefully; get a perfect score (bowling)
meter	the rhythm in a line of poetry	a machine that measures things; a unit of measurement in the metric system
grain	a crop such as wheat, which yields flour	a tiny particle of something; the natural shape within a cross-section of a log

Read the following sentences. Under each sentence, write the meaning of the boldfaced word. Use a dictionary to confirm or refine the definition you infer from the context. Then write another meaning of the word, using the dictionary as needed.

1. The professor showed me a machine that measured **waves** of electricity.
Definition:

Another Meaning:

2. When the blood tests came back, Susan learned that she did not have enough **iron** in her diet.
Definition:

Another meaning:

continued on next page

3. I was impressed, initially, with the size of the tiny computer's **memory**; it held a lot of information.

Definition:

Another meaning:

4. The sign of an experienced fisherman is that he knows how to pick a good **lure**.

Definition:

Another meaning:

5. Many people consider the most complex part of a stage production to be the building of the **set**.

Definition:

Another meaning:

Project-Based Assessments

Dramatic Scene

Work with a small group to write a scene that dramatizes a historical event from a famous person's life. Write a one- to two-page script that includes a narrator, dialogue, and an aside. For a greater challenge, include a chorus of actors. Then perform the scene for the class.

Here are some steps to help you:

1. Choose a historical event or person you find interesting or that you are currently studying in social studies or science.

2. Identify a meaningful event in the person's life and research the details. Note the main characters involved in the event.

3. Rewrite the facts into a script. Your script should include the following elements:

   - a narrator who introduces the scene and provides background. This may be one of the characters who steps in and out of the action.

   - dialogue between characters

   - an aside in which a character speaks directly to the audience

   - stage directions that explain where the characters should move, to whom they are speaking, and how the lines should be read.

4. Use the excerpt from this chapter as a guide for formatting your script, including writing the name of the character speaking in all caps followed by a colon and placing stage directions in parentheses or brackets.

5. Practice your scene following the stage directions you've written. Keep props and costumes simple, using a hat, glasses, or a cane instead of dressing in full costume.

6. Perform your scene for the class. Use appropriate speaking voices. Have your script in hand, but avoid being tied to it.

Use the following guidelines for your scene.	
To receive the highest score, the dramatic scene must meet all of these criteria.	Your dramatic scene • portrays a historical event or important event in the life of a historical figure. • is based on researched facts but presents the facts in a creative way. • includes a narrator, dialogue, stage directions, and an aside. • is presented in a professional manner. • is typed and formatted like a play. • includes the participation of all group members. • uses correct grammar, word usage, spelling, and punctuation.

Documentary

A documentary is a movie, television, or radio program that provides a factual record or report. Documentaries use text, images, and music to convey facts about a person's life. Write a script for a 3- to 5-minute documentary film about Blackwell's life. (Or choose another person who fought for human rights according to your teacher's guidelines.)

Although the goal of your documentary is to present facts, it should be as captivating to the viewer as a well-written piece of fiction. Think about how you can creatively communicate the events of Blackwell's life.

Use the following guidelines for your documentary script.	
To receive the highest score, the script must meet all of these criteria.	Your script • raises interesting questions about its subject. • presents provocative ideas about the time in which it takes place. • offers information in an entertaining and inviting manner. • uses correct grammar, word usage, spelling, and punctuation.

On Your Own: Integrating Ideas

1. Read several articles about 19th century medicine. Which of the advancements made since then have turned out to be the most significant?

2. Read about other women pioneers in medicine, such as Florence Nightingale, Elizabeth Anderson, Maria Montessori, Virginia Apgar, and Antonia Novello.

3. Research current female innovators in science, medicine, or technology. What do these women have in common with Elizabeth Blackwell?

Connect to Testing

In this chapter you practiced the skills of determining theme, analyzing structure, and identifying the author's purpose. You will be tested on these skills on reading tests. Answer the following questions to help you practice these skills.

Read the following excerpt from the play and then answer the questions that follow.

> **ELIZABETH:** *(With a dreamy enthusiasm)* I can see myself on a big, white horse, leading a charge into battle! Or painting a famous picture! Or . . . or . . . making a big, important speech while thousands of people cheer!
>
> **MAN 1:** *(Entering stage left)* As if women could say anything important!
>
> **MAN 2:** *(Entering stage right)* As if women could do anything important!

1. Which of the following best describes the central conflict of the scene in the excerpt above?

   A. business owners vs. employees

   B. women's desire for rights vs. men's ideas about women

   C. Elizabeth's dreams vs. society's expectations of women

   D. Mr. Blackwell's plans for his daughters' education vs. Mrs. Blackwell's plans

2. Write a paragraph describing the theme of the scene in this chapter. Refer to details in the text to support your answer.

3. **Part A:** In the passage, Mrs. Blackwell's character could best be described as

   A. terrified but aware of the need for women's rights.

   B. enraged at the injustice confronting her daughter.

   C. skeptical that her daughter will benefit from an education.

   D. angry that her husband was paying too much attention to her daughter.

   Part B: Which of the following provides the strongest evidence for the answer to Part A?

   A. (MRS. BLACKWELL steps forward. She's quieter than her husband and daughter.)

   B. **MRS. BLACKWELL:** *But, husband dear, our house is already bursting at the seams! How will we fit in one more person?!*

   C. **MR. BLACKWELL:** *We'll just have to try! The governess will teach our girls the same subjects the boys are learning in public school.*

   D. **MRS. BLACKWELL:** (With mild protest) *But, husband dear. What will they do with such knowledge?*

4. **Part A:** The purpose of the scene in the chapter is to

   A. provide a factual description of an event from Elizabeth's childhood.

   B. establish the setting of America in the 1800s.

   C. describe the poor working conditions people faced in the 1800s.

   D. explain the influence of Mr. Blackwell on his daughter's character.

   Part B: Which of the following provides the strongest evidence for the answer to Part A? Choose all that apply.

   A. **MRS. BLACKWELL:** *Husband! Elizabeth is far too young to have any idea what she wants to be.*

   B. **MR. BLACKWELL:** *I believe you will, Elizabeth! There's a special determination about you. A special spark.*

   C. **ELIZABETH:** (With a dreamy enthusiasm) *I can see myself on a big, white horse, leading a charge into battle! Or painting a famous picture! Or . . . or . . . making a big, important speech while thousands of people cheer!*

   D. **MAN 1:** (Entering stage left) *As if women could say anything important!*

   E. **MR. BLACKWELL:** (Speaking seriously) *Never forget, child. The greatest thing in life is to find a cause you believe in and fight for it!*

   F. **ELIZABETH:** *You take that back!*

   G. **MR. BLACKWELL:** *It's all right, Elizabeth. When you have new and different ideas, you're likely to take a lot of punishment! (with conviction) But the important thing is not to let the criticism bother you. Just keep on working for what you believe.*

Writing a Research Paper

*Those who cannot remember the past are
condemned to repeat it.*
—**George Santayana**

Study the past if you would define the future.
—**Confucius**

In this unit, you read a mixture of nonfiction and fiction on historical subjects ranging from the civil war to civil rights. In this chapter, you'll research and write about a historical figure to explore the qualities that led that person to advance a cause, right a wrong, or lead a nation.

WRITING PROMPT

Think of a person from history that you find intriguing. It may be a charismatic leader, someone who was the first to achieve something, an inventor, or an average person who spoke out against injustice. Research and write a biographical sketch of that person that captures both the actions and the character of the person. While the paper should include basic biographical facts, the central focus should be on an event or action that made history. In your conclusion, identify a lesson you learned by studying this person's life. Find five good sources to use for your research. Your final paper should be two to three typed pages and double-spaced. Use Times New Roman 12 point font.

Look over the prompt. Underline key words that explain the requirements of the task. Then fill in the following graphic organizer to identify what you must do.

Purpose	
Audience	
Content Requirements	
Additional Requirements	

The Writing Process

Brainstorm

First, gather some general ideas about people from history that you find interesting. Use the following questions to direct your thinking. Jot down notes in the margins.

1. Think about people you have studied in your history classes. Which people did you find intriguing and want to know more about?
2. What movies have you seen lately that made you want to learn more about a person who made history?
3. What historical fiction books have you read? Did any of the events or people make you want to learn more about them on the Internet to see if the movie was historically accurate?
4. To get more ideas, Google a topic that interests you. For example, *women scientists* or *who invented the computer*.

From your notes, create a list. Narrow down the topics to two or three. Then conduct some initial research online to make sure you can find five sources on the person. If you can't find enough sources, choose a different person.

Gather Ideas

Create an organizer similar to the one shown. Write the name of the person you have chosen to research in the center circle. Then note what event they were involved in or what action they took that made them worthy of study. In the circles surrounding the center circle, write details about the person and the event that you currently know about.

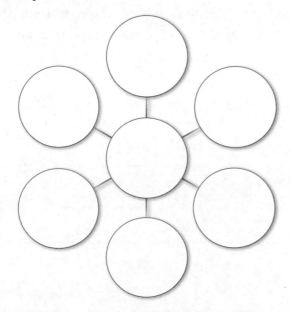

After completing the graphic organizer, you'll have a better idea of what questions need to be answered about your topic. Write the *who, what, when, where, why,* and *how* about your subject and event below. Then write one question you have about each of these points. If your answer is "I don't know," that's okay. That's the point of the exercise.

Who? _____

One question I would like to answer:

What? _____

One question I would like to answer:

When? _____

One question I would like to answer:

Where? _____

One question I would like to answer:

continued on next page

Why? _____

One question I would like to answer:

How? _____

One question I would like to answer:

Conduct Research

Use the questions you generated to guide your research. Many sources can be found online, but not all sources are equal in quality and reliability.

Evaluate sources carefully to make sure the author or creator is reliable. Websites that end in .gov (published by the government) or .edu (sponsored by a college or other educational facility) are generally trustworthy. The following questions will help you evaluate the quality of your sources:

1. Who wrote it? Is the author an expert on the topic? Was the writer an eyewitness to the events described? Sources written by someone who witnessed or was involved in the events are called primary sources. Sources written by someone who was not directly involved in the events are referred to as secondary sources. Reading primary sources such as letters, diaries, and biographies can offer new perspectives on historical figures and challenge your assumptions about events of the past.

2. What is the purpose? Websites that are trying to sell a product or make money may misrepresent information to persuade viewers. Books or magazines published by political institutions may only present one side of an issue or contain bias.

3. When was it written? Sometimes new information is discovered that impacts what we know about history. Check for the copyright year or year of publication. More recent information is usually better than something written 25 years ago, unless it is a primary source.

Take Notes

As you read your sources, take notes on key ideas you want to include in your paper. Notes can be recorded in a word processing file, a note-taking program, or on paper note cards.

When taking notes, either:

- write the information in your own words—paraphrase what the source says, or

- quote the source word for word. Be sure to put the quoted information in quotation marks.

This will help you avoid plagiarizing, or taking someone else's work as your own, when you write your paper. When writing about a person, include quotations to share important things the person said or wrote. However, using too many direct quotations can make your writing choppy.

Always include source information under the note—author's name, title of the article or book, website name, publisher, and date of publication. At the top write a short description of the information.

Sample note for direct quotation

Lost Opportunities for Girls' Education —————————————— **Description**

"A lost opportunity for education not only hurts the girls forced into early marriage, but has far-reaching and long-lasting repercussions for their children and communities." — **Quotation**

—Agnes Odhiambo, women's rights in Africa researcher

Odhiambo, Agnes. "Why Keeping Girls in School Can Help South Sudan" www.hrw.org.HumanRightsWatch. 10 Oct 2014. Page 95. — **Source Information**

Organize Ideas

Your paper should open with an introduction that includes a thesis statement or a main idea statement. This sentence should include the name of the historical figure and the impact he or she had on the world. For example, if you were writing about Elizabeth Blackwell, your thesis statement might be *Elizabeth Blackwell was the first woman to graduate from medical school, proving that women could be effective doctors.*

Before you begin writing, make a plan for your paper. Think about how to logically organize your ideas. When writing about the life of a person, chronological order makes sense. Provide background information, facts about main accomplishments, and impact on history. Use the order of the graphic organizer on the next page to help you organize your notes into a logical order.

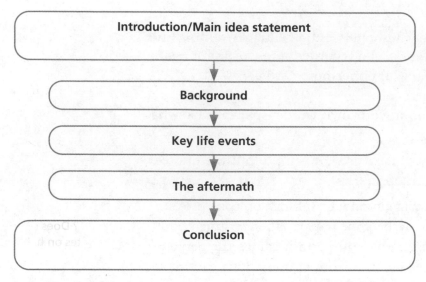

Organize the notes you've taken and put them in order according to the topics on the graphic organizer. You may find that you don't have enough information for some of the main ideas. Conduct more research so that you have strong facts and details about each point.

First Draft

Use your outline to write a first draft of your paper. Here are some tips for drafting:

- Refer to the order in the graphic organizer.

- Write quickly. You will revise and proofread later.

- Write on every other line or double-space if working on a computer. This will make it easier to make revisions.

- If you take a break and then return to drafting, reread what you have written before continuing. This will help you resume the flow of thought.

- Mark this paper Draft #1.

- Make sure to include your citations in your draft.

As you write your paper, include the sources from your notes. These in-text citations usually record the author's last name and a page number: (Odhiambo 95). Formats vary, so follow your teacher's instructions carefully. Including citations in your draft will save time later. Also, compile a list of all the sources used in your research and follow your teacher's instructions for formatting.

Revision

When you complete your first draft, show it to others. Here are three ways to revise your paper.

First Peer Review

This review will evaluate whether your ideas are interesting and whether they flow together in a logical order. With a group of two to three people, complete the following steps.

Steps for Peer Review

1. Select a timekeeper. Each writer gets ten minutes. Stick to the time.
2. One person begins by reading aloud his or her introduction while other members listen.
3. Pause. The same writer reads the introduction aloud a second time.
4. Writer asks, "Does the introduction of my research paper make you want to know more? Does it clearly explain what my paper is about?" Each member responds, as the writer takes notes on his or her draft.
5. Writer reads the entire paper, pauses, and then reads it again.
6. As writer reads, members take notes.
7. Writer asks, "What questions do you have about the person I wrote about? What else do you want to know about him or her?" Writer jots down replies.
8. Repeat Steps 1–7 with the next writer.

As soon as you've finished the peer review, look over the feedback you received. Revise, or edit, the paper now, changing it according to these comments. Mark this Draft #2.

Second Peer Review

Second Review: Teacher/Parent Review

Ask an adult or older sibling to read your paper and evaluate it using the following rubric.

Thesis statement
Is my main idea clearly stated in the introduction?

Content
Is there enough information given about the person and their contribution to history?
What information or ideas are missing?
Do any points need to be more developed?

Organization of Ideas
Are the main points logically organized?
Are good transitions used between paragraphs? between ideas?

Conclusion
Does my conclusion reinforce the thesis statement?
Does it bring the paper to a satisfying close?

Grammar, Usage, Punctuation, and Spelling
Are there any mistakes in grammar, usage, punctuation, and spelling?

When you finish, label this Draft 3.

Final Peer Review

Ask a classmate to read your paper. Have him or her give it a rating using the rubric below.

Use the following guidelines for your research paper.	
To receive the highest score, the narrative must meet all of these criteria.	Your research paper should • discuss a historical figure and his or her involvement in an important historical event. • include engaging description of the life and personality of the person and the events surrounding his or her contributions to history. • be logically organized and include good transitions. • have a clear and interesting writing style that includes a variety of sentence types. • cite sources to avoid plagiarism and include a list of all sources consulted for the paper. • use correct grammar, word usage, punctuation, and spelling.

Proofread

Proofreading is important. Before you turn in your paper, check for mistakes in punctuation and grammar. Make sure, as well, that you didn't leave any words out of sentences. Check for mistakes that your spell check program won't find, such as using *there* instead of *their* and other easily confused words.

Final Essay

Share your completed essay with audiences beyond your classroom. Read it to your family and friends. Upload your finished digital copy to your class website. Find an appropriate website and ask the editors to publish it. If you have a school or personal blog, share it with your readers.

Practice Performance Task

A performance task determines how well you understand literary and informational texts. The task may start with multiple-choice or short answer questions. These questions usually cover the main ideas of the passages and also important vocabulary. The questions prepare you to complete a writing assignment.

Complete the following performance task based on selections from this unit.

Source #1

Read the following excerpt from *The Lions of Little Rock*.

"I thought things settled down at Central once they called the soldiers in."

"Somewhat," said Daddy. "At least that was the official story. But things were not ever pleasant for them there. Minnijean Brown got expelled."

She was the colored girl who'd dumped a bowl of soup on the boys who were picking on her. That was something Liz would do.

"If they were still being harassed, why didn't they complain?"

Daddy shrugged. "Maybe they did and nothing was done. Maybe they thought if they showed any weakness, it would only get worse. In any case, last year the pictures from Central told the whole world Little Rock is filled with hate. And now the town's gone and voted against opening the schools. We are not just a town of racists, but those of us who believe in integration . . ." He shook his head. "We can't seem to find our voice."

Daddy was so upset, for a minute I thought he was going to cry. That scared me as bad as anything he'd said.

continued on next page

I knew what it was like to have trouble finding your voice,

so I reached over and patted his arm. He didn't look at me.

"I mean it, Marlee. I don't want to scare you too

much—I'll keep you safe—but I do want you to be careful.

Which means you stay away from Liz."

I nodded to show him I understood what he was

saying.

But I didn't promise that I would.

1. What is most likely Marlee's point of view about integration?

2. What could you infer about Marlee's father's opinion of his community?

   A. He is ashamed that the community has voted against integration.

   B. He is neutral about his community's decision.

   C. He wishes he lived in another community.

   D. He wants integration to happen at a slower pace.

3. What is the connotation of the phrase *find our voice* in the passage?

   A. It suggests that no one is sufficiently interested in integration.

   B. It suggests that people in favor of integration aren't effectively organized.

   C. It suggests that integration is too difficult to achieve in the United States.

   D. It suggests that integration advocates haven't been able to communicate well.

Continue the performance task by reading this passage and answering the questions that follow.

MR. BLACKWELL: Everyone is <u>entitled</u> to earn a decent living!

WOMAN 1: Stop your jabbering about decent wages. You'll take away some of the profits from my husband's cloth factory.

MR. BLACKWELL: Good!

WOMAN 2: Mr. Blackwell also wants to make our hospitals cleaner and better run!

MAN 2: And he wants to raise our taxes to do it!

ELIZABETH: *(Proudly)* My father believes that women should be free and equal citizens. They should not be considered just the property of their husbands!

MAN 1 and MAN 2: Balderdash!

MAN 1: Mr. Blackwell, you are a crackpot!

ELIZABETH: How dare you say such things about my father! He's a very great man!

MAN 2: He's crazy as a loon!

(Marching determinedly to MAN 2, ELIZABETH gives him a kick in the leg.)

ELIZABETH: You take that back!

4. Write a short summary of this passage.

continued on next page

5. What could you infer about Elizabeth's feelings about men and women being paid equally?

   A. She most likely feels it is important that everyone be paid equally.

   B. She most likely feels wage amounts have to be decided by managers.

   C. She most likely feels that factory workers need to be paid more.

   D. She most likely feels that she needs to consider the effects of wage equality further.

6. Based on the context, the word *entitled* most nearly means

   A. to provide the means to

   B. to give a right to

   C. to give a title to

   D. to guarantee

Your Assignment

WRITING PROMPT

Use *The Lions of Little Rock* and the play "Elizabeth Blackwell" as your two sources. Compare them as portraits of strong female characters who face opposition from family and their communities. Return to each source as needed. As you write your comparison, support your main idea with details from the passages.

Before you begin your comparative essay, fill in the graphic organizer on the next page to organize your thoughts. Consider the main characters, the conflicts they are facing, and their relationship with their fathers based upon the excerpts you read. Return to the texts to find evidence to support the similarities in the texts.

	Lions of Little Rock	Elizabeth Blackwell
Similarity 1/ Evidence		
Similarity 2/ Evidence		
Similarity 3/ Evidence		

Explanation

Read the prompt carefully before you begin writing. Underline key words that explain what you are required to do. Study the rubric on the next page before you being writing.

Use the information from the graphic organizer to write your essay. Before you begin, sketch out an outline on a sheet of paper. Explain the evidence carefully and thoroughly. Arrange your ideas so they flow together logically.

Rubric

Your response will be scored using the following criteria:

Reading Comprehension
- How well did you understand the texts?
- Did your writing reflect your understanding of the sources?

Writing Expression
- Does your writing address the requirements of the prompt?
- Does your comparison reflect the content of both sources?
- Is your comparison well organized with reasons that flow logically?
- Does the writing style contain precise, accurate language and content?
- Is your writing appropriate for the purpose, task, and audience?

Writing Conventions
- Does your writing follow the rules of standard English with few errors in grammar, word usage, and spelling?

When you are finished writing, evaluate your essay using the rubric above. Revise your writing as needed.

Acknowledgments

Pages 10–12, Decety J and Cowell J (2016) OUR BRAINS ARE WIRED FOR MORALITY: EVOLUTION, DEVELOPMENT, AND NEUROSCIENCE. Front Young Minds. 4:3. doi: 10.3389/frym.2016.00003.

Pages 48–51, ZOO COMPLICATED: ARE CAPTIVE ANIMALS HAPPY? by Kathryn Hulick from Muse magazine, © by Carus Publishing Company. Reproduced with permission. All Cricket Media material is copyrighted by Carus Publishing Company, d/b/a Cricket Media, and/or various authors and illustrators. Any commercial use or distribution of material without permission is strictly prohibited. Please visit http://www.cricketmedia.com/info/licensing2 for licensing and http://www.cricketmedia.com for subscriptions.

Pages 83–85, "Why I am a Vegetarian" by Matthieu Ricard from A PLEA FROM THE ANIMALS. Copyright 2014 by Matthieu Ricard. Previously published in French as "Plaidoyer pour les Animaux: Vers une Bienveillance pour Tous." English copyright 2016, from A Plea for the Animals: The Moral, Philosophical, and Evolutionary Imperative to Treat All Beings with Compassion. Published by Shambhala Publications. Used by permission.

Pages 89–91, VEGETARIANISM by Judy Krizmanic from Muse magazine, © by Carus Publishing Company. Reproduced with permission. All Cricket Media material is copyrighted by Carus Publishing Company, d/b/a Cricket Media, and/or various authors and illustrators. Any commercial use or distribution of material without permission is strictly prohibited. Please visit http://www.cricketmedia.com/info/licensing2 for licensing and http://www.cricketmedia.com for subscriptions.

Pages 120–123, Excerpt(s) from CATCH ME IF YOU CAN: THE TRUE STORY OF A REAL FAKE by Frank W. Abagnale, copyright © 1980 by Frank W. Abagnale. Used by permission of Broadway Books, an imprint of the Crown Publishing Group, a division of Penguin Random House LLC. All rights reserved.

Pages 140–143, Reprinted from Guy P. Harrison, THINK: WHY YOU SHOULD QUESTION EVERYTHING (Amherst, NY: Prometheus Books, 2013), pp. 61–64. Copyright © 2013 by Guy P. Harrison. All rights reserved. Used with permission of the publisher;
www.prometheusbooks.com.

Pages 159–162, THE FACT CHECKER'S GUIDE FOR DETECTING FAKE NEWS. From *The Washington Post*, November 22, 2016, © 2016 *The Washington Post*. All rights reserved. Used by permission and protected by the copyright laws of the United States. The printing, copying, redistribution, or retransmission of this content without express written permission is prohibited.

Pages 178–181, DEBUNK IT! HOW TO STAY SANE IN A WORLD OF MISINFORMATION

Pages 197–200, Excerpt from THE GIVER by Lois Lowry. Copyright © 1993 by Lois Lowry. Reprinted by permission of Houghton Mifflin Harcourt Publishing Company. All rights reserved.

Pages 234–237, Excerpt(s) from SMARTER THAN YOU THINK: HOW TECHNOLOGY IS CHANGING OUR MINDS FOR THE BETTER by Clive Thompson, copyright © 2013 by Clive Thompson. Used by permission of Penguin Press, an imprint of Penguin Publishing Group, a division of Penguin Random House LLC. All rights reserved.

Pages 251–253, "All Watched Over by Machines of Loving Grace" from THE PILL VERSUS THE SPRINGHILL MINE DISASTER by Richard Brautigan. Copyright © 1968 by Richard Brautigan. Reprinted by permission of Houghton Mifflin Harcourt Publishing Company. All rights reserved.

Pages 270–272, ROBOTS WILL ELIMINATE 6% OF ALL U.S. JOBS BY 2021, REPORT SAYS" by Olivia Solon. Copyright Guardian News & Media Ltd. 2017

Pages 275–276, ROBOTS ARE SLOWLY TAKING OVER THE JOB MARKET

Pages 288–292. FEED. Copyright © 2002 M.T. Anderson. Reproduced by permission of the publisher, Candlewick Press, Somerville, MA.

Pages 306–308, "It's 'digital heroin': How screens turn kids into psychotic junkies" by Dr. Nicholas Kardaras was originally published in the *New York Post* on August 27, 2016. Reprinted with permission from the author.

Pages 312–314, WHY CALLING SCREEN TIME 'DIGITAL HEROIN' IS DIGITAL GARBAGE by Rachel Becker,originally published on The Verge on August 30, 2016. Copyright Vox Media, Inc. Used by permission.

Pages 342–346, "Talking to Daddy" from THE LIONS OF LITTLE ROCK by Kristin Levine, copyright © 2012 by Kristin Levine. Used by permission of G. P. Putnam's Sons Books for Young Readers, an imprint of Penguin Young Readers Group, a division of Penguin Random House LLC. All rights reserved.

Pages 350–354, THE HISTORY BEHIND THE LITTLE ROCK NINE from the Arkansas Department of Parks & Tourism at arkansas.com. Used by permission.

Pages 365–368, THE DRUMMER BOY OF SHILOH by Ray Bradbury. Reprinted by permission of Don Congdon Associates, Inc. Copyright © 1960 by the Curtis Publishing Company, renewed 1988 by Ray Bradbury.

Pages 371–372, DRUMMER BOYS by Stephen Currie from Cobblestone magazine, © by Carus Publishing Company. Reproduced with permission. All Cricket Media material is copyrighted by Carus Publishing Company, d/b/a Cricket Media, and/or various authors and illustrators. Any commercial use or distribution of material without permission is strictly prohibited. Please visit http://www.cricketmedia.com/info/licensing2 for licensing and http://www.cricketmedia.com for subscriptions.

Pages 382–384, "Our Jacko" by Michael Morpurgo from THE GREAT WAR: STORIES INSPIRED BY ITEMS FROM THE FIRST WORLD WAR. Reprinted by permission of Candlewick Press. All rights reserved.

Pages 396–399, From FALLEN ANGELS by Walter Dean Myers. Copyright © 1988 by Walter Dean Myers. Reprinted by permission of Scholastic Inc. (Digital rights) Reprinted by permission of DeFiore and Company, on behalf of the Estate of Walter M. Myers. Copyright © 1988 by Walter Dean Myers.

Photo Credits: iStock: pp. 379 (middle), 384; Library of Congress: p. 176 (middle), NPS Photo: p. 367; Thinkstock.com: all other photos